THE RACIAL MUNDANE

The Racial Mundane

Asian American Performance and the Embodied Everyday

Ju Yon Kim

NEW YORK UNIVERSITY PRESS

New York and London

NEW YORK UNIVERSITY PRESS
New York and London
www.nyupress.org

References to Internet websites (URLs) were accurate at the time of writing. Neither the author nor New York University Press is responsible for URLs that may have expired or changed since the manuscript was prepared.

ISBN: 978-1-4798-9789-6 (hardback)
ISBN: 978-1-4798-4432-6 (paperback)

For Library of Congress Cataloging-in-Publication data, please contact the Library of Congress.

New York University Press books are printed on acid-free paper, and their binding materials are chosen for strength and durability. We strive to use environmentally responsible suppliers and materials to the greatest extent possible in publishing our books.

Manufactured in the United States of America

10 9 8 7 6 5 4 3 2 1

Also available as an ebook

CONTENTS

ACKNOWLEDGMENTS

I was drawn to Maxine Hong Kingston's novel *Tripmaster Monkey: His Fake Book* as a frame for the introduction of this book because of its portrayal of the messy, dynamic community that forms around its protagonist, Wittman Ah Sing. Wittman's community occasionally disappoints and aggravates him, but it also propels him to create a unique theatrical experience. Like Wittman, I saw what I had envisioned as a solitary project become an exciting collective enterprise. I was fortunate enough, however, to write *The Racial Mundane* with the support of a community of friends, mentors, and colleagues who always inspired, and never disappointed.

David Palumbo-Liu and Harry Elam, Jr. have read and reread my scholarship, bringing out its best and challenging me to make it better; they have given me time without hesitation, even when time was short; and they have provided models of pedagogy and scholarly engagement to emulate. No words can adequately convey my appreciation. I owe immense thanks as well to Paula Moya for her astute feedback on my research and for her wise and discerning advice, both of which continue to influence how I approach my work. Gordon Chang, Shelley Fisher Fishkin, and Stephen Sohn provided invaluable support and counsel during my time at Stanford University. Cherríe Moraga's life-sustaining words, guidance, and faith in my writing have motivated me to seek ways to connect art, politics, and scholarship; my admiration and gratitude run deep.

The Modern Thought and Literature Program (MTL) and the Center for Comparative Studies in Race and Ethnicity (CCSRE) were important homes for me at Stanford. I am indebted to Monica Moore for the care with which she shepherded us through the Modern Thought and Literature Program; as many will concur, she is the heart of MTL. Celine Parreñas Shimizu and Kyla Wazana Tompkins were departing the program as I was joining it, but they immediately became trusted mentors when our paths crossed several years later. At Celine's suggestion, I spent an invigorating quarter as a lecturer at the University of California, Santa Barbara. Kyla generously advised me on this book, and her suggestions moved it in exactly the right direction. CCSRE supported my research with a teaching fellowship and gave me the opportunity to attend a range of talks on the latest scholarship in race and ethnic studies. The center is a testament to the vitality and importance of this research, and my year as a fellow was crucial to the development of this project. I am grateful as well to the Mellon Foundation for funding two years of study and research.

I found an incomparable community of friends and colleagues at Stanford. Sarah Richardson and Nirvana Tanoukhi, with their brilliance and loyalty, have encouraged me to be a better scholar and a better friend. My memories of San Francisco are filled with the many conversations and meals I had with Mike Benveniste and Karen Paik. I benefited from friendships with Harris Feinsod, Nigel Hatton, and Jayson Sae-Saue, who made me laugh and think. The women of my writing group, Allison Carruth, Heather Houser, Michael Hoyer, Ruth Kaplan, and Claire Seiler, have reviewed countless versions of the following pages, always with enthusiasm, and always with keen insights. They are my true collaborators in this project, which is all the more meaningful because of the traces of their queries, comments, and encouraging words that lie across it.

The English Department at Harvard University has been a stimulating and collegial place in which to develop my research. The book became bolder as well as more expansive and nuanced through conversations with colleagues who have been equally gracious and rigorous in their questions and suggestions. I am especially grateful to Stephen Burt, Glenda Carpio, Amanda Claybaugh, Marjorie Garber, Martin Puchner, James Simpson, Werner Sollors, and Nicholas Watson for their mentorship and engagement with my research. I thank Deans Diana Sorenson and Heather Lantz for ensuring that I had the support necessary to finish this book. I am appreciative as well of Caroline Elkins, Kay Shelemay, and Tessa Lowinske Desmond of the Committee on Ethnicity, Migration, Rights, and Sun Joo Kim and the Korea Institute for their steady support. Robin Bernstein has offered keen advice on our many shared research interests. The extraordinary peers I met my first few days at Harvard have remained my closest friends: Alex Bloemendal, Kerry Chance, Nicholas Harkness, Keerthi Madapusi, Emily Madapusi Pera, Laurence Ralph, and Emily Riehl have made Cambridge home.

The Everyday Life working session that Robin Bernstein and Kyla Wazana Tompkins began at the American Society for Theatre Research (ASTR) conference has been a key forum for exchanging scholarship on performance and the everyday, and I am thankful to all of the participants for their feedback on my papers. Esther Kim Lee and Ron West's ASTR working session on Asian American theater was an important introduction into the field. I am grateful to Josephine Lee for her generous mentorship of emerging scholars, among her many contributions to the study of Asian American theater. I approached Karen Shimakawa several years ago about acting as an early reader for this project, and her feedback and support have been critical to its development, as well as my development as a scholar. Her insights have improved this book, and her confidence in my work has sustained me through its writing.

I completed work on *The Racial Mundane* while I was a visiting scholar at the American Academy of Arts and Sciences. The fellowship enabled me to finish revisions while beginning a second book project. I am grateful to John Tessitore and Hilary Dobel for their support of the fellows, and to Mary Dunn and Patricia Spacks for their perceptive questions about my research and offers to read my works in progress. For many lively conversations, I thank the other fellows at the academy: Kornel Chang, Jillian Hess, Heather Houser, Gretchen Purser, Crystal Sanders, Stephen Tardif, Colin Williamson, and Bernardo Zacka.

I cannot imagine a better experience working with a publisher than the one I have had with NYU Press. Eric Zinner has been an ideal editor, offering input and latitude at exactly the right points. I owe many thanks to Alicia Nadkarni and Dorothea Halliday for ushering the manuscript from review to production. Two anonymous reviewers provided thorough, subtle assessments of the manuscript that helped elevate the book. I am deeply appreciative of their careful reviews and suggestions. Portions of the manuscript previously appeared in *Theatre Journal* and *Modern Drama*, and I am grateful to the publishers of the two journals for allowing me to reprint them here. An earlier version of a section of Chapter 1 was published as "Trying on *The Yellow Jacket*: Performing Chinese Exclusion and Assimilation," *Theatre Journal* 62.1 (March

2010): 75–92; a section of Chapter 3 was published as "The Difference a Smile Can Make: Interracial Conflict and Cross-Racial Performance in *Kimchee and Chitlins," Modern Drama* 53.4 (Winter 2010): 533–56. The anonymous reviewers for the two articles offered many helpful comments, the benefits of which are also evident in this book.

My interest in Asian American theater began with a performance group at Yale University called Jook Songs. I thank the members for their friendship and inspiring writings, and Nelson Wong and T. J. Nguyen in particular. I continue to benefit from conversations with Suyun Kim, Tammy Kim, and Nina Rastogi about everything from politics and theater to careers and life priorities. I have the unique fortune of having an extended family of friends from high school as well as their partners. Many of the same friends who helped me celebrate my sixteenth birthday were in the audience when I received my doctorate, and I know that they will be in my life for decades to come. My friendships with Laura Chang, Kathleen Chen, Hanie Lee, Mamta Mehta, Jane Park, Doris Yang, Stella Yang, and Tina Yao have spanned almost twenty years; they have my unwavering trust, affection, and admiration. Brian Choi, Kent Hu, Johann Lau, Ken Lee, Stephen Lee, Bosun Min, and Joel Sangria brighten my life with their presence. They are in many of my warmest memories. Casey May, Scott Takano, Jason Wang, Sam Yoon, and Andrew Hou, who is profoundly missed, have enlivened trips and gatherings through the years, and I hope we never stop laughing together.

Larson Hogstrom brought much happiness into my life as I finished this book, and made the days easier with his cheerful and calm support. Even the most difficult times have become joyful thanks to him. Finally, I dedicate this book to my family: my grandparents Kim Byoung Sik, Jang Keum Ok, Seo Seok Ho, and Lee Jong Pil, my brother Seung Gon Kim, and, especially, my parents Young Ho Kim and Won Ok Kim, who have provided constant love and encouragement.

Introduction

Ambiguous Habits and the Paradox of Asian American Racial Formation

It is in the everyday and its ambiguous depths that possibilities are born and the present lives out its relation with the future.
—Henri Lefebvre, *Critique of Everyday Life*

Anybody American who really imagines Asia feels the loneliness of the U.S.A. and suffers from the distances human beings are apart. Not because lonesome Wittman was such a persuader but because they had need to do something communal against isolation, the group of laststayers, which included two professional actors, organized themselves into a play.
—Maxine Hong Kingston, *Tripmaster Monkey: His Fake Book*

Wittman Ah Sing, the restless, inspired, and oft-raging protagonist of Maxine Hong Kingston's novel *Tripmaster Monkey: His Fake Book* (1990), is immersing himself in a typing frenzy when a familiar problem confronts him: "And [he] again whammed into the block question: Does he announce now that the author is—Chinese? Or, rather, Chinese-American? And be forced into autobiographical confession. Stop the music—I have to butt in and introduce myself and my race."[1] Although explicitly stating his "race" seems unappealing to Wittman, he also resists the obvious alternative, to leave himself and his characters racially unidentified.[2] He muses, "'Call me Ishmael.' See? You pictured a white guy, didn't you? If Ishmael were described—ochery ecru amber umber skin—you picture a *tan* white guy" (34). Stymied as soon as he begins to write, Wittman feels he must either assert his racial identity or allow a presumptive whiteness to assert itself. He suspects, moreover, that in making this choice, he alone would carry responsibility for insisting on the significance of race, or denying its importance.

As Wittman ponders—or rather, fumes about—this dilemma, he decides to circumvent it by choosing a different literary form: "By writing a play, he didn't need descriptions that racinated anybody. The actors will walk out on stage and their looks will be self-evident. They will speak dialects and accents, which the audience will get upon hearing" (34). Moving from textual description to embodied performance,[3] Wittman disperses responsibility for racial identification among the various actors and spectators who will make theater from his writing. Although he avoids explicitly "racinating" his characters, he nevertheless assumes that identifications will happen in the encounters between those who look and speak and those who see and hear in historically informed and socially meaningful ways. Rather than write race, Wittman decides to let it materialize in the dynamic exchanges that constitute a performance.

In picturing this theatrical event, however, Wittman hastily ascribes a transparency to what the audience "will get" and see as "self-evident." Namely, he assumes that the performance itself will erase the fraught issues of racial identification raised by his attempt to write. He consequently evades questions of whether the walks, looks, dialects, and accents presented on the stage will be those of the actors, or those of the characters they are assigned to play; whether any friction might exist between performer and role; and whether the audience's perception of bodies and behaviors will align with the intentions of those staging the performance. In other words, Wittman ignores theater's uncertain mingling of the real and the fictive, and the possible conflicts between representation and reception that might produce something *other* than what he envisions. With this turn to performance, the novel becomes a lesson—for Wittman and the reader—on theater's unruliness.

Following Wittman into the theater, *The Racial Mundane: Asian American Performance and the Embodied Everyday* delves into the very ambiguities that not only elude *Tripmaster Monkey*'s restive artist but ultimately trump him as well—a glorious defeat with which this introduction will close. Although Wittman imagines that simply having his actors walk in front of an audience will allow their features and mannerisms to speak for themselves, he neglects to consider the transformation that occurs at the threshold of the stage. Behaviors carried out with nonchalance in the everyday acquire a new context and style when they move into the spotlight of the theater. In the language of performance studies, performative reiterations become "twice-behaved behaviors."[4] However neatly a performance might attempt to align the look (appearance) of the actor with the look (gaze) of the spectator, the necessary gaps that emerge between actor and role and between the stage and the seats are spaces of dynamic interaction, spaces where social boundaries consolidate and dissolve, where affiliations emerge and shift. They are, moreover, sites where everyday behaviors shed their ordinariness to become subjects of marked interest, consequently revealing their unregistered importance, or taking on an altogether new significance.

The displacement of quotidian behaviors from anonymity into public scrutiny more broadly has played a crucial role in shaping Asian American racial formation. From the nineteenth century to the present, everyday scenes of eating, working, shopping, and studying have buttressed competing views of Asian Americans as ideal and impossible Americans. Even as the Asian body has remained persistently alien vis-à-vis the American national imaginary, the behavioral proclivities attached to that body have had a more flexible career. These everyday enactments are what I refer to as "the mundane" to underscore a fusion of the corporeal and the quotidian. Whether set in direct opposition to American living or regarded as particularly amenable to it, the presumed habits of Asian Americans have provided powerful if unreliable support for competing arguments about the permeability of racial and national delineations. For those who study Asian American racial formation, its vacillations between the extremes of the "yellow peril" and the "model minority" constitute an enduring paradox. The minutiae of daily life not only imbue these opposing characterizations of Asian Americans with an illusory precision, but also play a vital role in managing their contradictions. As this book elaborates, the paradox of Asian American racial formation is sustained through the mundane's ambiguous relationship to the body: it is enacted *by* the body, but may or may not be *of* the body.

From inflections of speech and gesture to daily routines, the mundane is the slice of the everyday carried—and carried out—by the body.[5] Although reading a newspaper in the morning might seem quite different from physical tendencies such as an accent or a gait, they share a repetitive, consistent quality that places them at the limits of conscious action. It is not that the mundane proceeds completely unconsciously, but that it seems in some measure programmed into the body. At the same time, it leaves open the possibility of transformation through the repetition of alternate behaviors, a process that in one context is called assimilation, and in another, theatrical rehearsals. Different motions can suggest different levels of attachment to the body, with small mannerisms appearing more deeply embedded than quotidian practices of work and leisure, and therefore more resistant to change. Yet across the spectrum, the mundane manifests a bodily training that makes modification seem both plausible and difficult. Its equivocal relationship to the body lies in this tension between the endurance of previously acquired habits and routines, and the possibility that such behaviors are open to alteration.

In the long historical production of racial categories and hierarchies, the mundane has played dual roles, insisting, on the one hand, on the truth of difference (demonstrated not just in selected physical features but in ostensibly distinct ways of being in the world), and offering, on the other, a vehicle for erasing or ameliorating difference (through assimilation as a national or colonial subject). Richard Dyer's argument that whiteness has been conceived as "something that is in but not of the body" contrasts the abiding belief that those who are white can transcend their bodies with the perception that those who are racially marked are reducible to their bodies.[6] These beliefs, Dyer further contends, sanction the former to control the latter.[7] The mundane, as something enacted by the body that is not necessarily of the body, inserts a productive uncertainty whereby the prerogative to manage racial others can be channeled into efforts to change their behaviors. Yet the presumed incompleteness of these endeavors, exemplified by Homi Bhabha's "almost the same, but not quite" colonial subject, affirms the very boundaries that such efforts are meant to erase.[8] American sociologist Robert E. Park thus mused in studies from the first half of the twentieth century that although people of Asian descent were capable of adopting American customs and mannerisms, an incongruity lingered between their conduct, which seemed typically American, and their physical appearance.[9] The body may move differently, but the conglomeration of features used for racial classification continues to prompt questions about whether these new habits supersede or merely mask prior tendencies. The project of assimilating racial minorities therefore sets the possibility of transforming people by modifying their everyday behaviors in tension with the inexorable corporeality that burdens those who are racially marked. Seductive but never satisfying, the mundane serves as a wedge between absolute difference and its complete unraveling.

In emphasizing this nebulous relationship between habitual behaviors and the body, I am not posing an epistemological problem or soliciting a biological explanation, but instead calling attention to the social usefulness of this ambiguity. Beliefs about the body are crucial to structuring the world, and even dated or contradictory beliefs (those that empirical or historical study could potentially discount) can have important effects. As Dyer demonstrates, the notion that a certain quality is not "of" the body but instead resides "in" the body has had, and continues to have, wide-ranging social consequences. Alternately, uncertainty has its own force, and it has been particularly effective in managing racial boundaries through the mundane. This book is therefore concerned not with habits and routines per se, but rather with the social significance attached to certain everyday practices and to the possibility of adopting and transferring those practices across racial lines.

These interests resonate with Pierre Bourdieu's disquisitions on the habitus and Judith Butler's theory of gender performativity, but I diverge from these works in putting ambiguity at the core of the racial mundane. In describing, respectively, the transmission of practices through the habitus, conceived as "embodied history . . . internalized as second nature,"[10] and the reiterated citations of norms that perform or "do" gender, Bourdieu and Butler argue that the enactment of conventional behaviors perpetuates the social stratifications and divisions that it seems merely to reflect. By appearing innate, bodily repetitions naturalize identity, status, and institution, legitimating, for example, the king's authority or binary conceptions of gender. The transhistorical scope of these theories sets them apart from studies of the everyday that specifically link it to the experiences of modernity. For instance, in her recent study of Asian American literature's engagement with capitalist modernity, Yoon Sun Lee observes that the writing of the everyday "tends to show the draining away of significance through the phenomenon of repetition."[11] The repetitions that concern Butler and Bourdieu, by contrast, are those that are significant and efficacious precisely because of their continual, perfunctory embodiment. The normative identities and practices that they dissect propagate quietly through the body, their longevity and impact tied to their discreet rhythms.

Because of their interest in challenging accepted notions of the natural and the essential, however, Bourdieu and Butler are less concerned with the quotidian force of ambiguity, which draws attention to itself as the evasion or disruption of certainty. Ambiguity emerges when unfamiliar bodies take up familiar behaviors, when the relationship between body and behavior becomes an open question and consequently takes on a *theatrical* character: as the subject seems to split into actor and role, questions of imitation and authenticity surface. These more dubious performances, in Bourdieu and Butler's frameworks, are either innocuous because they lack a rote, compulsory quality or potentially subversive because they call norms into question.[12] Ambiguity and theatricality nevertheless constitute the commonplace of the racial mundane: denaturalizing everyday behaviors (as strange, spectacular, quaint, or dangerous) is fundamental to naturalizing racial difference.

The association of theatrical performance with the willful playing of false roles generates a misleading opposition between the everyday and the theatrical that obscures their intimacy in the production of racial boundaries. In elaborating his theory of the habitus, for example, Bourdieu sets theatrical performance as its foil. Arguing that the habitus is "a practical *mimesis* (or mimeticism) which implies an overall relation of identification and has nothing in common with an *imitation* that would presuppose a conscious effort to reproduce a gesture, an utterance or an object explicitly constituted as a model," Bourdieu stresses that when it comes to the habitus, "The body believes in what it plays at: it weeps if it mimes grief. It does not represent what it performs, it does not memorize the past, it *enacts* the past, bringing it back to life."[13] Bourdieu implies that whereas theatrical performances involve self-reflexive, intentional acts, the habitus is the body's involuntary enactment of history. Yet in asserting that "the body believes in what it plays at," Bourdieu insinuates that the habitus is, in some ways, *like* theatrical performance. He suggests that the difference between mimesis and imitation is one of degree, and it is measured by the extent to which an actor believes in her or his role.

As sociologist Erving Goffman points out, however, individuals can move between belief and disbelief as they perform various social roles.[14] Ultimately, the efficacy of a presentation depends on the performer's ongoing interactions with an audience. Analogies to theater allow Goffman to conceptualize daily social interactions in terms of information exchange: everyday performances are efforts by their various participants to influence one another.[15] By assuming the intentionality of participants, Goffman's model sits uncomfortably with some poststructuralist critiques of the subject,[16] but it nonetheless usefully envisions everyday performances as sites of ongoing struggles to control meaning and behavior, sites of asymmetries and disruptions as well as measures from all sides to maintain a common understanding of the scene. At the simplest level, Goffman's model conceives of performance as an individual asking an audience to believe in her or his presentation. While the concept of the habitus focuses on the alignments of belief—the body and its audience believing together—that sustain the authority of established roles, the *mis*alignment of belief can also affirm social hierarchies and distinctions.

Exemplary in this regard, racial difference maintains its credibility through performances in which beliefs are incongruent, when a body believes in its performance but the audience does not share this belief, or when a performance that should stretch belief is taken as natural and authentic. Audiences as well as actors draw the line between mimesis and imitation, and not always at the same point. This is the lesson embodied by Bhabha's imperfect colonial mimic, and conveyed in W. E. B. Du Bois's description of racial double consciousness as a "sense of always looking at one's self through the eyes of others, of measuring one's soul by the tape of a world that looks on in amused contempt and pity."[17] Pressed to meet standards that are simultaneously used to cast their efforts as poor role-playing, racial and colonial others are trapped between two kinds of performances. Recognizing the complex imbrications of race, theatricality, and the everyday, Saidiya Hartman develops an expanded sense of "performing blackness" in her study of racial domination in the nineteenth century to reflect the blurry lines between racial performance and performativity.[18] Whereas Bourdieu turns to theatrical performance to draw a contrast to the habitus, theories of racialization turn to theatrical analogies to describe the experience of being racially marked. The racial mundane, which joins the repetition of habitual behaviors with the production of racial difference, is theatricality made ordinary, and everyday enactments made ambiguous.

If the racialization of nonwhite bodies renders them theatrical, it is not because race is a role willingly played, and not only because such bodies become the objects of spectacle or surveillance. Both racialization and theatrical performance rely on a productive tension between what could be termed the "actor" and the "role," a doubling that is mediated by "the eyes of others." Rather than focus on the agency of the actor, theater scholar Bert O. States and philosopher Umberto Eco choose involuntary performers—a dog and an intoxicated man—to explicate, respectively, the phenomenology and the semiotics of theatrical performance. States argues, "A dog on stage is certainly an object . . . but the act of theatricalizing it—putting it into an intentional space—neutralizes its objectivity and claims it as a *likeness* of a dog."[19] To theatricalize a dog is to make it double as itself and its effigy—a simultaneous splitting and drawing together of the real and the representative. Explaining that in theater, "image and object, pretense and pretender, sign-vehicle and content, draw unusually close,"[20] States implies that performance depends on both a centripetal and a centrifugal movement: "pretense" and "pretender" converge on one body, but without ever fully collapsing into each other. Eco similarly describes an inebriated man used by the Salvation Army to preach against intemperance as, at once, real and representative, singular and typical: unwittingly cast to perform the evils of alcohol, he enables and exceeds symbolization.[21] To the extent that all objects represent types, the exceptionality attributed to theatrical performance may seem arbitrary. The point, however, is that theatrical performance makes explicit a tense union between the body or the object that is present and the concept that it represents. Richard Schechner refers to this relationship as the "double negativity" of performance: an actor is "not" herself, but she is also "not not" herself.[22]

The questions raised by these paradigms of theatrical performance point to questions that one might also ask about racialization, particularly at a historical moment when the notion of race as a social construction is gaining acceptance, but continues to chafe against beliefs about the indelibility of racial differences. When a person is "theatricalized," which traits lend a reality to the performance and which ones exceed the designated role, thereby disappearing into insignificance, challenging the "truth" of the performance, or extending the scope of the role? To ask similar questions about racialized bodies is to underline the social construction of race and to insist on an awkward fit between body and role, while taking seriously the drive to make them converge. What aspects of the body as a material presence moving through time and space are used to sustain or undermine the credibility of race, and what, conversely, does racialization make visible or obscure?

Many evocative parallels join them, but the critical relationship among racialization, theatricality, and the mundane in this book might be summed up thus: when racialized, the mundane takes on a theatrical quality that accentuates its ambiguous relationship to the body. The motions of the body throughout a day are innumerable, and not every gesture becomes racially representative. The racial frame instead captures certain mannerisms and behaviors, and in doing so draws them closer to the marked body while also turning their relationship into a question, a paradoxical dynamic familiar to theatrical performance, which, as States and Eco describe, holds actor and character in productive suspense.

Yet however useful theater might be as a paradigm for social interactions and processes, it is also a distinct cultural form with the potential to affect—as well as represent and explicate—those dynamics. Its privileged place in this book among various modes of representation and performance reflects its special relationship to the mundane. As I argued above, although theater and the mundane seem to be antitheses, they share an important feature: their aesthetic and social possibilities derive from the body's ambiguous relationship to the behaviors that it enacts. However, this attribute of the mundane becomes evident only when it sheds its perfunctory character to become something that is scrutinized or actively reshaped. By contrast, theatrical performance explicitly manages the relationship between body and behavior—or more precisely, the convergence on one body of the mannerisms of both actor and character—as formal practice, even if this process is not always evident in the final production. Method acting, for example, encourages closing the gap between actor and character, whereas Brechtian alienation effect emphasizes the distance between them. In theatrical performances, more than in film and television where the ideal is often seamless integration, the space between body and behavior remains a practical problem and a point of experimentation. As Karen Shimakawa argues, "As a medium theatre, by definition, depends on and exposes the fragility of identity (sexed/gendered, racialized, and national) and the complex, dynamic relations between subjects, objects, and the abject."[23] The performances considered in the following chapters purposefully intensify this quality of theater, its playful suspension and rupture of unitary selves, through devices such as role-doubling and cross-racial role-playing. Although these devices occasionally appear in other forms, they are primarily—and inherently—theatrical in their manipulation of the possibilities of the live body.[24] In theater, the interstices between body and behavior bridged by the mundane have the potential to break open into palpable, unstable fissures that exert aesthetic and social force.

Performing the Asian American Mundane

The relationship between Asian American racial formation and the mundane is both historical and theoretical. As I establish below and elaborate in the following chapters, debates about Asian American immigration and assimilation have persistently located national controversies in the subtle motions of the body, in the minor dramas of doing chores or greeting a customer. These seemingly trivial behaviors have been fundamental to maintaining Asian Americans as what Shimakawa calls the "national abject"—that which must be continually expelled in order to maintain a coherent national identity.[25] Reflecting a pervasive and abiding curiosity about how others live, the scrutiny of everyday behaviors is not exclusive to Asian American racial formation. Most racial stereotypes implicate the mundane, which enlivens their flattened portraits with the small details of how people walk, speak, eat, or hold their bodies. Furthermore, as mentioned above, projects of assimilation and colonization have long been preoccupied with how to change the tendencies of those deemed racial others. Nevertheless, the sheer extremes of idealization and alienation that constitute the paradox of Asian American racial formation illustrate with particular clarity the social and cultural efficacy of the mundane's ambiguous relationship to the body. Likewise, this quality of the mundane is critical to elucidating how apparently inconsistent characterizations of Asian Americans remain persuasive.

At the turn of the last century, calls to end Chinese immigration put a spotlight on the habits of Chinese laborers. For those advocating immigration restrictions, these habits seemed to demonstrate the inability of the Chinese to assimilate, as well as the unfair advantage they might have over white workers. Lurid descriptions of the unsanitary practices and meager living standards of the Chinese filled government reports and fed fears that although Chinese immigrants could not adopt American ways of living, they would spread their tendencies to others. Everyday behaviors—considered intractable when it came to Chinese workers and dangerously vulnerable when it came to white Americans—offered a particularly expedient means of protesting Chinese immigration. The mundane could be called on to manifest racial difference and support claims of a fundamental incompatibility, but also arouse anxieties by suggesting the potential for traversal.

After the United States moved to restrict immigration from Asia and attenuated fears that "Chinese" habits would spread, the mundane—ever flexible—came to serve an opposing project, that of exploring the possibility (previously rejected) of transferring "American" habits to those of Asian descent already residing within the nation, and thus assimilating them. This project took on an added urgency as World War II ended and both the United States and Canada confronted the question of how to integrate Japanese North Americans after their release from internment camps. Each state pursued policies to hasten assimilation by dissolving ethnic communities: while for a short period the U.S. government encouraged voluntary relocations to various parts of the country, the Canadian government forcibly dispersed Japanese Canadians to areas east of the Rocky Mountains. These efforts assumed that separating Japanese North Americans from one another would compel them to absorb (white) American and Canadian tendencies, and result in the dissipation of difference. Japanese women who immigrated to the United States in the postwar era as wives of American servicemen became unwitting exemplars of this process: living in communities scattered throughout the country, they reportedly carried out domestic tasks just like regular American housewives. Yet if they seemed to fulfill a particular vision of individually willed integration, the curiosity they provoked for their adoption of American lifestyles simultaneously affirmed their alienation by pointing to a disjuncture between their racialized bodies and their everyday behaviors. The mundane slyly tendered evidence of both the capacity of racial minorities to become model Americans *and* their abiding strangeness.

This indeed constitutes the signature duality of the model minority myth, which emerged in the 1960s with stories of the success of Japanese Americans and eventually encompassed Asian Americans as a wider demographic. The stereotype has elicited wary responses from activists and scholars who argue that in touting the apparent achievements of Asian Americans, it masks class disparities and ethnic diversity, fuels interracial resentment and anxieties, and falsely justifies cuts in public funding.[26] In the late 1980s and early 1990s, friction in inner-city neighborhoods belied the innocuousness of the model minority myth, as Korean American merchants and black customers in economically depressed areas became engaged in a struggle over limited resources that was exacerbated by racial stereotyping of both groups. During this time, the daily practices of running a business (managing goods, interacting with customers, exchanging money) gave credence to divergent perceptions of Korean immigrants as hardworking Americans and unwelcome strangers. Although Korean Americans were lauded as bootstrapping minorities who succeeded without government support, their tendency to pass change in a certain way or to avoid eye contact also raised concerns about their "cultural difference." Transforming these behaviors, rather than addressing economic inequities, became the focus of efforts by community and government organizations to alleviate hostilities. Set as the cause of and the solution to antagonisms, the mundane became the site where racial divides could be crossed—or not.

Just as the daily practices of Korean American merchants elicited criticism as well as praise in discussions of the "Black-Korean conflict," recent accounts of high-achieving Asian American youths characterize their routines as models to emulate and causes for concern. Although activities like completing one's homework, preparing for exams, and practicing musical instruments might seem unremarkable in themselves, the style with which Asian Americans purportedly carry out these activities (excessively, automatically, ceaselessly) casts them as signs of an un-American lack of creativity and playfulness. Deftly portraying Asian American students as *hyper*assimilated, such representations turn behaviors that seem to promise the erasure of difference into further evidence of racial distinctions. Although ostensibly divergent characterizations of the Asian American mundane bookend the century with early depictions of the "bad" habits of Chinese immigrants and recent depictions of the "good" habits of Asian American students, in both cases public interest in the practices of these groups circled around questions of whether such habits were intrinsic to Asians or could be transmitted to others. Woven into arguments about whether or not "Asian American" is really "American" are arguments about whether or not habitual behaviors are separable from the bodies they set in motion.

As immediate, tangible embodiments of social and historical pressures, everyday enactments seem to make persuasive claims. Differing assumptions about what those claims *are* have allowed the mundane to support the paradox of Asian American racial formation. By setting the mundane at the center of the contradictory dynamics of national abjection, however, I do not intend to privilege it as the primary medium for shifting racial and national boundaries, or to neglect the force of other factors. Chapters 1 and 4 show that a focus on quotidian behaviors has at times moved public discourse away from thorny political concerns and issues of economic disparities. Nevertheless, the efficacy of small behavioral tendencies in shaping conversations about who can cross certain lines (economic, racial, national, or gendered) and who cannot—as well as their more subtle perpetuation of identities and social relations in the form of Bourdieu's habitus or Butler's performative citations—makes them crucial to investigations of how difference and inequity are sustained. Furthermore, because habitual behaviors seem to enact culture reflexively through the body, they bridge body-centered conceptions of race and a contemporary discourse of cultural difference. References to cultural differences often serve today as a euphemism for racial differences, yet they also imply the potential detachment of culture from racialized features. In joining the cultural and the corporeal, the mundane flexibly substantiates conflicting notions about how and where racial lines are drawn.

In probing the significance that everyday behaviors assume in debates about race, immigration, and assimilation, this book does not claim to describe the actual habits of Asian Americans. In other words, the day-to-day practices of those who might identify or be identified as Asian American are less my concern than how and why specific behaviors associated with Asian bodies attract attention. The racial mundane is always charged with spectacle—whether on the stage, in a magazine article, or in a government report—and only gives the illusion of representing the quotidian experiences of those who are racialized. As I stressed above, the everyday body is never reducible to a racial frame: its numerous motions catch and evade attention, shifting between the typical and the singular, the conscious and the unconscious. To the extent that this study is about habits and routines, it is expressly about habits and routines as *mediated* by various cultural forms. When selected behaviors and mannerisms become the object of public interest, they become more intelligible, but they also become estranged from the subtle unfoldings of the everyday. Thus dislocated, they pulsate with new consequence and potential, posing, to borrow Henri Lefebvre's phrasing, complex problems that are both aesthetic and ethical.[27]

The critical potential of defamiliarizing the everyday, or making it strange, has been a primary concern of scholars and artists in the twentieth century. In theater, this inquiry is commonly associated with Bertolt Brecht, especially his work on the alienation effect and the *gestus*. Attentive to the possibilities offered by performances outside the theater as well as in it, theorists such as Butler and Elin Diamond propose that blatantly imitative, inappropriate, and excessive performances of naturalized behaviors might have a subversive force.[28] Indeed, film, literature, and the visual arts, as well as theater, have all been part of investigations into the political efficacy of disrupting the ordinariness of the everyday. As Lefebvre puts it, such projects seek "to make [the everyday's] latent conflicts apparent, and thus to burst them asunder."[29] Lefebvre himself chooses Charlie Chaplin's "Tramp-figure" to illustrate his concept of the reverse image, "an image of everyday reality, taken in its totality or as a fragment, reflecting that reality in all its depth *through* people, ideas and things which are apparently quite different from everyday experience, and therefore exceptional, deviant, abnormal."[30] The reverse image is not the opposite of the everyday, but rather the everyday as reflected by and mediated through what appears to be its opposite. Breaking through the tightly patterned surface of the everyday to reveal its contradictions, the reverse image depends on both formal techniques of defamiliarizing the everyday and social delineations of otherness.

Like Chaplin's Tramp, figures of geographic displacement—refugees, exiles, immigrants—have served as devices for critiquing the everyday. Representing the experience of migration, forced and voluntary, often involves envisioning the everyday of a particular place from an alienated perspective. Thus, the strange animals, dreamlike landscapes, and cryptic signs that greet the immigrant (and the reader) in Australian artist Shaun Tan's graphic novel *The Arrival* (2006) convey the bewilderment that accompanies basic activities of sleeping, eating, and working in a new space. The immigrant can also be invoked to shed light on alternatives to conventional practices. Michel de Certeau, for example, explains his theory of everyday "tactics" by referring to the practices of the Kabylian immigrant in France, who finds "*ways of using* the constraining order of the place or of the language."[31] Yet de Certeau is also sensitive to the dangers of critiquing the everyday through its others, and faults Bourdieu for depending on a "remote foreign element" to develop his theory of the habitus.[32]

The risks and challenges of estranging the ordinary through those regarded as "exceptional, deviant, abnormal" become especially clear when it involves those marked as racially different. To the extent that practices of defamiliarizing the everyday depend on a common understanding of the familiar, how might their force and meaning change when enacted by unfamiliar bodies? How do such strategies reflect back (as Lefebvre hoped) the alienation of the audience, rather than simply affirm the alienness of others? Although stylistic manipulations such as excessive repetitions or alienation effects might disrupt our sense of the everyday by troubling the relationship between the body and its routine motions, the production of racial difference relies on similar strategies to make the quotidian enactments of certain bodies seem exaggerated, unnatural, and imitative. Aesthetic modes advanced with the explicit goal of critiquing established conventions can therefore have contradictory effects when they involve racialized bodies.

The cultural productions examined in the following chapters press into this complex juncture, defamiliarizing everyday behaviors specifically in order to unsettle racial delineations. They accordingly engage (and engage with) two key projects of modernity: endeavors by artists and theorists to render the everyday strange, and wide-ranging efforts to substantiate racial distinctions. While public debates about Asian Americans have turned to small, recurrent behaviors as evidence of either the permeability or the inflexibility of racial lines, various works of theater, film, and fiction have experimented with the porousness of social boundaries by playing with the relationship between habit, body, and identity. The mundane's uncertain attachment to the body thus becomes an opportunity to try different practices, to stage an exchange of bodies and behaviors, and to formalize and stylize quotidian activities.

Set within a larger discursive network composed of newspaper and magazine articles, government reports, and sociological studies, performances and works of literature intimately concerned with performance form the center of the following case studies. The mundane serves as a vehicle for managing racial and national identifications as these works integrate aggressively nonrealist performance modes, including ritual, mime, cross-racial role-playing, and caricature, with ethnographic and documentary elements. By mixing and moving between styles, they draw attention to *how* the mundane sheds or acquires its anonymity. They moreover show that as everyday behaviors move between ordinary and exceptional, racial boundaries concomitantly harden, shift, and dissolve. With the exception of the afterword, each of the following chapters pairs works of theater, film, and literature that put pressure on existing conceptions of racial difference by using parallel strategies of defamiliarizing habitual behaviors. By comparing two key works in each chapter, I investigate why, as they grapple with issues of immigration, assimilation, and interracial relations, they share not just a keen interest in the mundane, but similar modes of presenting it as well. Furthermore, I find in the *discrepancies* that emerge between the paired works new possibilities for performing the mundane differently, that is, for realizing alternate practices on the stage that might illuminate and reshape practices in the everyday.

In the era of prohibitions on Chinese immigration to the United States, when the line between "Chinese" and "American" was strictly maintained, a drama that purportedly offered Broadway audiences an authentic experience of the Chinese theater was hailed as a pioneering American play. Now largely forgotten, J. Harry Benrimo and George C. Hazelton, Jr.'s *The Yellow Jacket* (1912) nimbly accommodated a dual identity as an amusing spectacle of racial otherness and an important work of modern American theater. In particular, the scripted property man's execution of routine tasks while "managing" the stage lent the performance an ethnographic verisimilitude that made possible its passages between entertainment and art, and moreover, enabled its viewers to conceive of themselves as both Chinese and Western spectators. Chapter 1 compares *The Yellow Jacket* to a dramatic work that bears its echoes: Thornton Wilder's iconic *Our Town* (1938). Like *The Yellow Jacket*, *Our Town* defamiliarized everyday behaviors to encourage audiences to identify with *and* to distance themselves from the world depicted on the stage. The two plays' use of non-naturalistic theatrical conventions to present the mundane challenged established social demarcations by inviting multiple, sometimes competing identifications. At the same time, their projection of a distinct spectatorial position set limits on the crossings that they promised.

Chapter 2 further explores the potential for performances of quotidian behaviors to forge unlikely affiliations, but in the context of the broad pressures faced by Japanese North Americans after World War II to reject ethnic ties. Setting midcentury depictions of Japanese North Americans against retrospective accounts of their experiences of displacement, the chapter moves between "archives of racial representation" and "archives of ethnic self-expression," an approach that Colleen Lye argues may "[put] into practice a fully social (and nonessentialist) consciousness of race."[33] In a striking convergence, Velina Hasu Houston's drama *Tea* (1987) and Joy Kogawa's novel *Itsuka* (1992) envision the everyday performance of community by Japanese North Americans as a rejection of post–World War II imperatives to disperse. Their characters materialize tenuous yet vital connections to one another by turning activities such as recycling, taking tea, and completing basic organizational tasks into shared rituals. Pairing a Canadian novel and a U.S. American play, Chapter 2 extends the book's analysis of the mundane both geographically and formally. It considers crucial parallels and differences between the postwar treatment of Japanese Canadians and Japanese Americans, and assesses the distinct formal limits that drama and fiction impose on the project of "ritualizing" routines.

Cross-racial performances of the mundane, while a recurring interest in the book, are the focal point of Chapter 3, which interrogates the claim that the minor behavioral tendencies of Korean American merchants were a major cause of antagonisms during the so-called Black-Korean conflict. Whereas community and government efforts encouraged merchants to adopt nicer conduct, Elizabeth Wong's play *Kimchee and Chitlins* (1990) and Anna Deavere Smith's solo show *Twilight: Los Angeles, 1992* (1993) asked instead what kind of change might result from assuming the gestures, mannerisms, and accents of those positioned as one's enemy. *Twilight* and *Kimchee and Chitlins* together demonstrate that despite the risk of replicating stereotypes and further aggravating relations, performing the mundane across lines of race, gender, and class has the potential to bring to light the elusive networks of influence that make resolving conflicts across those lines so difficult.

Moving from cross-racial performances to those that cross divides *within* Asian America, Chapter 4 elucidates the contradictory desires incited by the model minority stereotype through an analysis of Justin Lin's 2002 film *Better Luck Tomorrow* and Lauren Yee's 2008 play *Ching Chong Chinaman*. These works feature characters who appear to be diligent, privileged high school students, but simultaneously seek to be the model minority's "others"—either the yellow peril gangster or those whose hardships are obscured by tales of Asian American triumphs. As these characters attempt to expand their lives by doubling as their others or taking them on as surrogates, the mundane alternately enables these performances and upholds their material limits. Whatever doubling is made possible by borrowing and delegating everyday tasks, their obligatory physical execution and unpredictable social impact restrict the characters' efforts to play different types of Asian Americans.

In recent years, the online video has become the quintessential form of the everyday, capturing life's smallest moments and disseminating them globally through websites such as YouTube. It has also become a major vehicle for Asian American cultural production, as Asian American artists, actors, and entrepreneurs have become some of the most popular providers of online content. As the afterword demonstrates, their videos assert the ordinariness of Asian Americans, not only by focusing on the banalities of snacking, dating, and applying eyeliner, but also by strategically inserting spectacular performances of everyday practices. Set against these exaggerated depictions, the Asian American performer takes the position of the interested subject, rather than the interesting object. Yet in seizing on quotidian activities as a medium for dissolving racial peculiarity, the videos also risk advancing a narrow conception of the Asian American ordinary as exclusively middle-class and heterosexual. Their informal quality nonetheless allows a tension to emerge between the ordinary body and the live one, the former arranging itself into accepted patterns and the latter perpetually escaping their strictures.

The following chapters largely revisit events and issues (Chinese exclusion, Japanese internment, the Los Angeles riots, and debates over affirmative action) that have held a significant place in accounts of Asian American history and racialization. By linking these critical episodes to shifting conceptions of the racial mundane, the book establishes the embodied everyday as a vital lens through which to reexamine the supposed paradox of Asian American racial formation. Instead of offering a comprehensive historical and cultural survey, the book lingers at sites where well-documented controversies about race that implicate the mundane meet works of theater, film, and literature that engage related issues through their estranged presentations of everyday behaviors. Attending to what might be considered high-density subjects in Asian American studies, *The Racial Mundane* replicates the field's initial focus on Chinese and Japanese Americans in Chapters 1 and 2. The analysis in Chapter 3 of representations of Korean American merchants during the Los Angeles riots and the explorations in Chapter 4 and the conclusion of less ethnically defined performances (in other words, Asian American performances without a strong connection to a specific ethnic group) widen the compass and reflect the demographic changes that followed the 1965 immigration reforms.

The book nevertheless confronts the perennial challenge of doing justice to the diverse affiliations subsumed by the designations "Asian American" and "Asian North American."[34] The myriad qualifications that must accompany these terms draw attention to their provisional quality and the historical and political contexts in which they are used. This inherent definitional ambiguity, however unsatisfying, is a valuable corrective to axiomatic thinking. The theoretical elasticity of the book's conception of the racial mundane, developed through readings of a necessarily finite set of texts and performances, is therefore meant to accommodate, rather than elide, the nuances that should follow any effort to conceptualize Asian American racial formation. One might note, moreover, that the importance of the embodied everyday to representations of diasporic experiences exceeds the focus here on a distinct set of national controversies. Carlos Bulosan's short story "The Story of a Letter" (1946), for example, conveys the impact of migration through a stylistic shift in how the narrator recounts his day-to-day activities in the Philippines and in the United States. In Wendy Law-Yone's novel *The Coffin Tree* (1983), the narrator's brother, Shan, becomes a kind of Lefebvrian "Tramp-figure" in the United States, where his continued disorientation after suddenly leaving Burma/Myanmar makes it difficult for him to carry out the basic tasks needed to maintain his life. Chapter 3's discussion of *Tea* and the trilogy that it concludes touches on similar depictions of characters who must respond to abrupt changes in their quotidian practices as they move globally. These examples point to other potential areas of analysis outside *The Racial Mundane*'s primary interest in exploring the interface between national debates about Asian Americans that hinge on claims about racialized bodies and everyday behaviors, and performances that test those claims through their unconventional presentations and enactments of habits and routines.

To the extent that all notions of racial difference are comparative and articulate distinct understandings of the relationship between bodies and behaviors, the relevance of the racial mundane extends beyond its role in constituting the Asian American as a paradoxical figure. In the contemporary moment, recognizing its impact can help offset hasty pronouncements of an emergent postracial era. Although much of this book focuses on cases in which the public scrutiny of habitual behaviors heightened a sense of racial difference, *obscuring* the impact of race on everyday interactions and possibilities can also preserve existing distributions of privilege. During his first presidential campaign, Barack Obama made this point when he responded to a question about whether he was "authentically black enough" by joking, "When I'm catching a cab in Manhattan, in the past, I think I've given my credentials."[35] In its appropriate if awkward shift between past and present tenses, Obama's quip turns from the exceptionality of his campaign to the everyday encounters that manifest the continuing force of racial stereotypes and discrimination. As legislative actions in the United States move increasingly toward color-blind policies that insist, as Patricia J. Williams puts it, on hearing no evil, seeing no evil, and speaking no evil,[36] they raise the stakes of making the daily impact of race legible without further turning racialized bodies into spectacles.

Tracing the intimate relationship between the embodied everyday and Asian American racial formation, the following chapters map a thick dialogue on the racial mundane. Each study brings together popular, canonical, and "minor" texts and performances of differing public reach and aesthetic cachet. Such categories of distinction, however, are also contingent, changing as the works move through time and space. Exemplified most spectacularly by The Yellow Jacket, many of the cultural productions discussed in The Racial Mundane have taken on different identities in front of different audiences. Such transformations pertain equally to the "archive" of written texts and recorded performances as well as the "repertoire" of embodied performances and practices, to borrow Diana Taylor's distinction.[37] Nevertheless, even when veiled by darkness, the audience impresses on the live performance a physical presence that has direct effects and cannot easily be discounted. Alain Badiou thus proposes, "Cinema counts the viewers, whereas theatre counts on the spectator."[38] As Chapters 1 and 3 illustrate, an actor's effort to shift between roles by adjusting her or his physical bearing and the spectators' attendant discomfort or pleasure can momentarily crystallize the interactive process by which social demarcations become more or less salient. Such encounters make tangible the mundane's role in facilitating—or resisting—passages across those divides, and reveal the mutual involvement of audience and performer in adjudicating the lines between mimesis and imitation, propinquity and estrangement. In addition, theater necessarily (if not uniquely, as the afterword illustrates) exposes the impossibility of completely capturing and fixing the mundane, even as it asks actors and spectators to participate in that very project. Even when a performance puts the mundane under scrutiny, makes it unfamiliar, or strives to replicate it as closely as possible, it must contend with the tendency of the living body to strain against its form, or to slip past its perimeters. Theater therefore involves a process that parallels the production of racial difference in its attempts to frame and capture the mundane (thus, the redundancy of racial spectacle), while continually manifesting the limits of such efforts.

An audience's relationship to a performance might well be conventional, conforming to the predictable shape that such exchanges have taken over decades, even centuries. As Wittman Ah Sing learns at the end of *Tripmaster Monkey*, however, performances can also move in unexpected directions. Contingent and conventional, actual and historical, theatrical performance turns the body into a machine of spatial and temporal compression. Elin Diamond argues, "Performance, even in its dazzling physical immediacy, drifts between present and past, presence and absence, consciousness and memory . . . each performance marks out a unique temporal space that nevertheless contains traces of other now-absent performances, other now-disappeared scenes."[39] When Wittman turns to theater believing that a performance will enable him to avoid "racinating" his characters, he hopes to take advantage of this convergence of the past and the present: "The actors will walk out on stage and their looks will be self-evident. They will speak dialects and accents, which the audience will get upon hearing." Wittman fails to consider, however, that in the "dazzling immediacy" of the performance, what the audience will grasp may diverge from what he assumes is obvious. After the spectacular conclusion of his masterwork, a frenetic, exuberant medley of Chinese American history and mythology, Wittman pulls out reviews of the performance printed by local papers. Reading descriptions of the show as "East meets West" and "Exotic," he rails at his audience, "Quit clapping. Stop it. What's to cheer about? You like being compared to Rice Krispies? Cut it out. Let me show you, you've been insulted. They sent their food critics. They wrote us up like they were tasting Chinese food" (307). Wittman begins a long tirade explaining the offensiveness of the reviews and ranting against racism and racial self-hatred. Livid that the reviewers missed what he had intended to convey through the performance, he sets out to reinterpret the show and educate his audience.

And yet, at the end of Wittman's long speech, his audience similarly transforms his monologue into something unexpected: "Out of all that mess of talk, people heard 'I love you' and 'I'll always love you' and that about dying and still loving after a lifelong marriage. They took Wittman to mean that he was announcing his marriage to Taña and doing so with a new clever wedding ritual of his own making. His community and family applauded. They congratulated him" (339). Despite Wittman's attempts to explicate his political views, the audience ignores his social critique and turns his angry performance into the paradigmatic performative: the declaration of marriage. His exercise of authorial privilege thus falls short when confronted with the unpredictable chemistry of the performance as the competing interests and expectations of its participants intersect. Joining his community's festivities, the once isolated tripmaster monkey concedes that there are no last words without an audience to celebrate them in unintended ways.

1

Trying on *The Yellow Jacket* at the Limits of *Our Town*

The Routines of Race and Nation

On the nearly bare stage of Thornton Wilder's *Our Town*, the New England village of Grover's Corners attains a tangibility, if not a visibility, through the bodies of the actors as they mime the daily activities of residents. Delivering milk, preparing meals, reading the newspaper, or doing homework, they carry out the routine tasks that give the unseen town its life, rhythm, and shape. Guided by these gestures, theatergoers are asked to fill the stage with their own vision of a particular place and time. Between the empty stage and the details supplied immediately by the Stage Manager (the town's name, the town's latitude and longitude, and the exact date),[1] the actors and the audience must create a community from embodiments of the mundane.

Yet who exactly constitutes the community realized by these performances? The question of how far the borders of "our town" actually stretch has troubled critical assessments of Wilder's drama. Much like its juxtaposition of a blank stage with the minutiae of geographic coordinates, the play splits possible answers between the abstract and the specific. Although *Our Town* opens with the birth of twins to a "Polish mother" (6), this family remains at the periphery of Grover's Corners: offstage and "by the tracks" (6), they await incorporation into a community that is mostly populated, a character later explains, by those who come from "English brachiocephalic blue-eyed stock" (22). Wilder's own writings about the play, however, suggest a desire to imbue daily life in Grover's Corners with a universal significance, to "set the village against the largest dimensions of time and place."[2] What mediates between the specificities of life in Grover's Corners and the drama's more centrifugal tendencies are the quotidian activities that allow the audience to "see" the town without props or scenery. As actors simulate the motions of the townspeople, the degree of familiarity they bring to their roles and evoke in viewers generates relationships of affiliation and estrangement that modulate the expansiveness of the community articulated by the performance.

In the early twentieth century, the potential for routine behaviors to manifest social and cultural boundaries was weighed in heated political disputes, investigated in foundational sociological studies, and dramatized as part of a new movement in American theater. Each of these sites placed competing pressures on the mundane to enable passages between established racial and national demarcations, and to impede such crossings. Beginning with restrictions on immigration from China in the late nineteenth century, the United States set entry limits that targeted nations in Asia as well as Southern and Eastern Europe. In the debates leading up to the Chinese Exclusion Act of 1882 and subsequent efforts to implement the new immigration laws, supporters of Chinese exclusion and government agents tasked with enforcing the border called on small behavioral tendencies to distinguish those who could enter the United States from those who could not. The embodiment of particular habits and the potential to assimilate new ones could position applicants for entry on either side of the U.S. perimeter. As I establish in the next section of this chapter—and trace across the book—the mundane offers only fleeting and capricious support when called on to make such distinctions; indeed, it threatens to undermine the very truths it presumably discloses and raises questions about the reliability of perception.

In an era when immigration restrictions attempted to draw strict lines between "Chinese" and "American," a drama purporting to replicate Chinese theater was hailed an American classic, and likely inspired the staging of Wilder's *Our Town*. In 1912, J. Harry Benrimo and George C. Hazelton, Jr's *The Yellow Jacket* offered Broadway audiences a supposedly authentic experience of the Chinese theater, including elaborate costumes, minimal sets, props that served multiple functions, and a "property man" who openly managed the stage during the performance. Mildly successful when it opened in New York, the drama became a favorite among prominent European and Russian directors during its international tour and returned to the United States as an aesthetically sophisticated and influential American play, rather than an amusing imitation of the Chinese theater. Despite the acclaim bestowed upon *The Yellow Jacket* and the revivals that continued to the midcentury, it has since slipped from classic to curiosity, leaving only secondhand traces on the American dramatic canon through its echoes in *Our Town*. In examining the two works together, I am less concerned with charting a line of influence than with comparing how they integrate the performance of quotidian activities with emphatically nonrealistic stage conventions. As the plays invite their audiences to trespass (or surpass) certain boundaries by seeing and not seeing the mundane, their experiments with Chinese theatrical practices become explorations of the relationship between habitual behaviors and social delineations—the site of so much contestation in debates about Chinese immigration.

Bad Habits and Exclusion Acts

In 1885, the San Francisco Board of Supervisors appointed a special committee to investigate and evaluate living conditions in the city's Chinatown. Appended to the yearly municipal report, the committee's assessment, which covers a variety of subjects including housing, crime, prostitution, and health, offers a stark picture of the neighborhood and its residents. It bluntly states, "Here [in San Francisco's Chinatown] it may truly be said that human beings exist under conditions (as regards their mode of life and the air they breathe) scarcely one degree above those under which the rats of our water-front and other vermin live, breathe and have their being. And this order of things seems inseparable from the very nature of the race."[3] Emphasizing that crowding, grime, and a general lack of hygiene are endemic to Chinatown, the report catalogues the habits of Chinese immigrants deemed responsible for creating living conditions akin to those of rats. It moreover ventures a connection between the "order of things" in the neighborhood and "the very nature of the race": the immigrants' way of living, it suggests, might be essential rather than circumstantial, and thus unchangeable.

Even as it repeatedly proposes an abiding bond between race and behavioral tendencies, the report's hesitation to claim a *definitive* link reveals a lingering uncertainty about their relationship. Tracing this uncertainty across seemingly disparate arguments about Chinese immigration, I contend that the ambiguous attachment of bodies to habits allowed the mundane to play dual roles in these debates. While calls for restricting Chinese immigration in the late nineteenth century stressed the intransigence of particular modes of living and the incompatibility of "Chinese" and "American" habits, the potential for those of Chinese descent to adopt different habits—whether as part of the process of assimilation or as part of an attempt to foil immigration officials—became a matter of serious consideration in the decades after entry limits were imposed. The mundane helped to substantiate claims of racial difference, but also served, through its performance in interrogation rooms as well as on the theatrical stage, as a vehicle for testing borders of race, nation, and class.

In the mid-nineteenth century, the gold rush and the building of the transcontinental railroad drew thousands of Chinese immigrants, largely from Canton, to the United States. These opportunities in mining and railroad construction had faded by the 1870s, however, and Chinese immigrants found themselves in competition for jobs with white Americans and European immigrants during a time of economic recession. The potential threat that Chinese labor posed the white working class became a central part of campaigns to regulate immigration. In his study of the factors that led to the passing of Chinese immigration restrictions, Andrew Gyory argues that the national labor movement played a much smaller part in the enactment of these laws than the politicians who found immigration an expedient issue for building political support.[4] Protecting white American labor nevertheless became a major justification for the first U.S. law limiting immigration from a particular nation. The Chinese Exclusion Act, first passed in 1882, was continually renewed until it was superseded by the Immigration Act of 1924, which closed immigration from Asia. The initial restrictions on Chinese immigration, however, were less expansive in scope, and specifically distinguished Chinese laborers, who were barred, from merchants, scholars, diplomats, and leisure travelers, who were permitted temporary access. The government made other exemptions for entry and reentry for those who had immediate family in the United States and for those who were citizens by birth, although Chinese immigrants could not become naturalized citizens.

In defending their position, proponents of exclusion stressed that the Chinese could not assimilate: their living habits were too different from those of Americans and, moreover, could not be changed. In 1877, the California State Senate presented an address to Congress that declared,

"The Chinese have now lived among us, in considerable numbers, for a quarter of a century, and yet they remain separate, distinct from, and antagonistic to our people in thinking, mode of life, in tastes and principles, and are as far from assimilation as when they first arrived."[5] The alleged problem was not just that the Chinese "mode of life" was too different, but that it seemed innate and unchangeable as well. Connecting the particular state of Chinatown to the particularities of the Chinese people, the 1885 report (cited above) similarly stated that forcing residents to abide by American standards of living by enforcing municipal regulations would probably not change them; it would, however, induce them to leave because of their deep *resistance* to changing. It claimed, "The fact that the race is one that cannot readily throw off its habits and customs, the fact that these habits and customs are so widely at variance with our own, makes the enforcement of our laws and compulsory obedience to our laws necessarily obnoxious and revolting to the Chinese."[6] Thus, it was not just the habits themselves but also the supposed fixity of these habits that affirmed the obduracy of racial difference. Any conflict between this depiction and prevailing contemporary stereotypes of the Chinese as quintessentially imitative could be resolved by differentiating between the temporary adoption of acceptable behaviors—for example, while working as a servant in a white household or while under scrutiny by municipal officials—and the ingrained habits to which the Chinese would always return.[7]

Yet if the possibility that the Chinese could assimilate was widely dismissed, the potential for Chinese habits to infiltrate and reshape American behaviors loomed over debates about Chinese immigration. In his study of San Francisco's Chinatown, Nayan Shah explains that anxieties about the Chinese "contaminating" the American way of life were connected to fears that they would bring dirty and unsanitary conditions to cities, as well as force white workers to lower their standard of living. The comparison of Chinese immigrants to vermin, seen in the 1885 report on Chinatown, was a prevalent one in the late nineteenth century, in popular culture as well as in government-sanctioned studies. Shah observes, "In health reports and journalistic reports of health inspections, Chinese were likened to a wide array of animals, including rats, hogs, and cattle. The choice of animals underscored a relationship to waste and an imperviousness to crowding."[8] The San Francisco report, for example, is thick with sensory details that convey the deplorable living conditions of Chinatown and the baffling habits of its residents: it describes "open cess-pools, exhalations from water-closets, sinks, urinals and sewers tainting the atmosphere with noxious vapors and stifling odors," and "people herded and packed in damp cellars, living literally the life of vermin, badly fed and clothed."[9] "Herded and packed" into rooms like animals, the residents of Chinatown as depicted by this report are surrounded by similarly crowded receptacles of excrement. Multiple public health investigations of Chinatown stirred fears that such living practices and conditions would spread.[10] Reports about white prostitutes living in the neighborhood recounted that their "mode of life seems to be modeled after that of the Mongolian, to a larger extent than after the manners and customs of the race to which they belong."[11] These public studies hinted that white Americans were in danger of taking up the behaviors of the Chinese, who, by contrast, remained impervious. Habits—as well as disease—could be contagious, but apparently moved in only one direction.

Anxieties about economic competition intensified trepidation about contact and contagion: supporters of immigration restrictions argued that because the habits and customs of the Chinese allowed them to subsist on much lower wages than white workers and their families, the latter would be forced to adopt similar practices just to compete. Shah contends that as unions advocated for better working conditions and living standards, "the so-called American standard of living, or more bluntly 'the white man's standard,' was defined in resolute opposition to the 'Asiatic' or the 'coolie' standard of living."[12] The San Francisco municipal report determined of the Chinese, "Their habits and mode of life render the cost of support less than one-fifth of that of the ordinary American laborer who exercises what is commonly recognized as the strictest rules of economy and thrift."[13] Among the tendencies that supposedly enabled the Chinese to live on so little, dietary choices emerged as key. Erika Lee notes that "Chinese immigrants' purported diet of 'rice and rats' was . . . cited as a clear sign that they had a lower standard of living, one that white working families could not (and should not) degrade themselves by accepting."[14] The California State Senate elaborated on the potential consequences of these different eating practices in "An

Address to the People of the United States upon the Evils of Chinese Immigration":

> Our laborers require meat and bread, which have been considered by us
> as necessary to that mental and bodily strength which is thought to be
> important to the citizens of a Republic which depends upon the strength
> of its people, while the Chinese require only rice, dried fish, tea, and a
> few simple vegetables. The cost of sustenance to the white is four-fold
> greater than that of the Chinese, and the wages of the whites must of ne-
> cessity be greater than the wages required by the Chinese. . . . To compete
> with the Chinese, our laborer must be entirely changed in character, in
> habits of life, in everything that the Republic has hitherto required him
> to be.[15]

The address connected eating practices to the very vitality of the nation. Dietary preferences were not simply a matter of taste, but intrinsic to the American worker's "character," and essential to fulfilling the responsibilities of a republican government. Offering its own theory of consubstantiation, the state senate located the body politic in the very meat and bread consumed by the nation's citizens. The presumed irreconcilability of "meat" and "rice" as metonyms for American and Chinese ways of living set distinct racial limits on the struggle for workers' rights by suggesting that the very "stuff" of Chinese and American labor differed.

Political addresses and government reports such as these attached the "problem" of Chinese immigration to the mundane, and their minute considerations of living habits lent their statements an ethnographic weight. Although polemic anti-immigration speeches made stronger claims about the relationship between the (racialized) body and its habits, municipal reports had the added purchase of being official, government-sanctioned studies. Moreover, their breadth in covering numerous corners of Chinatown life suggested a comprehensive examination of this community.

Yet arguments against Chinese immigration that appealed to the embodied everyday rested on an unstable base. The scrutiny of habitual behaviors, which helped to justify the exclusion acts, later became the basis for *challenging* their reliability as expressions of social distinctions. Reflecting both forceful calls to protect white workers and fears among U.S. business interests that immigration restrictions would endanger trade relations with China, the initial exclusion act forbade only Chinese laborers from entry. The limited scope of the law, however, meant that the government needed to develop a system to distinguish those who were from the exempt classes (merchants, scholars, diplomats, tourists, U.S. citizens, and immediate family members of existing residents) from those who were falsely claiming an exempt status. Adam McKeown argues that what was remarkable about these immigration restrictions was less their barring of a category of people from immigration than "their goal of sifting through migrants one by one and applying a status to each that determined his or her right to enter."[16] With paper certificates considered vulnerable to misuse and forgery, the daily enforcement of the exclusion acts relied heavily on interactions between those attempting to enter the United States and those assigned to verify the identities of these applicants.

The performance of the mundane—the physical and verbal articulation of one's habits and routines before an inquiring audience—was critical to these evaluations. Kitty Calavita emphasizes that much weight was placed on the judgment of individual enforcement agents, "in part because formal definitions could never cover the infinite variety of actual cases, but . . . largely because only those who were face to face with the applicant were thought to be capable of discerning his essential nature."[17] Identifying the "essential nature" of applicants involved looking for physical inscriptions of everyday behaviors associated with specific classes. Enforcement officials assumed, McKeown explains, that the "proper categorization of each person was not knowable through social relationships but through marks directly perceivable in the body and bearing of each individual: his mode of speaking, expression, the condition of his hands, his gait."[18] While arguments for exclusion insisted on the (stubbornly fixed) bad habits of the Chinese, enforcing the acts required a more nuanced examination of bodily tendencies as bearers of an individual's social status.

Since the initial exclusion laws were intended to filter out Chinese laborers, evaluations paid particular attention to whether or not applicants embodied distinct class markers. As Erika Lee recounts, "If [Chinese laborers] were supposed to be cheap, servile workers who competed with white workingmen, then Chinese merchants, officials rationalized, should be wealthy, educated, and refined gentlemen who posed no threat either to white labor or to American society in general."[19] Yet making such distinctions proved more difficult in practice, as everything from literacy tests to the texture of hands and feet contributed to assessments of whether an applicant was a merchant or a laborer.[20] For example, Calavita describes how calluses, along with sunburns and large joints, became an important indication that a person was a laborer because they ostensibly manifested the kind of work that occupied him on a regular basis.[21] Calluses, however, also became a point of contention in one case, in which an applicant won admission by arguing that his hands were callused because merchants in China used hammers to mark their coins.[22] However dependable physical expressions of repetitive behaviors might have seemed, enforcement agents' incomplete knowledge of the customs of different classes *in* China meant that applicants could contest the connections they made among body, habits, and identity.

Applicants who based their right to enter on their U.S. citizenship or on family relations also had to establish their identity through the mundane, namely through their familiarity with the prosaic details of the lives they claimed on paper. American citizens had to demonstrate their status partly through clothing and mannerisms that evinced their time in the United States. Despite depictions of the Chinese as resolutely unable or unwilling to assimilate, those who could show some signs of "American" habits, proficiency in English, and knowledge about the United States built a stronger case for admission.[23] Officials also attempted to confirm citizenship and kinship by asking applicants and the witnesses who came forward on their behalf questions to verify their identities. These questions often focused on the trivia of the villages in which the applicants allegedly lived, the people with whom they would have interacted, and the daily activities in which they would have engaged. They were asked, for example, to recall the number of doors, windows, or clocks in a house, the distance between landmarks, and the age and the location of neighbors.[24] These questions, like the attention paid to calluses, assumed that even if applicants could forge documents or enlist false witnesses, the truth would come out with the mundane. When convincingly articulated, such details could help them gain entry;

by contrast, the inability to demonstrate, physically and verbally, that they performed these routines and thus lived as they professed could mean that their application would be rejected.

Despite the confidence placed in the deep cognitive and physical inscriptions of the everyday, officials had access only to the applicants' narration and performance of their "paper" lives in a specific institutional context. Richard Schechner's conception of performance as "restored" or "twice-behaved" behavior is applicable here as potential entrants had to reenact their identities for immigration officials. In this setting, the fissure between the everyday and its performance opened up by the former's "restoration" enabled those who were not from exempt groups to adopt the attributes of merchants, educators, and diplomats. Once inspectors identified a set of features as signs of a particular class or occupation, applicants could attempt to replicate those same features, with more or less success. Coaching books, for example, provided detailed notes to help those who falsely claimed familial connections answer the extensive list of questions asked by officials.[25] Calavita therefore argues that "Chinese immigrants were able to exploit the contradiction between cultural assumptions about the intrinsic nature of identity and the reality of its social construction."[26] I would add that they also exploited the uncertain attachment of the mundane to the body. As I elaborated in the introduction, this ambiguity allows the mundane to bridge contradictory conceptions of identity as intrinsic and constructed.

Given the importance placed on an agent's ability to read and assess the statements and physical attributes of those attempting to enter, the determining "truth" of any case took shape in an eminently theatrical exchange between applicant and official. The embodiment of minute, habitual behaviors and the recollection of the world in which they would have been enacted needed to be convincing only to a limited audience— and for a limited time—to serve their purpose of facilitating immigration and reentry. In relying on the everyday to manifest the truth of an individual's identity, inspectors paradoxically made it available for "restored" performances and fictional recitations. Crossing national borders when one was Chinese, or suspected of being Chinese, ultimately required a persuasive performance of the mundane.

Those of Chinese descent who were already residing in the United States, were born within its borders, or managed to enter despite such arduous procedures saw some of the vehement anti-Chinese sentiments subside through the early decades of the twentieth century. According to Shah, even San Francisco's Chinatown—the subject of lurid reports in the late nineteenth century—became a "sanitized tourist destination for middle-class white families" by the late 1930s.[27] He notes that within the community, some families made an effort in the 1930s and 1940s to demonstrate their assimilation of middle-class American habits in order to show their worthiness for public assistance.[28] Furthermore, although debates continued about whether or not Chinese immigrants and their children could assimilate into American society, the tenor of such queries changed. In 1885, the special San Francisco municipal report on Chinatown had asked, "What shall we do with these Chinese children born upon our soil, though partaking in no respect of the proclivities and habits of any other known race except those of their own progenitors?"[29] In answering this question, the report rejected the idea that these children should be admitted to American public schools: while such an opportunity might indeed encourage them to adopt other (more American) proclivities and habits, it was also likely to incite "a blaze of revolution" from white parents.[30] The report nevertheless continued, "If these [Chinese American] children could be separated from their parents and scattered among our own people, away from the populous centers, the question involved would be perhaps easy of adjustment."[31] The report therefore proposed that assimilation might be possible for the children of Chinese immigrants, but only if they were taken from their communities and dispersed. The slight distinction made in the report between the children's race and the "race . . . of their own progenitors" left room for a shift in behavior between generations. Yet the report finally resigned itself to accepting that integration was implausible, and that the children were consequently doomed to replicate their parents' ways of living.

The possibility that assimilation might well take place among the descendants of Chinese immigrants received more serious consideration several decades into the era of exclusion, when the issue had lost the fiery edge of immediate political quarrels and become a subject of sustained academic inquiry. Robert Ezra Park and other sociologists trained at the University of Chicago took up the so-called Oriental problem of assimilating Asians as a major part of their investigations of race relations in the United States in the first half of the twentieth century. According to Henry Yu, "The 'Oriental problem' became an intellectual construction—a set of questions, definitions, and theories about Asian immigrants and citizens of Asian ancestry in the United States—which provided the vocabulary and the concepts for scholarly discussions about Chinese Americans and Japanese Americans between 1920 and 1960."[32] Yu argues that the "Oriental problem" bridged the Chicago sociologists' interest in the relationship between black and white Americans, and their study of immigrant assimilation.[33]

In his writings on race, Park was adamant that the children of Chinese and Japanese immigrants could indeed assimilate typically "American" behaviors and mannerisms. He argued that "the Oriental who is born in America and educated in our western schools is culturally an Occidental, even though he be racially an Oriental."[34] For Park, habits that are "conventionalized, sanctioned, and transmitted" were what comprised and continued a specific culture.[35] Thus, his contention that someone could be culturally "Occidental" and racially "Oriental" implied that habitual behaviors were not racially intrinsic, and split race from the mundane. In contrast to the claims made in the San Francisco municipal report, Park asserted in 1925, "Children do not inherit the cultural complexes of their parents and when children of immigrants grow up in the country of their adoption they inevitably take over all the accents, the inflections, the local cultural idioms of the native population. This is true of the Chinese in America, even though they are reared—as most of them are—in a ghetto. Most of the native sons among the Chinese in California are outrageously American in their manners and in their sentiments."[36] While the municipal report gloomily mused that only the dubious separation of children from their parents might lead to their assimilation, Park contended that whether or not they grew up in ethnic enclaves, the children of immigrants—even the Chinese—would adopt "the accents, the inflections, the local cultural idioms" of the country in which they were raised. Offering an example of the "outrageously American" manners of U.S.-born Chinese Americans, he asserted, "The native sons are likely to be brusque and familiar. If they enter your house at all, they use the front door, not the back."[37] Rejecting stereotypes of the Chinese as subservient (or sneaky), Park stressed the straightforward, almost defiant style of the later generations—a style characterized as quintessentially American. In both their insistence on using the front door and their nonchalance, the "native sons" declared their place in the American home.

Yet if, as Park believed, the children of Chinese immigrants were just as likely to adopt the "brusque and familiar" behaviors of Americans as other ethnic and racial groups, then the continued marginalization of people from China and Japan in the United States was a puzzle. Explaining this apparent contradiction, Park suggested that the external, physical signs of "race," which forced blacks and Asians to wear an irremovable "racial uniform,"[38] hampered the otherwise natural process of assimilation by making them *and* white Americans more conscious of their difference. He argued that "the ease and rapidity with which aliens, under existing conditions in the United States, have been able to assimilate themselves to the customs and manners of American life have enabled this country to swallow and digest every sort of normal human difference, except the purely external ones, like the color of the skin."[39] The physical traits that serve as markers of racial otherness therefore remained "indigestible," however much the immigrant incorporated "the customs and manners of American life." The flexibility of habits and conventions—what Park regarded as the vital substance of culture—collided here with the apparent fixity of corporeal features associated with different "races."

Park echoed the faith of the San Francisco municipal report in the revelatory powers of the mundane, its capacity to reflect an individual's degree of assimilation or a group's potential to assimilate, even as he rejected the idea that those of Chinese descent could not adopt American ways of living. For Park, it was the "racial uniform" worn by certain groups—and not their habitual behaviors—that imposed a limit to integration. Assessing Park's contention that the external markings of race doomed Asians to be seen as abstractions rather than as individuals, David Palumbo-Liu remarks that he "completely bypasses the socioeconomic apparatuses that perpetuate and manage racism."[40] Within the constraints of Park's analysis, however, what emerges vis-à-vis the embodied everyday is the recognition of a tension between seeing race and seeing the mundane. The question is not how closely racial identifications align with habitual behaviors, but how racial identifications shape the *perception* of habitual behaviors. The spectator therefore becomes visible as a constitutive—even determining—force in performances of the racial mundane.

Thus, during the era of Chinese exclusion from U.S. immigration, the mundane played an important role in efforts to sustain racial and national boundaries, as well as attempts to probe their permeability. Calls for immigration restrictions, interrogations of applicants for admission, and studies of those within U.S. borders after the gates were shut all propounded their own theory of the relationship among identities, physical traits, and habitual behaviors. Mannerisms and routines came to emblematize what resisted change, and thus embodied racial essences; what allowed for useful differentiations *within* racial groups; and what held the possibility of effacing difference—up to a point. Because habits seemed eminently cultural *and* physical, and their form (repeated enactments) suggested both stability and the potential for modulation, they could stand at the crossroads of opposing imperatives to uphold and contest social distinctions. For two major American plays, *The Yellow Jacket* and *Our Town*, this duality enabled experiments with theatrical form and audience perspective that concomitantly tested the fungibility of racial and national identity.

Seeing and Playing in Yellowface

Advertised as a "Chinese Drama Played in [the] Chinese Manner,"[41] J. Harry Benrimo and George C. Hazelton, Jr.'s *The Yellow Jacket* opened at the Fulton Theatre on Broadway in 1912 to enthusiastic reviews by critics who were unhappy with the naturalistic sets then dominating American theater. After a mediocre first run on Broadway, the play began a highly successful international tour, during which leading theater directors in Europe lauded the performance. Multiple Broadway revivals followed, and by the time Benrimo passed away in 1942, his obituary declared the drama "a classic of the American theater."[42]

Set in China, *The Yellow Jacket* begins with a provincial governor's fateful decision to kill his first wife and their son, Wu Hoo Git, to rid himself of the physically deformed child and elevate his second wife. The farmer charged with executing the murders secretly spares and raises Wu Hoo Git, who later pursues his birthright and the yellow jacket befitting his privileged social position.[43] Depictions of Chinese characters on the American stage were not uncommon in the nineteenth and early twentieth centuries, and ranged from spectacular portrayals of China in various productions of *Aladdin* and the Ravel family's *Kim-ka!* (1847) to plays featuring Chinese characters in the United States, which appeared after the midcentury rise in immigration.[44] The latter included Western melodramas such as Bret Harte and Mark Twain's *Ah Sin* (1876) and Chinatown plays such as Francis Powers's popular realist drama *The First Born* (1897), in which Benrimo performed. In these productions, as in *The Yellow Jacket*, white actors played Chinese characters.

The Yellow Jacket was unusual, however, in claiming to adopt the stage conventions of the Chinese opera as well as Chinese settings and characters. The conventions that it supposedly borrowed included a stage decorated with "Chinese banners," "signs of good cheer," and "huge lanterns";[45] the use of chairs, tables, cushions, sheets, and other basic properties to represent settings, actions, and objects within the dramatic plot; a visible orchestra playing cymbals and gongs; and a "Property Man" who moves about the stage during the performance to manage the set. The Property Man's tasks include providing swords to fighting characters, tossing shredded paper to represent snow, and holding a pole to represent a weeping willow. In addition, he reads a newspaper, smokes, and eats at specific moments when he is not supervising the stage. According to James Harbeck, "Reviews often spent half of their length on the staging and gave more column inches to the property man than to all other performers combined."[46] Carrying out his work with apparently little concern for whether or not he interrupted the performance, the Property Man became one of the most popular aspects of the production.

Just as debates about Chinese immigrants fueled scrutiny of their mannerisms and everyday practices, *The Yellow Jacket* invited its audiences to attend to the Property Man's smallest behaviors. Yet Benrimo and Hazelton's drama offered viewers an opportunity not simply to discern the presumed alienness of the Chinese, but also to simulate the experience of Chinese spectatorship. Even as the play reiterated notions of racial peculiarity and white normativity through theatrical devices that affirmed the estranged perspective of its European American viewers, it also encouraged spectators to see differently by seeing *as* the Chinese. The play's integration of nonrealistic "Chinese" staging with the

Property Man's realistic enactments of the mundane made it possible for its audiences to engage—alongside the actors—in provisional racial crossings. While discussions of Chinese immigration assumed that habits themselves manifested intractable racial differences or the dissipation of those differences, performances of *The Yellow Jacket* illuminated how the act of *looking* at typically unremarked behaviors could activate or undermine racial boundaries. When the drama became an international success, however, its apparent imitation of Chinese theater troubled efforts to establish it as an American creation, leading Benrimo to insist that audiences were seeing only the American invention of Chinese difference.

Despite claiming to follow Chinese theatrical practices, Benrimo and Hazelton were selective in the elements they chose to adopt for *The Yellow Jacket*. For example, the performance differed from the Chinese opera by having the actors speak, as opposed to sing, the majority of their lines.[47] The Chorus is another key divergence from its "Chinese manner." In a foreword to *The Yellow Jacket*, Benrimo and Hazelton explained that the character of the Chorus replaces signs normally used in Chinese theater to establish scenes (232). The role of the Chorus nonetheless exceeds that of a marker: as both character and guide, he explains different aspects of the performance and provides abstruse remarks and pseudo-philosophical commentary. He advises the audience with statements such as, "Observe well with your eyes and listen well with your ears. Be as one family, exceedingly happy and content. Heaven has no mouth. It makes men speak for it" (234). Such nonsensical "wisdom" and exaggerated erudition turn the Chorus into a humorous caricature of a "Chinese scholar," in a racialized adaptation of the Greek chorus. Hardly unique to *The Yellow Jacket*, the figure of the Chinese wise man has become a persistent stock type. He makes an appearance, for example, in Eugene O'Neill's 1928 drama *Marco Millions*, the Charlie Chan detective films that were popular from the 1920s to the 1940s, and a range of recent martial arts movies.

Whatever comparisons might be made between Benrimo and Hazelton's drama and the Chinese opera, *The Yellow Jacket*'s most significant distortion is the fixity it ascribes to Chinese theatrical practices and forms. Colin Mackerras notes that Chinese opera went through significant changes during the Qing dynasty (1644–1911/12), including the decline of the aristocratic *kunqua* drama, the rise of the popular regional theaters, and the increasing politicization of theater.[48] Although each enactment of *The Yellow Jacket* might have exhibited live performance's immediacy and ephemerality,[49] Benrimo and Hazelton arrested Chinese theater's diverse and changing performances into a single, comprehensively scripted show that envisioned the East as perpetually archaic. Krystyn Moon argues that the popularity of quaint images of China in the decades around the turn of the century reflected contemporary anxieties about modernization.[50] The radical transformations occurring in China, however, belied such images. A year before *The Yellow Jacket's* premiere, a major revolution began in China and eventually led to a republican government replacing the Qing dynasty. Actors were deeply engaged in these struggles, mobilizing supporters through the stage and even participating in armed missions.[51] Although the basic plot of *The Yellow Jacket* traces a regime change, the performance's static presentation of a "traditional" Chinese drama obscured the aesthetic vitality and political import of the Chinese theater during this period.

Furthermore, to the extent that Benrimo and others involved in the production of *The Yellow Jacket* were, as they claimed, inspired by Chinatown theaters in the United States, they were drawing from diasporic Chinese performances, primarily in the regional Cantonese style. These theaters were important centers of immigrant society and, according to Nancy Rao, "took an active role in defining the historical, geographical, and social positions of Chinese Americans."[52] Emerging in the mid-1800s, these immigrant theaters became popular tourist attractions in San Francisco and New York. The first Chinese theater in New York opened in 1893 but closed just a year before *The Yellow Jacket's* first run. Despite growing public interest in Chinese drama in the late nineteenth century,[53] and the importance of these performances to the immigrant community, more than a decade passed before another theater devoted to Chinese opera opened in New York.[54]

The absence of both a significant Chinese immigrant population and a Chinese theater in New York at the time of *The Yellow Jacket's* first two Broadway runs was likely crucial to the play's success. Pointing to a shift in American representations of the Chinese at the turn of the century from sly cheats to refined mandarins, Dave Williams observes that hostility toward the Chinese declined somewhat after the passage of the exclusion act.[55] Moon similarly tracks a shift from "unconditional hatred" to "fascination" prompted by the exclusion acts, the revolution in China, and the return of popular depictions of Chinese culture as (charmingly) backward.[56] If, as Robert G. Lee observed of the mid-1800s, the increasing presence and proximity of Chinese immigrants led to enmity and representations of the Chinese as menacingly alien rather than safely foreign,[57] their shrinking numbers at the turn of the century seem to have motivated a reverse movement: distanced both spatially (through the exclusion acts) and temporally (through representations of an unchanging East), the Chinese could be quaint and inspiring once more.

Not only did the physical barring of Chinese immigrants clear a space for less blatantly derogatory representations, the subsequent closure of Chinatown theaters in New York allowed *The Yellow Jacket* to open without the competing presence of stages where the property men would go about their tasks without a script stipulating indifferent behavior, and where no Chorus would explain to the audience how they should see and understand the performance. Despite the decline of Chinatown theaters before *The Yellow Jacket*'s premiere, their popularity as tourist destinations and subjects of books and articles at the end of the nineteenth century meant that Americans were not entirely unfamiliar with the kind of performance emulated by the play. Chinese opera produced primarily for Chinese spectators, however, offered a much less mediated and comfortable experience for Western audiences than *The Yellow Jacket*. In a 1903 account of a visit to a Chinese theater, for example, E. M. Green described the uneasiness of American tourists attending the performance: "A row of Americans extend on either side from the rear wall to the front of the stage. The faces of these onlookers bear that stupid expression always noticeable in people listening to a language they do not understand. The hideousness of the occidental costume is made glaringly apparent by the somber color, yet graceful lines, of the every-day dress of the old men and children who lounge about on the stage behind them and by the exceeding beauty of the costumes of the actors."[58] Whereas performances of *The Yellow Jacket* offered a space for Western audiences to observe the foreign without actually confronting the foreign bodies that might disturb the integrity of their vision of self and other, Green's account highlights the awkwardness of these encounters in less controlled spaces where Chinese spectators made little effort to ease the discomfort of tourists and could potentially return their gaze to scrutinize their expressions and clothing as inappropriate or strange.

Produced with white actors in yellowface, that is, in makeup and costumes that signal "Asianness," Broadway performances of *The Yellow Jacket* also ensured that only the semblance of Chinese bodies would appear on the stage.[59] In their respective studies of early yellowface performances, Robert G. Lee and Sean Metzger link the practice to anxieties about contamination and assimilation. Metzger, for example, argues that the use of a queue, or a braid of hair, by the actor Charles Parsloe when he played Chinese characters fixed the Chinese as indelibly different.[60] Gaining popularity during the mid-1800s, yellowface performances persisted through the twentieth century, and in the early decades became part of what Moon describes as "a more totalizing racialization on the stage": the integration of increasingly more facets of a production, including makeup, costumes, sets, and music, to represent racial otherness.[61]

Adopting "Chinese" stage conventions as well as fashions and melodies, *The Yellow Jacket* exemplified this trend of creating an integrated theatrical experience. Yet performances of the drama extended its "totalizing racialization" even further, past the stage and into the audience. With Chinese immigration no longer the heated political issue it was before the exclusion acts, the complex racial identifications activated by Benrimo and Hazelton's drama were closer to the contradictory mix that Eric Lott finds in blackface minstrelsy, where "transgression and containment coexisted."[62] *The Yellow Jacket* specifically cultivated this dynamic by encouraging spectators to conceive of themselves as yellowface *viewers*. The Property Man's casual mannerisms and execution of daily tasks were critical to enabling the audience to assume dual—but not equal—roles as white and "Chinese" spectators. In an inversion of anxieties about Chinese immigration, in which fears of becoming like the Chinese led to increased observation of the Chinese, *The Yellow Jacket* asked its audience to watch its presentation of the Chinese in order to enjoy both the possibility of being like them and the certainty of not being like them. Simply by ignoring or paying attention to the Property Man, spectators could straddle racial divides without upsetting them.

Although less blatantly comical than Bret Harte and Mark Twain's Ah Sin in the eponymously named (and much less successful) drama, the

Property Man bears some resemblance to this earlier character. Through much of Harte and Twain's frontier melodrama, Ah Sin handles objects (often pilfering them) and manages the "set" as a laundryman and domestic. For example, he spends almost the entire third act setting up a table. When asked at one point what he picked up while attending the theater, Ah Sin enters with a carpet sack and "takes out gorgeous costume and odds and ends of dramatic properties."[63] Ah Sin's display of stolen riches not only emphasizes his sticky fingers, it also calls attention to the work of moving stage properties that preoccupies him throughout the play. Usually at the edges of dramatic action, Ah Sin observes more than he participates, except when managing objects. This initially peripheral role enables Ah Sin to prove a man's innocence at the end of the play—despite being unable to testify in court—by displaying a bloody jacket that he had stashed away.

The Property Man also occupies a liminal position in *The Yellow Jacket*, one that similarly involves keeping an eye on the play and moving properties around, sometimes with comic as well as practical effects. Ah Sin's marginal status, however, is explicitly connected to racial discrimination, which limits the kinds of occupations available to him, forbids his legal testimony, and prevents him from forming more substantial relationships with other characters. Harte and Twain depict those who treat Ah Sin harshly as unsympathetic, yet they also characterize Ah Sin as imitative and hapless through his relentless collection and mishandling of objects. Ah Sin's performances of the mundane therefore serve to perpetuate as well as critique stereotypes of Chinese immigrants common in the late nineteenth century. In *The Yellow Jacket*, by contrast, the Property Man's exact activities while managing the set or taking a break are less important than their presentation in full view of spectators who understand that they should not be seeing these activities—whether because of Western dramatic conventions that hide them, or Chinese dramatic conventions that assume the audience will ignore them. Although activities such as using chopsticks and perusing a Chinese-language newspaper help to indicate the Property Man's difference from the audience, his apparent disinterest in viewers while eating and reading enables the audience's *interested* gaze to affirm their distance from the culture depicted on the stage and from the Chinese theatergoers invoked by the performance—even as they occasionally come to identify with these other (imagined) spectators.

In its presentation of the "Chinese theater," *The Yellow Jacket* explicitly addresses viewers who would find the performance mystifying. For example, it makes frequent references to the audience's inability to understand the conventions and narrative traditions of Chinese drama. The performance opens with the Property Man "enter[ing] indifferently from the opening at center of curtain, strik[ing] thrice on a gong and exit[ing]" (233). The Chorus then addresses the audience, introducing the play and warning, "Much of our acting will be strange" (233). In declaring that the performance will *be* strange, as opposed to suggesting that it may *seem* strange, the Chorus accepts as normative the perception of those who *do* find it strange. He then continues to remind audience members of their estrangement from the culture presented on the stage by offering explanations and lofty soliloquies. In similar fashion, Wu Hoo Git's father Wu Sin Yin, who is the first character of the enacted narrative to speak, explains, "I am the most important personage in this play. Therefore, I address you first. By your gracious leave, with many apologies, I will state in all modesty, for your edification only, for of course I know who I am and how great and august I am, while you are not so favored, that I am Wu Sin Yin, the Great" (235). In convoluted language, Wu Sin Yin, like the Chorus, speaks directly to the audience and takes for granted their lack of familiarity with the performance.

Consequently, although *The Yellow Jacket* implies two possible audiences, Chinese spectators who would have assimilated its conventions as the norm and Western spectators who would find them strange and incomprehensible, it assumes that the latter constitutes the actual viewership of the performance. Erika Fischer-Lichte observes that "the performance does not presuppose the existence of a 'natural' bond between perception and meaning as established by a common, generally accepted discourse or an effective theatrical norm such as, for example, that of realistic theatre."[64] Yet even as *The Yellow Jacket* defamiliarizes discursive and theatrical norms by deviating from established conventions, the overt acknowledgment of a disjuncture between the assumed (Western) audience's perceptual habits and those of imagined Chinese theatergoers also affirms the former's disorientation as natural and encourages a sense of tangible cultural difference.

While less explicit than the Chorus or Wu Sin Yin's remarks to the audience, the Property Man's performance of the mundane helps foster an alienated perspective of Chinese theater. The Chorus informs the audience early in the play, "Ere departing my footsteps hence, let me impress upon you that my property man is to your eyes intensely invisible" (234). The Chorus thus instructs viewers on how to see the character's behaviors "properly," that is, as an audience accustomed to the Chinese opera might. Yet in asserting the invisibility of the Property Man, the Chorus only effects the opposite, highlighting his visibility and the peculiarity of the convention, which he must clarify for the audience. As Dave Williams argues in his reading of *The Yellow Jacket*, "[Chinese theatrical] conventions, wrenched from their theatrical and cultural context, do not fit organically into the performance as they would in a Chinese theatre. Instead, they become quaint distractions from the story, the exact opposite of their original function."[65] Whereas a similar "property man" in the kind of Chinatown theater presumably visited by Benrimo would have a purely practical role managing the stage and would not be considered part of the performance itself, Benrimo and Hazelton scripted, in great detail, the behaviors and mannerisms of *The Yellow Jacket*'s Property Man. Their stage directions, as I mentioned above, not only call for the Property Man to arrange the set, but also direct him to smoke, read a newspaper, hurt himself accidentally, eat a bowl of rice with chopsticks, and put a cushion in the wrong place before fixing his mistake; they even specify his attitude, mainly "indifferent" (233) or "complacent" (234) (Figure 1.1). Performances of *The Yellow Jacket* therefore do not simply *use* Chinese stage conventions; instead, they *mimic* the application of these conventions, reenacting—and continually reproducing—a specific staging of a "Chinese drama."

The Property Man's enactment of the mundane, however, generates a sense of intimacy as well as difference between the performance and the audience. As a carefully scripted impersonation, the Property Man is, at once, the most stylized and the most ethnographic aspect of the play. Replicating minor mannerisms, habits, and even "mistakes," the actor relies on the mundane to imbue his performance with an air of authenticity. In other words, the apparent banality of his performance reinforces its realism. An article on Arthur Shaw, who originated the role, stressed the skill required to play the part faithfully: "For two hours

Figure 1.1. The Property Man, Wu Sin Yin, and Tai Fah Min, the father of Wu Sin Yin's second wife. *Scenes from the Play Called The Yellow Jacket by George C. Hazelton and Benrimo.* Photograph by Arnold Genthe. Courtesy of the Library of Congress, Prints & Photographs Division, Arnold Genthe Collection: Negatives and Transparencies.

and a half this property man moves among the actors as though invisible to them and to the spectators. The slightest bit of overplaying, the least stooping to buffoonery, the merest suggestion of theatricals on his part would ruin his impersonation and mar the whole play."[66] The writer thus emphasized that the actor must convey the impression that he is an actual property man as opposed to a scripted character. Shaw reiterated this point when he explained why his part was more difficult than it appeared: "Suppose I took a notion to get interested in somebody out in the audience! Can't you see how quickly the whole illusion would blow up! Or even suppose that I became excited about the play or anything save my work as a property man, can't you imagine how soon I'd be fired? . . . I don't dare do anything except loll around and pretend to do nothing in a nonchalant, lackadaisical, celestial way. But in reality I am working all the time."[67] Referring to his work as an "illusion" that he must carefully maintain, down to the "nonchalant, lackadaisical" attitude assumed to be the natural manner of the Chinese or "celestial," Shaw explained that his performance had to seem unaffected in order to replicate the experience of Chinese theaters and offer the audience an "authentic" presentation.

The Property Man's apparently indifferent execution of and occasional deviations from his duties therefore heighten the sense that the audience is witnessing a realistic representation of Chinese drama. In doing so, the performance generates two—ostensibly opposing—effects. On the one hand, it accentuates a divide between viewers who would be equally indifferent to the Property Man, and those who would find his behaviors the most fascinating aspect of the production. In reviews of the play, writers stressed this difference in perception, reiterating that Chinese audiences familiar with the theatrical conventions replicated in *The Yellow Jacket* would not see them as strange or comic. Reflecting on the drama's first production on Broadway, the *New York Times* explained, "[The Property Man's] menial assistants are supposed to follow him in sublime invisibleness. And the effect, to our eyes, should be merely amusing, whereas to the Celestial it is all taken in deadly earnest."[68] Watching the Property Man doze off or apathetically kick away a prop, Broadway audiences could take pleasure in seeing what would remain "unseen" to a Chinese viewer habituated to such conventions. While the very banality of the Property Man's behaviors augments the play's claim to ethnographic verisimilitude, their careful replication every night before curious audiences makes his enactments of the mundane notable, as opposed to ordinary. The performance's double movement of implying the "naturalness" of the Property Man's behavior to Chinese spectators and affirming its strangeness to Western audiences therefore materializes racial particularity as a way of *seeing*, as well as a way of being.

On the other hand, even as performances of *The Yellow Jacket* promoted a sense of racial difference, they also allowed viewers to dabble with the prospect of looking differently (without looking different). The accounts of theater critics who attended the 1912 and 1916 productions on Broadway suggest that they vacillated between identifying with and distancing themselves from the enacted drama. Clayton Hamilton asserted in the *Bookman*, "They [the play's producers] have invited their American audience to laugh at these [Chinese theatrical] conventions;

and they have forced their audience, by this very act of laughing at them, to grow so familiar with the Chinese conventions as to accept them ultimately as media for the expression of delicate poetry and poignant pathos."[69] In Hamilton's assessment, the performance both affirmed the audience's view of Chinese culture as strange *and* allowed theatergoers to "grow so familiar" with its conventions that they were able to appreciate the drama's compelling qualities. In other words, the audience ultimately came to assume the perspective of Chinese spectators habituated to such performances. Alexander Woollcott similarly observed in the *New York Times* that *The Yellow Jacket*, then in its first revival, allowed for both amusement and absorption: "The curious thing about this Celestial drama is that we are augustly asked not merely to accept the conventions but to be amused by them at the same time. And it is the amazing thing about 'The Yellow Jacket' that entering into the spirit of the adventure, we do just this. We not only laugh delightedly at the detached boredom of the efficient property man and the comic insufficiency of his snowstorm, but we follow with bated breath the humiliation of the Daffodil and submit utterly to the unforgettable enchantment of the languorous flower boat."[70] According to these critics, audience members experienced *The Yellow Jacket* as an American *and* a Chinese spectator, the former laughing at the strange conventions and the latter engrossed by the dramatized narrative. In these performances, Woollcott's bored and efficient Property Man served as a crucial interface between the stage and the seats, and between Western spectators and "Chinese" ones. Circulating between the "real" world of his daily labor and the "imagined" world of Wu Hoo Git, the Property Man moved in and out of the audience's center of vision, and through these partial appearances and disappearances, facilitated the viewer's shifts between different modes of spectatorship.

These performances of *The Yellow Jacket* therefore enabled white American audiences to see the Chinese and to see *as* the Chinese, simulating a racial crossing while making unnecessary the presence of anyone who might be Chinese. The yellowface of the actors onstage found its reflection in the yellowface of the audience members as they imaginatively inhabited the spectatorial position of the other without sacrificing a distanced perspective. The performance could therefore safely transmute anxieties about becoming like the Chinese, which had prevailed during debates about immigration at the turn of the century, into the pleasures of temporary racial masquerade.

Yet while *The Yellow Jacket* allowed Broadway audiences to delight in the possibility of trying on Chinese spectatorship, its success abroad led its creators and supporters to obscure their initial endorsement of the performance as an authentic portrayal of the Chinese theater. Instead, they moved to establish it as an exclusively American contribution to modern theater by diminishing its debt—however loose the borrowing—to Chinese performances. The play's partial replication of the Chinese theater, which initially lent it the impression of authenticity, later allowed Benrimo to claim that it actually evinced a calculated *inauthenticity*. Much like the Chorus's insistence on the "invisibility" of the Property Man who is clearly present to the audience, the playwright's claim in a 1928 *New York Times* article that "'The Yellow Jacket' is not a Chinese play" asked that the public blind itself to the production's imitation of the Chinese theater.[71]

The Yellow Jacket's success in the United States presents the puzzle of how a play first advertised as a "Chinese drama" became heralded as "a classic of the American theater"[72]—particularly in an era when immigration exclusions enforced strict boundaries between "Chinese" and "American." Illustrating how social and aesthetic distinctions emerge and shift in relation to each other, the drama's ultimately short-lived transformation from amusing Chinese spectacle to modern American masterpiece reflects its flexible participation in contemporary debates about theatrical realism and experimentation, popular culture and high art, and acceptable and unacceptable "foreignness." Although *The Yellow Jacket* straddled apparently conflicting cultural categories, it did not subvert existing binaries so much as act as a kind of filter, initiating negotiations of what could cross certain lines and what could not. In particular, dual conceptions of Asian peoples and cultures as objects of curiosity and sources of aesthetic inspiration enabled *The Yellow Jacket* to appeal to predilections for both ethnographic voyeurism and avant-garde experimentation. The Property Man, as a purportedly authentic impersonation of similar figures in Chinese theaters *and* a deviation from Western dramatic conventions, was vital to accommodating the play's multiple identities.

By the early twentieth century, the use of "illusionistic" stage sets that strove to replicate real milieus had reached its height in the United States, particularly in the hands of director David Belasco. By the time of *The Yellow Jacket*'s premiere, however, a backlash had developed. For example, in July 1912, Clayton Hamilton attacked Belasco's sets as distracting, expensive, and unimaginative.[73] The complaint against Belasco was just one among many directed at American theater during this period by critics who lamented the emphasis on entertainment and novelty over aesthetic development. In an article titled "What Is Wrong with the American Drama?" which appeared between *The Yellow Jacket*'s first two Broadway runs, Hamilton argued that the American public's taste for invention was incompatible with the cultivation of profound and imaginative plays.[74]

Much of the initial publicity surrounding *The Yellow Jacket* suggested that it would feed rather than correct the tendencies in American theater deplored by critics. Advertisements for the production proclaimed that it was "The Laughing Novelty"[75] and "The Sensational Novelty of the Year!!"[76] Articles on the play reiterated this point with headlines identifying it as "Something New and Strange in Drama."[77] A review printed immediately after the 1912 Broadway opening enthused,

It has been a long time since Broadway has seen anything as quaintly entertaining as "The Yellow Jacket," shown for the first time at the Fulton Theatre yesterday afternoon. The play aims to present the drama of the Chinese in a manner intelligible and attractive to our audiences and it succeeds most admirably in its purpose. For besides reflecting a very great deal of charm and sentiment it contains no end of good fun. In fact, the first audience alternated between loud laughter at its grotesquerie and hushed awe at those portions of the play which developed the more serious motives.[78]

Characterizing the play as "quaintly entertaining" and providing "no end of good fun," the article stressed the popular appeal of the production. The audience's enjoyment, it further explained, was enhanced by its shifts between "loud laughter" and "hushed awe"—in other words, by its vacillations between alienation and engrossment.

Describing *The Yellow Jacket* as novel and entertaining, advertisements and reviews focused on the very traits that Hamilton would decry in "What Is Wrong with the American Drama?" Yet Hamilton himself was an admirer of *The Yellow Jacket* and raved, "*The Yellow Jacket*, on the other hand, deserves to be recorded as the most remarkable artistic achievement of the present season. This is a veritable Chinese play devised and written and produced by Mr. J. Harry Benrimo and Mr. George C. Hazelton Jr. . . . To achieve such an eloquent effect as this by means so primitive and childish is a scarcely precedented triumph of theatric art; and the critic can merely toss his hat aloft in praise of the imaginative prowess of Mr. Benrimo and Mr. Hazelton."[79] Hamilton clearly placed *The Yellow Jacket* in the category of the truly "artistic" and "imaginative," as opposed to the simply entertaining. His glowing response is not surprising, however, given his attack on Belasco. Praise of *The Yellow Jacket* could imply or explicitly include a jab at illusionism. A *New York Times* article on the play remarked, "Modern producers, on the other hand, paint it all and leave nothing to the imagination. Which is not flattering to the audience."[80] *The Yellow Jacket* provided these critics with an opportunity to vent their frustrations with existing theatrical practices while suggesting new paths for American drama: Belasco's realism was outdated, and American theater now needed drama that excited—even demanded—the audience's imagination.

The Yellow Jacket's "novelty" thus merged popular entertainment and artistic innovation: critics could latch onto it for its creative use of non-Western theatrical conventions, while the general public could enjoy its "strangeness" and "quaintness." The drama could feasibly occupy both roles because even as it seemed to reject verisimilitude in its staging, it asserted an overarching realism in its representation of Chinese culture. As Fischer-Lichte points out, the performance is invested in maintaining an "illusion of reality," "But in this case, the illusion of reality is proclaimed to be the reality of *another* stage: the Chinese stage."[81] Although *The Yellow Jacket* employs "nonrealistic" devices and staging, its basic conceit is that its spectators are watching a realistic representation of a Chinese drama. However unfamiliar and stylized the conventions deployed, the double framing of the play as both an imaginative representation of the dramatic narrative and an accurate reproduction of

Chinese theater allowed it to lay claim to both aesthetic experimentation and ethnographic fidelity.

While Hamilton might have appreciated *The Yellow Jacket*'s metatheatrical conventions, he nevertheless understood it as a faithful depiction of the Chinese theater, referring to *The Yellow Jacket* as "a veritable Chinese play" and explaining, "It may probably be stated as a fact that Mr. Benrimo knows more about the Chinese stage than any other American today. It occurred to him that it would be interesting to devise a play out of the traditional materials of the Chinese theatre and to present it precisely in accordance with the conventions of the Chinese stage."[82] Hamilton thus embraced the play's "precise" reproduction of Chinese theater, if not the meticulous details of Belasco's sets. The preview article in the *New York Times* similarly underscored the "authenticity" of its representation, from its adaptation of "several real Chinese dramas" to efforts by the actors "as far as possible . . . to duplicate the methods of Chinese performers."[83] *Current Opinion* claimed that "Mr. Benrimo's observations of the Chinese theater in San Francisco have enabled him to steep his pen in realism."[84] Stressing that the performance exemplified an ethnographic, if not dramatic, realism, reviews of and advertisements for the original production advanced a distinct mode of looking at the performance: namely, as an authentic representation of the Chinese theater.

Although the play's initial New York run was too short for any specific understanding of its significance to concretize, its European tour and subsequent revivals in the United States established it as an important work of modern American drama. *The Yellow Jacket*'s international tour began when Benrimo took the play to London after a critically lauded but financially unsuccessful production on Broadway. Max Reinhardt's subsequent decision to produce it at his Berlin theater and Konstantin Stanislavski's sponsorship in Moscow secured its new reputation at home as an exceptional American play embraced by major theater artists. Productions in Madrid, Vienna, and Budapest followed performances in major German and Russian cities, leading the *New York Times* to dub *The Yellow Jacket* the "Play That Went Round the World."[85] Returning to Broadway for a short run in 1916, it achieved the domestic success that its supporters thought it had deserved the first time around.[86] Attesting to the drama's continued popularity, additional revivals followed in 1921, 1928, 1934, and 1941.[87]

Given that European theater artists such as Reinhardt, Jacques Copeau, and Edward Gordon Craig, among others, espoused an interest in Asian theater that preceded *The Yellow Jacket*,[88] their enthusiasm for the play is unsurprising. In the early twentieth century, directors in Europe developed stylized theatrical productions and simplified stages that drew inspiration from a range of performance traditions, including the English Renaissance stage, Greek theater, Chinese opera, and Japanese *noh* and *kabuki*. Arthur Feinsod recounts that these developments in European theater gradually made their way across the Atlantic and began to have an impact on American artists and critics around the time of *The Yellow Jacket*'s opening in 1912.[89] The early twentieth century was, more broadly, a time of burgeoning intercultural exchanges in theatrical performance. The Kawakami Theatre Troupe from Japan toured the United States and Europe from 1899 to 1902, attracting the interest of English actors Henry Irving and Ellen Terry, as well as Paris-based dancer-choreographer Loie Fuller. Peking opera star Mei Lanfang similarly made celebrated international trips in the 1930s, and Bertolt Brecht drew from Mei's performance to explain his theory of the alienation effect. W. B. Yeats wrote a *noh*-inspired drama, *At the Hawk's Well* (1916), which his collaborator Michio Ito brought to the United States,[90] and Antonin Artaud found inspiration for his theater of cruelty in Balinese performance. Artists in Asia adapted and produced realist plays, developing *shingeki* in Japan and *huaju* in China.

The attention that *The Yellow Jacket* received while abroad, however predictable in this context, further validated the praise it received from domestic critics as a welcome departure from existing practices in American theater. As the first American play to receive such a widespread and favorable response in Europe,[91] *The Yellow Jacket* seemed to represent a possible turning point in American drama—its emergence from the shallowness of second-class entertainment to establish itself as a national art that deserved international recognition. Yet the play needed to shed its old clothes as an entertaining novelty and authentic imitation in order to assume this new role. Its evocation of Chinese "otherness" presented a particular challenge to its assimilation into a nascent American dramatic canon.

Praise of *The Yellow Jacket* as an accurate depiction of Chinese theater could imply that it was an uncreative imitation, a characterization made even less desirable by its supposed representation of Chinese, rather than European, theater. According to Jack Tchen, by the time of the Chinese exclusion acts, the "American imitation and emulation of Chinese luxuries" evident in colonial times had been replaced by its opposite: "With the rise of a destined sense of American civilization, the Chinese were cast as the embodiment of slavish imitators— the opposite of the free and happy Americans."[92] Despite the play's self-declared replication of the Chinese theater, which would seem to belie stereotypes of the derivative Chinese and the inventive American, an article in the *New York Times* on *The Yellow Jacket's* return to Broadway reveals a striking resistance to seeing China as a source of inspiration:

This tardy appreciation of a beautiful example of native dramatic literature will be seized as capital by those who love to proclaim that America is a nation of imitators, incapable of appreciating its own art until it bears the stamp of alien approval. In this case they will be wrong, for the circumstances are misleading. It is probably true that the mass of theatergoers is ignorant of the wide popularity of "The Yellow Jacket," and that the true explanation of the belated enthusiasm is that it arrived four years before its time—before the leaven of the new stage movement had begun its upheaval of the native stage.[93]

Given the play's elaborate presentation of a "Chinese drama," the author's prediction that its success would lend credence to claims that the United States is "a nation of imitators" would seem to allude to its "Chinese" story and staging. Yet the subsequent reference to the "stamp of alien approval" reveals that the alleged imitation is not of Chinese but *European* theater practitioners, those who enthusiastically endorsed the play after its modest first run on Broadway. Emphatically claiming *The Yellow Jacket* as a "native" creation, the writer does not consider the possibility that its apparent reproduction of a Chinese performance would also confirm accusations of American mimicry.

The refusal of such writers, at the height of *The Yellow Jacket's* success, to acknowledge that the drama owed much to an appropriation of

Chinese theater fits into the tradition of "American orientalisms," identified by Tchen, which "began with some admiration or fascination for an actual Chinese thing, idea, or person, then went through a phase of emulation and mimesis, and ended with European American mastery and dominance."[94] Although the temporary incorporation of *The Yellow Jacket* into the ranks of important American plays might seem to suggest a broadening of cultural borders to encompass Chinese influences, efforts to establish it as an expressly American contribution to modern theater revealed instead that its "emulation and mimesis" of Chinese opera became a problematic point necessitating a complicated set of circumventions and erasures.

The performance's success in Europe indeed led to a refigured understanding of its "Chinese" and "American" elements, with the former relegated to the less significant decorative or "atmospheric" aspects of the play. Celebrating *The Yellow Jacket*'s international success, one article explained, "Reinhardt, that German magician of stage effects, snapped it up for Berlin soon after it swam into the astonished and delighted ken of American playgoers, and a young Frenchman fixed it up for Paris, and then Spaniards seized upon it, this 'Yellow Jacket' of American parentage, Chinese trappings, and cosmopolitan appeal, and introduced it to Madrid and later to many cities of Spain and Spanish America."[95] According to this account, the superficial "trappings" of the play may be Chinese, but its "parentage" is American. Similarly, in welcoming the drama back to Broadway in 1916, Woollcott characterized it as "a Chinese play, wrought *somewhat* in the Chinese way" (emphasis added), simultaneously identifying it as Chinese and casting doubt on that very identification. He elaborated, "But here is an additional aesthetic pleasure—the pleasure some of us always feel in the deliberate recapture for the moment of some ancient or alien accent, a pleasure we feel in our innocence whether the re-creation be authentic or not. It is authentic enough for our purposes."[96] In contrast to the emphasis placed on *The Yellow Jacket*'s ethnographic realism during its first run, Woollcott's review of its revival dismissed questions of authenticity, and suggested instead that the drama's aesthetic merit lay in the authors' active reworking of the mere "accent" or inflection of a foreign culture.

Assessing the accuracy of the play's representation became entirely moot when Benrimo later declared in the *New York Times*, "'The Yellow Jacket' is not a Chinese play."[97] Benrimo's article, which appeared in 1928, on the occasion of the drama's second New York revival, was titled "Legend and Truth: The Facts about 'The Yellow Jacket,' Again in Revival Here."[98] Benrimo explained,

> We borrowed not so much from the Oriental theatre as from the Chinese philosophy of life. In looking for a plot that would lend itself to Chinese treatment, we hit upon the underlying theme of "Pilgrim's Progress," substituting Chinese morality for that of Puritan England. In other words, we carried a boy from the cradle to the grave in a fashion plausible to the Occidental mind, and yet developed the tale in an Oriental atmosphere. We made use of Chinese imagery, symbolism and morality, but the basic vitality of the play was American. It is not a translation nor an adaptation, only clothed in Chinese garments.[99]

The "truth" about *The Yellow Jacket*, according to Benrimo, was that it was an American play, not a Chinese one. Despite repeated descriptions of the work as a translation of three Chinese dramas in newspapers and magazines sixteen years earlier, Benrimo insisted here that the origin of its plot was European American and specifically aligned it with the English *Pilgrim's Progress*. Meanwhile, he relegated the "Chinese" aspects of the play to the superficial "garments" surrounding a core of American "vitality." Locating his successful drama in an Anglo-American literary tradition, Benrimo assumed—and reaffirmed—the irreconcilability of Chinese and American.

Insisting that the play was American and not Chinese, however, also required that Benrimo admit to fraud. In the article, he acknowledged, "I am not, in the second place, a Chinese scholar. The legend that I am, like that which created the impression that 'The Yellow Jacket' was a translation from the Chinese, was the invention of the press department sixteen years ago. My collaborator, George C. Hazelton, wasn't a very good showman and refused to pretend that he knew Chinese. So the responsibility fell on me."[100] With this confession, Benrimo invalidated much of the publicity surrounding the play and made endorsements of his expertise (like Hamilton's statement that "Mr. Benrimo knows more about the Chinese stage than any other American today") seem ridiculous in retrospect.[101] Thus, in a head-spinning disappearing act,

Benrimo attempted to erase from the drama all substantial traces of "Chineseness" by stating that they were never actually there.

Extending the praise that critics bestowed on *The Yellow Jacket* for asking viewers to use their imaginative capacity, Benrimo claimed that the entire production was, for the playwrights as well, an exercise in invention. Characterizing the Chinese elements of the play as "trappings" and "garments," or in terms of an "ancient or alien accent" that is authentic "enough," both Benrimo and admirers of his drama pushed to dissolve the performance's presumed referent. Whether or not this affected how most theatergoers regarded *The Yellow Jacket* is difficult to establish, although Benrimo's decision to publish his "confession" suggests that the prevailing view then was that it was a Chinese drama. Furthermore, even Benrimo's overt attempt to change public perception may not have affected how audiences *experienced* the performance: as Woollcott's 1916 article on the Broadway revival makes clear, recognizing that *The Yellow Jacket* does not accurately represent Chinese theater does not necessarily deprive the audience of a pleasure that comes from the impression or "accent" of authenticity.

Few critics today would dispute the accuracy of Benrimo's claim that the play is more American invention than careful imitation. Yet I would also propose that insofar as the Property Man joins two definitions of performance—"doing" and "representing"—his onstage activities obstinately resist dissipation as the mere flavor or inflection of Chinese theatrical practices. However scripted and rehearsed his handling of the stage, the Property Man must manage the objects that prompt the audience and the actors to "see" a snowstorm or a weeping willow. In other words, in addition to his work as an actor, he must actually do some of the work of property men, and this work is what enables the rest of the performance to exercise—or be an exercise of—the American imagination. Whether or not the Property Man faithfully replicates those who manage the stage in Chinese theaters, his "doing" of common tasks connects them not through mimesis, but through practice. In this sense, Arthur Shaw was correct in remarking about his role as the Property Man, "I am working all the time."[102] In the slippage between representation and practice, playing a role and working a job, the Property Man bears a material affinity—albeit one that is always transient and partial—with the property men whom he evokes. Shades of the mundane Chinese body linger on the stage, even when distorted to serve as an effect of American ingenuity: they emerge not in the play's exotic accoutrements or in the Property Man's humorous "Celestial" expressions, but in those (never fully registered) moments of the performance when he is simply unrecognized labor.

The story of the "Play That Went Round the World" might be encapsulated as a chronicle of travels taken, imagined, and forbidden. In its treks from New York to Moscow and back, *The Yellow Jacket* also moved (if always partially) from amusement to art, authentic to fake, Chinese to American, while serving as a medium through which actors and audiences could try on racial otherness (and Benrimo could try on the hats of expert and fraud). Yet the play's mobility stands in contrast to its static portrayal of China as a distant, unchanging world, as well as the contemporaneous barring and segregation of immigrants from China. In a final twist, however, *The Yellow Jacket* lost much of its vitality after the mid-twentieth century, slipping out of the ranks of prominent American plays. Meanwhile, post–World War II changes to U.S. immigration policy overturned restrictions on Asian immigration. Despite the play's many circulations, its depiction of Chinese theater, which in hindsight practically solicits critique as an Orientalist caricature, might well preserve it as a fascinating object for analysis, but makes unlikely future travels as an enduring theatrical production.

The Mundane and the Metaphysical: Defining the Borders of "Our Town"

Despite *The Yellow Jacket*'s ultimate failure to live up to the eminent status bestowed upon it after its travels abroad, Feinsod observes that the play had an impact on subsequent dramatic works in the United States, as comparable staging practices are evident in productions that appeared between 1912 and 1922.[103] Thornton Wilder's use of similar conventions in *Our Town*, which opened in 1938, did not go unnoticed by contemporary writers. Wilella Waldorf of the *New York Post* commented that the staging reminded her specifically of *The Yellow Jacket*.[104] This connection would not have been a dubious one to make as Wilder had apparently read *The Yellow Jacket* at a young age.[105] He also attended

Mei Lanfang's performance in New York in 1930,[106] and was generally familiar with Chinese and Japanese theatrical practices.

Arguments for *The Yellow Jacket*'s exact influence on *Our Town* remain speculative, but the similarities between the two plays suggest, at the very least, that they drew from the same dramatic conventions attributed to the Chinese opera. Parallels include the lack of scenery, basic props serving multiple functions, the use of pantomime to indicate invisible objects, and analogous metatheatrical characters. Uniting the Property Man and the Chorus in one role, *Our Town*'s Stage Manager sets up scenes, moves props, and speaks directly to the audience about the performance. Echoing Benrimo and Hazelton's scripting of the Property Man's behaviors, Wilder stipulates in his stage directions that as the audience arrives, it should see the Stage Manager, "hat on and pipe in mouth" (3), placing chairs and tables about the empty stage. While the Stage Manager does not begin eating or dozing off like the Property Man, *Our Town* also presents him as a character with one foot in the real world of the audience. Critics immediately linked the Stage Manager to Chinese theatrical practices, and one even referred to him as "a sort of idealization of the Chinese prop man."[107] Reminiscent of responses to *The Yellow Jacket*, articles and reviews from the first year of productions mention the play's novel and strange staging, and praise the imagination of those who put on the drama as well as the imagination that it demands of its audience.[108]

Although *The Yellow Jacket* and *Our Town* both draw attention to the mundane through nonrealistic theatrical conventions, they establish markedly different relationships with the audience through their staging of routine behaviors. Productions of *The Yellow Jacket*, as we have seen, accentuated the audience's sense of estrangement from the culture onstage even as they facilitated a temporary crossing over into otherness by encouraging viewers to assume the "yellowface" of Chinese spectators. Wilder's drama, by contrast, explicitly projects a sense of affiliation between the spectators and "our town." It does not so much entice crossings as assume commonalities. Yet this assumption can become a point of friction, however, when articulated through performances of the mundane. If, as the playwright claimed,[109] *Our Town* lacks conventional dramatic conflict, its attempt to stage "the largest dimensions of time and place"[110] through the everyday sets a different kind of conflict at its center: namely, a struggle between an aspiration toward universality and the resistance of the mundane.

Although critics have remarked from *Our Town*'s earliest productions that Wilder took inspiration from Chinese theatrical conventions,[111] the play's use of these elements to stage life in a New England village in the early twentieth century (1901–13) meant that, unlike with *The Yellow Jacket*, its supporters did not have to defend or deny the authenticity of its representation in relation to Chinese culture or society. Instead, the fidelity of its portrayal of small-town America has become a major point of contention. In contrast to *The Yellow Jacket*'s melodramatic tale of a hero seeking his birthright, *Our Town* examines "Daily Life," "Love and Marriage," and "Death," as its acts are titled, in a New Hampshire community. Whereas a desire to claim *The Yellow Jacket* as an unequivocally American play compelled Benrimo to admit to fraud, *Our Town* has acquired such a prevalent reputation as a sentimental depiction of a certain kind of American way of living that those who seek to defend the play's critical value have felt it necessary to challenge this characterization. Responding to both reproachful and approving readings of the drama as a nostalgic affirmation of middle-class American values, Nancy Bunge argues that the play reflects "an anti-nostalgia for specificity in favor of a plea for a universal, shared understanding that erases borders and barriers, physical or mental."[112] Similarly, observing that a major anthology of American drama excluded *Our Town*, Christopher J. Wheatley admonishes the editors for missing Wilder's intentions, which were not to represent small-town America, but to signify the universal.[113]

Wilder himself acknowledged that his drama was sentimental and accounted for this quality by explaining that it presented a retrospective (and thus especially rosy) view of the time and place in which it is set.[114] Yet he was also quite explicit about his broader ambitions for the play. He explains in his preface to *Three Plays*, "*Our Town* is not offered as a picture of life in a New Hampshire village; or as a speculation about the conditions of life after death. . . . It is an attempt to find value above all price for the smallest events in our daily life. I have made the claim as preposterous as possible, for I have set the village against the largest dimensions of time and place."[115] While he avows, as Bunge and Wheatley insist, that the play has universal aspirations, he also emphasizes his interest in the relationship *between* the quotidian and the cosmic, the "smallest events in our daily life" and the "largest dimensions of time and place." He develops this idea in his preface to *Our Town*, in which he shares the questions that informed his writing of the play: "What is the relation between the countless 'unimportant' details of our daily life, on the one hand, and the great perspectives of time, social history, current religious ideas, on the other?/What is trivial and what is significant about any one person's making a breakfast, engaging in a domestic quarrel, in a 'love scene,' in dying?"[116] Wilder suggests that the attention given in the play to the routine happenings of Grover's Corners reflects a desire not to represent a specific space and time, but to situate the mundane in a larger historical and philosophical context. Paul Lifton states, "Wilder's entire dramatic vision is in fact suspended between the individual and the universal, the particular and the general, the trivial and the cosmic."[117]

Young Rebecca Gibbs explicitly articulates this dramatic vision in *Our Town* when she tells her brother George that a letter addressed to "Jane Crofut; The Crofut Farm; Grover's Corners; Sutton County; New Hampshire; United States of America; Continent of North America; Western Hemisphere; the Earth; the Solar System; the Universe; the Mind of God" (46) nevertheless made its way to the addressee. The Stage Manager also frequently calls attention to the broader implications of events—large and small—that take place in Grover's Corners; for example, he remarks before the marriage scene, "The real hero of this scene isn't on the stage at all, and you know who it is. It's like what one of those European fellas said: Every child born into the world is nature's attempt to make a perfect human being. . . . And don't forget all the other witnesses at this wedding,—the ancestors. Millions of them" (75). The Stage Manager therefore directs the audience to consider the wider temporal and spatial dimensions of these events.

The bare stage and the lack of properties are integral to how the play joins the trivial and the significant. Aside from a few chairs and tables and two arched trellises, the rest of the scenery and objects in the performance are imaginary, either described by the Stage Manager or inferred by the behavior of the characters, such as Joe Crowell "hurling imaginary newspapers into doorways" (8) or Howie Newsome "walking beside an invisible horse and wagon and carrying an imaginary rack with milk bottles" (10). In the preface to *Our Town*, Wilder relates, "I tried to restore significance to the small details of life by removing scenery. The spectator through lending his imagination to the action restages it inside his own head."[118] Wilder suggests that by forcing the viewer to envision the missing props, the play lends a gravity to the "small details of life" that often go unnoticed. Yet in the preface to *Three Plays*, he claims that he removed the remaining chairs and tables in the kitchen for the scene in which the deceased Emily relives her twelfth birthday in order to show that "our claim, our hope, our despair are in the mind—not in things, not in 'scenery.'"[119] Taken together, these seemingly contradictory statements suggest that the invisibility of the props and the scenery should serve two functions: to reflect the overlooked significance of everyday life, and to stress the insignificance of its material trappings. The removal of objects insists on their ultimate irrelevance while imparting, through the force of imagination, greater importance on the quotidian behaviors with which they are associated.

The scene of Emily's return from the grave to witness and reenact her twelfth birthday underscores this dual purpose, as the invisibility of objects moves from signifying their irrelevance to symbolizing the inability of people to appreciate the value of the everyday. When Emily asks to revisit her life, the Stage Manager warns her, "You not only live it, but you watch yourself living it" (99). As both participant and witness, Emily becomes a partial surrogate for the audience as they watch the people of Grover's Corners go about their daily routines. Wilder thus aligns audience members with the dead Emily and positions them to observe the scene that follows from the perspective of the dead. As Bunge argues, "Wilder constructs the play so that it coaxes the viewers to participate in Emily's vision, for the first act sets out the daily patterns Emily revisits as the play ends. . . . The familiar experiences, like the family breakfast that opened the play, now seem so rich it hurts to remember the distraction and dullness one usually brings to these rituals."[120] In an outburst before returning to her grave, Emily emphasizes her new appreciation for all that seemed routine and insignificant in life, and specifically calls attention to the very objects Wilder removed from the stage:

So all that was going on and we never noticed. Take me back—up the hill—to my grave. But first: Wait! One more look.

> Good-by [*sic*], Good-by, world. Good-by, Grover's Corners . . . Mama
> and Papa. Good-by to clocks ticking . . . and Mama's sunflowers. And
> food and coffee. And new-ironed dresses and hot baths . . . and sleeping
> and waking up. Oh, earth, you're too wonderful for anybody to realize
> you. (108)

In the context of Emily's sorrowful observations, the invisibility of the
food, coffee, dresses, and clocks simultaneously captures the blindness
of the living, who cannot properly see the value of these commonplace objects, and Emily and the audience's *estranged* view of the world
depicted onstage. For the dead Emily, life in Grover's Corners is no
longer real, and the bare set manifests her otherworldly perspective—a
perspective that the audience must share. Discussing Wilder's aesthetic
strategies, M. C. Kuner observes, "We are so lulled by the ordinary, it
seems so much part of our own lives, that we look no further. And when
we have become comfortable with its familiar things, suddenly they turn
into something else and become metaphysical symbols."[121] By thus disrupting the audience's viewing habits through the removal of scenery
and props, Wilder encourages spectators to see the routine as extraordinary, and the earthly as eternal. Director David Cromer's acclaimed
reinterpretation of *Our Town*, which was first staged in Chicago in 2008,
deviates from Wilder's script but remains faithful to its spirit by using a
full realist set for the moment when Emily revisits her life. The shock of
suddenly seeing everything Wilder had removed from the stage defamiliarizes this scene for contemporary viewers who are more accustomed to
nonrealist staging or already acquainted with the play.

In addition to imbuing the everyday with metaphysical significance,
Wilder's decision to leave most of Grover's Corners invisible assumes
that the audience will nonetheless be able to envision what is missing,
that they are at least somewhat familiar with the activities that the actors
mime. In order for the ordinary to become strange and take on a new
importance, viewers must share the play's sense of what constitutes the
ordinary. Whereas the presentation of the Property Man's routines of
work and rest in *The Yellow Jacket* stimulates a sense of racial and cultural difference by showing the audience what Chinese spectators would
disregard, the presentation of daily life in Grover's Corners insists on an

affinity with viewers by *not* showing them what they, presumably, can nevertheless imagine.

Furthermore, while remarks by the Chorus and other characters in *The Yellow Jacket* emphasize a disjuncture between the audience and the people and conventions depicted on the stage, comments by the Stage Manager reinforce the notion that the audience is already a part of "our town." Describing the landscape, he observes, "Naturally, out in the country—all around—there've been lights on for some time, what with milkin's and so on. But town people sleep late" (6). The Stage Manager's expectation that the audience would "naturally" know that country people are up before town people and that they would understand the activities implied in "milkin's and so on" generates a sense of identity between the community on the stage and the people in the seats. Explaining that George has been elected president and Emily secretary and treasurer at their high school, the Stage Manager similarly notes, "I don't have to tell you how important that is" (63), and wryly insinuates that the audience is aware of the significance that high school elections hold for adolescents.

Thus, despite their shared use of nonrealistic and metatheatrical conventions to accentuate the mundane, *Our Town* and *The Yellow Jacket* cultivate very different relationships with their audiences. While the latter emphasizes a racial and cultural divide, the former assumes likeness and community. Neither of these relationships, however, is without contradiction or tension. As I argued above, early productions of *The Yellow Jacket* affirmed distinct racial perspectives, but also encouraged viewers to "try on" Chinese spectatorship by imagining themselves as yellowface theatergoers. In Wilder's play, even as the bare set and the Stage Manager's remarks work to extend the compass of "our town" into the audience and beyond, other aspects of the drama make it clear that the community manifests the limits of its imagined historical setting. Various comments reveal, for example, that racial and ethnic "others" constitute the town's spatial and temporal boundaries. As discussed in this chapter's introduction, the birth of twins to a Polish family opens the play: setting up the first scene, the Stage Manager relates, "The only lights on in town are in a cottage over by the tracks where a Polish mother's just had twins" (6). Living "by the tracks," this family literally marks a line that cuts through Grover's Corners; kept at the edges of the seemingly close-knit community, they embody the limits of its inclusivity. The town is also defined against the Native Americans who occupied the space in the past. The Stage Manager calls upon a character, Professor Willard, to explain the town's demographic history: "Yes . . . anthropological data: Early Amerindian stock. Cotahatchee tribes . . . no evidence before the tenth century of this era . . . hm . . . now entirely disappeared . . . possible traces in three families. Migration toward the end of the seventeenth century of English brachiocephalic blue-eyed stock . . . for the most part. Since then some Slav and Mediterranean—" (22). Willard thus characterizes Grover's Corners as a largely white, Anglo-American town, its borders demarcated spatially by people from Eastern and Southern Europe, who would soon be subject to tighter immigration restrictions, and temporally by Native Americans, who have either "entirely disappeared" or left uncertain traces in "three families."

The question, then, is how to understand the clear delineation of town limits in relation to the play's concomitant drive to extend its bounds as far as the universal. Whereas Bert Cardullo argues, "Wilder is interested above all in *Our Town* in confirming, indeed glorifying, the eternal verities of family, country, and God, not in questioning or undercutting them,"[122] Bunge stresses that Wilder is critical of Grover's Corners, asserting that "when one looks closely at the community in this play, it undermines rather than supports its members."[123] The character of Simon Stimson, who suffers from alcoholism and eventually commits suicide, exemplifies the town's failure to take care of its own. Some of the Stage Manager's remarks also imply a denunciation of nationalism and social insularity. After associating efforts by people to "make sure they're Daughters of the American Revolution and of the *Mayflower*" with "layers and layers of nonsense" (87), the Stage Manager muses about the Civil War veterans buried in the Grover's Corners cemetery: "All they knew was the name, friends—the United States of America. The United States of America. And they wanted to die about it" (87). Although it is possible to construe and perform his comment as either cynical or patriotic, his ridiculing of the "Daughters of the American Revolution" implies a critical undertone.

Furthermore, when the Stage Manager describes the contents of the cornerstone built into a new bank for people to open a thousand years later, he emphasizes the importance of Western traditions to the town but questions the appropriateness of the selections: "Of course, they've put in a copy of the *New York Times* and a copy of Mr. Webb's *Sentinel* . . . . We're putting in a Bible . . . and the Constitution of the United States— and a copy of William Shakespeare's plays. What do you say, folks? What do you think?" (33). Much like the extended mailing address described by Rebecca Webb, the contents of the cornerstone connect the town to the northeastern region of the United States, the nation as a whole, Anglo-American culture, and Christianity. Yet while the Stage Manager begins by assuming that the audience would "of course" understand why these items were included, he ends by asking them to assess rather than simply accept their representativeness.

In his query to the audience, the Stage Manager comes close to articulating a viewpoint similar to that espoused by critic Mary F. Brewer, who suggests that opposing interpretations of *Our Town* are indicative of the differing social positions of its audience members: "The way in which *Our Town* is taken to be a reflection of American society, whether one considers it as a representative of the 'American-way-of-life,' or a radical critique of this dreamscape, depends in part on the spectator's particular relation to the dominant culture."[124] Brewer, however, goes on to argue that *Our Town* naturalizes and universalizes whiteness, except in its representation of white femininity. I would propose instead that if the contingencies of audience response determine the extent to which the play fulfills its aspirations toward a collective truth, performances of the drama serve less as an argument for the general representativeness of "our town," than as a test of the suppleness of the mundane. In other words, Wilder's script establishes a tension between the specificities of daily life in Grover's Corners and a sweeping vision of their significance; productions of *Our Town* then resolve, elide, or heighten this tension by engaging actors and audience members to realize (or not) its promised shift from the quotidian to the universal.

Innumerable productions of *Our Town* have followed its first performances in 1938, when it had a successful run on Broadway after brief stints in Princeton and Boston, and garnered a second Pulitzer Prize for Wilder. Widely produced outside the United States, it has also become a staple of American high school theater. More recently, performances such as the Wooster Group's experimental *Route 1 & 9* (1981) and the aforementioned production by David Cromer have defamiliarized *Our Town* for contemporary audiences. As critics have observed—sometimes with chagrin—the drama's reputation often precedes it. Its remarkable popularity has made it an icon of American life, and this status has keenly influenced the credibility (and the stakes) of its claim to represent common human experiences.

Brewer's reading of *Our Town*, for example, reflects both the play's iconic status and recent critiques of the discourse of universalism for obscuring differences and accepting the dominant as the normative. David Palumbo-Liu argues, "As 'universal,' the dominant erases the contingencies of time and space, history and location, and with the same gesture elides its operations of domination, projecting instead the appearance of being democratic."[125] Brewer associates *Our Town* with this tendency, even as she recognizes that popular and critical reception as much as authorial intention may be responsible for conflating the local, the national, and the universal in relation to the play: "Despite [Wilder's] insistence that the play explores universal human experience (itself a contentious category), spectators and critics have tended to read the production as an exercise in nostalgia, a soothing treatment of an idyllic small-town 'American way of life.' Indeed, given the custom among members of the dominant U.S. culture to conflate their experience with the universal, Wilder's claim may even encourage conservative readings."[126] Despite the Stage Manager's expressed ambivalence about national identifications, the play's reputation as the prototypical drama of the American everyday has set the national as the key framework for understanding its depiction of both the local and the universal: Grover's Corners becomes a metonym for the United States, which becomes a metonym for the universal. Whether defended or critiqued, this conception of *Our Town* obscures how the script's *provisional* alignment of one community's quotidian motions with the motions of the cosmos might generate performances of incongruence, friction, and disappointment that disrupt rather than affirm these associations.

As a conclusion, I focus on one such performance of *Our Town*, which illuminates the mundane's capacity not to manifest intrinsic differences, but to reveal the disparities that limit affiliations. In 1969, a performance in Harlem was the subject of a *New York Times* article titled "City Children Find 'Our Town' Alien."[127] Both Bunge's essay and David

Castronovo's book on Thornton Wilder refer to this article when they discuss popular and critical resistance to the play. These studies, however, do not address why the children interviewed by the writer might have found it difficult to identify with the people of Grover's Corners.

Although the world of *Our Town* is not any more real or authentic than that of *The Yellow Jacket* (an imaginative, retrospective view is central to Wilder's drama), spectators are nevertheless compelled by its concern for everyday trivia and universal experiences to measure it against their own world. By identifying their experiences with those presented on the stage, they lend the fictive town a corollary reality. Whether Wilder seems to be affirming or critiquing the society of Grover's Corners, his project of bringing together the mundane and the universal can be satisfied only through a corroborating audience that accepts their interpellation as a member of the represented community. Although Bunge asserts that some "critics mistakenly see a specificity Wilder never intended,"[128] if Wilder's goal was to create a work of universal scope and significance, an audience's sense of alienation from *Our Town* reflects not an erroneous reading of the drama, but the limits of its efforts.

According to the *New York Times* article, several of the children who performed in the Harlem production emphasized the contrast between the seemingly pleasant and simple life depicted in the play and the less-than-idyllic environment with which they were familiar: "'I wouldn't mind living in the country, away from all this,' a little girl in braids said plaintively. Eric, the 'town drunk,' stared at the black and white paper flowers decorating the wooden stage and remarked sadly, 'New York has the tallest buildings in the world, but the streets and the alleys are not very nice.'"[129] Construing these responses as a misunderstanding of Wilder's objectives not only overlooks the unavoidable specificity of his work—manifest in the play's attention to the details of the community and its daily activities—but also misses the specificity of the children's own living conditions, which make it difficult for them to accept the drama's generalizing claims. The children were moreover responding to a play that they were performing, and not just seeing. Given that at least some of the children were African American, Professor Willard's description of the primary demographic group of Grover's Corners as being of "English brachiocephalic blue-eyed stock" may have jarred with the identifications of those on the stage. This difference, much like the difference between the living conditions depicted in the drama and those familiar to the children, sits uneasily with the performance's more expansive impulses.

In both this particular staging of *Our Town* and yellowface productions of *The Yellow Jacket*, cross-racial casting (broadly construed and retrospectively named) emphasized a disjuncture between the society and culture represented by the plays, and the actors and audiences who materialized these performances. Yet whereas *The Yellow Jacket* perpetuated the physical exclusion of the Chinese while assimilating Chinese culture as a disembodied aesthetic, the Harlem production of *Our Town* highlighted material differences between the world of Grover's Corners and that of the performance's primary participants and spectators. Although Wilder could make the physical trappings of "our town" disappear, the reactions of the children suggest that other materialities do not dissolve as easily into the play's metaphysical ambitions. This does not mean, however, that the performance came up short in demonstrating the broader significance of "the countless 'unimportant' details of our daily life." The friction between script and production generated by the Harlem performance instead reveals how such "'unimportant' details" might enliven our sense of community, or illuminate the differences that matter.

By the time *Our Town* was produced in 1938, U.S. immigration restrictions had been continuously renewed and expanded, curtailing arrivals from Asia and Southern and Eastern Europe. In just a few years, however, the 1943 Magnuson Law overturned the Chinese exclusion acts, and the gradual reversal of U.S. immigration policy led to the elimination of quotas based on national origins in 1965. Meanwhile, the questions of race and assimilation taken up by Robert E. Park and his colleagues became a critical national concern after World War II, not just in the United States, but in Canada as well. Moving from the habits used to justify exclusion to those held up as proof of a minority group's quiet incorporation, the next chapter addresses postwar pressures on Japanese North Americans to erase racial difference.

2

Everyday Rituals and the Performance of Community

Six months after the U.S. Supreme Court's ruling in *Brown v. Board of Education* overturned *Plessy v. Ferguson* and its doctrine of "separate but equal," an article in the November 20, 1954, edition of the *Saturday Evening Post* announced the successful integration of Japanese "war brides" who had ostensibly vanished into American society after immigrating as wives of U.S. servicemen (Figure 2.1). The story's title, which asks, "Where Are Those Japanese War Brides?" encapsulates its tone of curiosity and surprise. According to the writer, William L. Worden, many of the women had assimilated into neighborhoods scattered throughout the country and adopted lifestyles typical of the American housewife: they drove automobiles, bought baby formula "containing no rice whatsoever," and debated the quality and price of groceries with other homemakers.[1] Worden claims, "This trick of disappearing as a group is one of the brides' outstanding characteristics,"[2] and observes, "few of the brides cling to Oriental communities."[3] Even as examples to the contrary appear in the article, Worden repeatedly downplays the impact of racial discrimination on the women's experiences, quoting sources who muse, "Apparently we Americans are losing our race prejudices,"[4] or insist, "Contrary to the general impression in Asia . . . the principal reason for the high ratio of unhappiness [in marriages between American military men and Japanese women] is not a racial problem."[5]

In a nation on the brink of a critical struggle over segregation and racial inequality, Worden's disappearing "war brides" offered a narrative of integration in which assimilation was the result of individual *gaman* (a Japanese word referring to the ability to endure hardship), and segregation was the result of an obdurate "clinging" to minority communities. Linking the disappearance of these women to the dissipation of racism, Worden proposes that the "racial problem" will wane with the dispersal of racialized groups and the gradual integration of willing individuals. In lauding the women's remarkable capacity for assimilation, however,

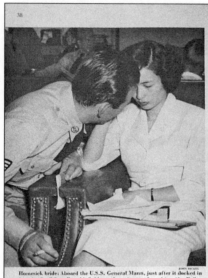
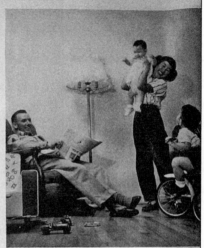

Homesick bride: Aboard the U.S.S. General Mann, just after it docked in Seattle, Staff Sgt. Ronald Goldsworthy tries to cheer his wife, Reiko.

M/Sgt. John Disharoon with his wife, Masayo (he calls her "Bonnie"), of Sasebo, Japan, and their kids, Mary Ann and Garry, at Fort Lewis, Wash.

Kishi Morrison and her twin daughters live near Albany, N.Y. Her husband is stationed in Europe.

In the last half dozen years, some 15,000 GI's have brought Japanese brides to this country. How have these mixed marriages worked out? What problems face the couples and their children?

Where are Those Japanese War Brides?

By WILLIAM L. WORDEN

THE house is large, two-storied and almost precisely like its neighbors in Seattle's slightly academic university district. Children's swings in the yard duplicate equipment up and down the street, and in the living room a visitor is likely to be shown school reports—two children doing very well—before the children's short and smiling mother will talk about anything else.

When the visitor notices a curious three-stringed instrument—a samisen—leaning in a corner of the living room, it is Mrs. Frederick Cotter who explains, "Michiko plays beautifully, and sings. In a musical play, she had an important part."

Perhaps this is nothing unusual: a mother-in-law proud of her daughter-in-law, Mrs. Conrad Cotter. The unusual aspect is that Mrs. Frederick Cotter is a tall and graying Caucasian; her son, Conrad Cotter, is a Cornell University graduate student study-ing governmental economics. The daughter-in-law, Michiko, and her two children are Japanese.

The existence of this unusual family provides an answer of sorts to the great question: Did the marriages of some 15,000 American soldiers to Japanese women in the last half dozen years work out? The answer is yes—provided that there was intelligence, willingness and plenty of guman.

The Japanese word guman translates, roughly, as "grin-and-bear-it." It has been important to Michiko, her husband and her mother-in-law, and to most of the Japanese brides who started to come to this country about 1949, and have continued to arrive, frightened, shy and confused, on almost every returning army transport since that time.

The Cotters' situation has been exceptional from the beginning. A Japanese-language student while he was in the service, Cotter met Michiko shortly

Figure 2.1. "Where Are Those Japanese War Brides?" Image from the *Saturday Evening Post*, November 20, 1954, 38. Courtesy of the *Saturday Evening Post*.

the article ignores the possibility that making the erasure of difference a condition for acceptance might speak to the persistence of "race prejudices," rather than promise their end.

A similar logic equating integration with dispersal and disappearance is evident in programs begun a decade earlier to resettle Japanese Americans and Japanese Canadians who were interned during World War II.[6] In both the United States and Canada, albeit with important differences that I discuss below, the state directed the dissolution of the very communities it had consolidated and segregated in wartime camps. After meeting strict eligibility requirements, including affirmations of loyalty to the United States, about nine thousand Japanese Americans were allowed to leave the internment camps and relocated to largely white, middle-class communities in various parts of the country. These efforts at resettlement, which were in effect from 1943 to 1945, suggest an early experiment in erasing difference and expediting assimilation through a geographic redistribution that was paradoxically coterminous with the continued internment of over a hundred thousand U.S. citizens and residents of Japanese lineage.[7]

Meanwhile, in Canada, such dispersals were compulsory rather than voluntary: at the end of World War II, the government released Japanese Canadians from internment but required them to choose between relocation east of the Rockies or Japanese "repatriation." Although the Canadian government admitted near the war's end that suspicions of treachery were unsubstantiated, it continued to insist that even if Japanese Canadians had not behaved in a way that justified their exclusion from the nation, they had not yet demonstrated that they belonged properly within it. In his August 4, 1944, speech to the House of Commons, Prime Minister Mackenzie King affirmed, "It is a fact no person of Japanese race born in Canada has been charged with any act of sabotage or disloyalty during the years of war."[8] This acknowledgment, however, preceded a case for dispersal that placed on Japanese Canadians the burden of eliminating the racism that fed wartime fears: "The sound policy and the best policy for the Japanese Canadians themselves is to distribute their members as widely as possible throughout the country where they will not create feelings of racial hostility."[9] Characterizing the dispersal policy as the government's attempt to look after the best interests of those whose lives it had just irrevocably upset, King argued that racism would fade only with the dissipation of racialized communities. Making overt the reasoning tacit in Worden's article, King's speech naturalizes racism as an inevitable reaction to the visible presence of minority groups, and implies that they must earn their acceptance and forestall enmity by being as inconspicuous as possible.

Despite crucial differences between the U.S. and the Canadian state and media's treatments of interned Japanese Americans, interned and forcibly separated Japanese Canadians, and recently immigrated Japanese "war brides," they collectively manifest the explicit and implicit demands placed on those of Japanese descent in North America during the postwar era to disperse and assimilate. These groups had to contend with both the persistence of racial hostilities spurred by wartime anxieties, and the insistence that they assuage racial animosity by effacing ethnic distinctions and rejecting affiliations with others who were of Japanese descent.

Produced several decades after World War II, Velina Hasu Houston's drama *Tea* (1987) and Joy Kogawa's novel *Itsuka* (1992) offer retrospective meditations on the impact of negotiating these dual pressures. Set in 1968 Kansas, *Tea* presents a group of women who gather to reflect on their lives over tea after a fellow Japanese "war bride" commits suicide. *Itsuka* shifts between the internment and dispersal of Japanese Canadians during and after World War II, and the later movement for redress, which culminated in 1988. The novel's narrator, Naomi Nakane, transforms through its pages from an isolated woman skeptical of the politics of redress to a committed member of a revived Japanese Canadian community. Moving from postwar conversations about Japanese North Americans to these later cultural productions, this chapter engages both "archives of racial representation" and "archives of ethnic self-expression."[10] The temporal shifts that characterize Houston's drama and Kogawa's novel facilitate this passage by building connections between the midcentury and the late century. The decades-long gap across which these works stretch includes, not insignificantly, a period in which claims of an Asian American identity—as opposed to classification as "Orientals"—gained traction. As part of the social movements of the 1960s and 1970s, newly self-identified Asian American activists and artists asserted a political and cultural presence. Their efforts included drawing attention to injustices like the internment and developing a distinctive body of Asian American literature.

Although Kogawa and Houston have come to occupy central places in conceptions of Asian American literature and theater, they also strain efforts to delineate the borders of an Asian American cultural corpus. Most obviously, Kogawa is a Canadian, not a U.S., writer. Asian American literary criticism's embrace of Kogawa's novel *Obasan* (1981), to which *Itsuka* serves as a sequel, has elicited wary reactions from scholars based in Canada who are concerned that it reflects an unthinking American appropriation of a Canadian text and elides differences between the U.S. and Canadian government's policies towards those of Japanese heritage, as well as differences among the experiences of Japanese North Americans.[11] As Donald Goellnicht points out, *Obasan* fills a noticeable gap within Asian American literature as a novel about internment by someone who directly experienced it.[12] Literary works set in internment camps by former internees—even those who were prolific writers—are few in number, a pattern that is unsurprising given the pressures of the postwar period. Wakako Yamauchi's play *12-1-A* (1982) and short stories such as Hisaye Yamamoto's "The Legend of Miss Sasagawara" (1950) and Lonny Kaneko's "The Shoyu Kid" (1976) stand as exemplary pieces next to memoirs from Jeanne Wakatsuki Houston, Monica Sone, and Mine Okubo. The tendency to include *Obasan* in this assemblage of Asian (U.S.) American writings raises a number of definitional, theoretical, and ethical questions: How do we define "Asian American," and to what end? What are the paradigms that best capture the complexity of identification? How do we avoid replicating a nationalistic logic of exceptionalism and a propensity to co-opt difference? Such questions have been generative for Asian American studies as occasions for critical self-reflection, and underscore the unwieldiness of the term "Asian American."[13]

As the editor of two anthologies of Asian American plays, *The Politics of Life* and *But Still, Like Air, I'll Rise*, Houston has actively participated in defining and promoting Asian American drama. Yet she has also put pressure on concepts of Asian American identity by drawing attention to the nebulous position of those who are mixed race. With a father of Native American and African American descent and a mother from Japan,

Houston has emphasized this background in her writings, both for the stage and in other public forums. During the 1990 controversy over the casting of a white actor to play the biracial character of the Engineer in the musical *Miss Saigon*, Houston wrote an article in the *Los Angeles Times* that was sympathetic to but slightly diverged from the position taken by Actors' Equity and Asian American theater artists. While she set the casting choice in a long history of privileging white actors in American theater (particularly in light of reports that the character was originally meant to be Vietnamese), Houston also criticized the debate for its tendency to assume an either/or conception of the Amerasian character and enjoined Asian American artists not to marginalize those who are mixed raced.[14]

Thus, while Kogawa and Houston's works have been crucial anchors for Asian American literature and theater, the complex implications of identifying their fiction and drama as Asian American expose the tenuousness of such designations. Their undecided status reflects ostensibly competing impulses: a desire for collective expression and a resistance to narrow categorization. The continuous negotiation of these inclinations constitutes a key concern of *Itsuka* and *Tea*, which set them in relation to the contradictory pressures faced by Japanese North Americans after World War II. Confronting the question of how to navigate between the sweeping claims of racial difference that justified the internments and the subsequent valorization of inconspicuous assimilation, the novel and the play posit the ritualization of everyday activities as a means of performing community and defying pressures to disappear. The ritualized mundane, as elaborated by these works, does not manifest "natural" or inherent racial bonds, or affirm accepted traditions; instead, it dynamically materializes communal ties as an oppositional response to the dual imperatives of racialization and assimilation. Furthermore, ritualization is not just a process that absorbs the characters of *Itsuka* and *Tea*; it also emerges as a technique of infusing the depiction and reenactment of banal behaviors with a ritual-inspired style and significance that aspires to engage the audience.

Ritualizing the Routine

An interdisciplinary field with links to research in anthropology, history, performance, and religion, ritual studies takes as its focus a particularly slippery object of inquiry. The difficulty of characterizing ritual with precision becomes immediately obvious not only in studies that directly tackle the problem, but also in introductory and theoretical works that foreground or circumvent the definitional challenges it poses.[15] Two aspects of rituals nevertheless require elucidation as a preface to illustrating the significance of mundane rituals in *Itsuka* and *Tea*: namely, ritual's relationship to the everyday, and its role in preserving and contesting established social relations. Both rituals and everyday behaviors realize specific societal arrangements and beliefs through repeated, embodied acts, and a fixed distinction between them remains hard to maintain in theory and in practice—a matter of degree and context more than absolute difference. Accordingly, the process of ritualizing the mundane at once draws out *existing* ritualistic aspects of the everyday, and imbues the everyday with more obviously ritualistic elements. Ritualizing quotidian activities makes their symbolic significance and social force explicit, thus bringing them closer to formally recognized rituals.

Notwithstanding debates about the specificities of ritual's attributes and effects, some of which I examine below, ritual is generally characterized as involving the repeated embodiment of a set of formalized, socially significant acts. In his study of collective memory, Paul Connerton stresses the "canonical" quality of rituals, which center on stylized repetitions of previous performances.[16] As reenactments of customary behaviors, rituals are patently social and historical, activating relationships among its participants as well as to the past. Furthermore, for Connerton, rituals are both symbolic and performative: in the repetition of highly meaningful acts, rituals realize social relations and have consequences beyond their obvious representative or practical significance.[17] Emphasizing the importance of direct, corporeal engagements to rituals, Bernhard Leistle argues, "It is by *doing* things, by handling objects, by performing standardized movements and gestures that ritual creates cultural meaning."[18] Ritual's efficacy depends on both cultural memory and physical immediacy.

The primary effects of performing rituals, however, are a topic of dispute. Since Émile Durkheim's influential association of ritual with social integration, scholars have debated its role in consolidating communal ties and beliefs. Victor Turner and Gerd Baumann are among those who have highlighted ritual's transformative possibilities and differentiating effects.[19] Baumann, for example, observes that rituals may promote social change rather than stability, and involve opposing factions and those considered "others" in relation to the performing community.[20] Reconciling divergent claims about ritual's impact on group solidarity, Catherine Bell concludes that "these loosely coordinated activities are constantly differentiating and integrating, establishing and subverting the field of social relations."[21] Rather than argue for ritual's either conservative or transformatory effects, Bell emphasizes that it dynamically configures and reconfigures matrices of social relationships, and moves for a shift in analysis from rituals to strategies of ritualization.

The question that remains, however, is what makes the repetition of conventional behaviors in a ritual different from the repetition of conventional behaviors in the everyday, particularly if we consider ritualization in terms of general practices rather than discrete events. In other words, how do we distinguish between rituals and routines? The emphasis on explicitly formalized acts in the works cited above suggests that the difference between ritual and the mundane might rest in their pitch rather than their rhythm: while the repetitions of the quotidian unfold, signify, and have social effects in a subliminal hum, rituals are more insistently patterned and symbolic.

For Bell, ritualization is a means of elevating certain acts as sacred: ritualization, she argues, is a way to "distinguish and privilege what is being done in comparison to other, usually more quotidian, activities."[22] If ritualization differentiates the extraordinary from the ordinary, however, it derives its meaning and efficacy from the specific relationship it generates *between* them. To the extent that ritualization organizes and manages social relations, its force depends on its intimacy with the quotidian, its capacity to infiltrate and shape the everyday. As Connerton observes, "Although demarcated in time and space, rites are also as it were porous. They are held to be meaningful because rites have significance with respect to a set of further non-ritual actions, to the whole life of a community."[23] Joseph C. Hermanowicz and Harriet P. Morgan assert that rituals intended to reinforce a group's identity are especially prone to co-opt the everyday: "the ritual draws upon the ordinary, intensifying and thus affirming it."[24] Furthermore, Jean Comaroff and John Comaroff warn against too rigidly dividing rituals from the everyday, as such distinctions tend to cast rituals as primitive and irrational.[25] Stressing instead ongoing, productive relations between formal and mundane practices, they argue, "The creative power of ritual . . . arises from the fact that . . . it exists in continuing *tension* with more mundane modes of action, of producing and communicating meanings and values."[26]

The dynamic relationship between ritual and the everyday finds rich elaboration in Velina Hasu Houston's *Tea* and Joy Kogawa's *Itsuka*, inspiring models of affiliation that oppose the dispersal of Japanese North Americans after World War II. Although rituals in the stricter sense (for example, formal political and religious events) appear in the play and the novel, both dwell on the everyday as a crucial site for forging social links, collectively constructing histories, and establishing a sense of belonging—thus, for performing community. In contrast to the imagined community of the nation theorized by Benedict Anderson, the communities that are the primary concerns of *Tea* and *Itsuka* are ambiguously situated at the very edges of the nation. The disavowed associations and disrupted histories that both splinter and unite Japanese "war brides" and Japanese Canadians stand in sharp contrast to the nation imagined, as Anderson argues, as a "deep, horizontal comradeship"[27] or a "solid community moving steadily down (or up) history."[28] Instead, the communities performed in these works are continuously negotiating, on the one hand, racialization as treacherous "Japs" and, on the other, demands that they quietly disappear. In a revealing convergence, *Tea* and *Itsuka* propose that the ritualization of quotidian activities can offer a way of mediating between these pressures. Exploring the generative possibilities of fusing ritual and the mundane, they draw from a performance form that is especially well suited to accommodate the contradictory situation of Japanese North Americans in the postwar era. According to Ronald L. Grimes, "Ritualizing enactments operate dialectically under circumstances in which polarities are too important to be chosen between. Participants seek some third way on a plane different from that occupied by the first two alternatives. . . . Ambivalence is at the heart of a ritualizing attitude."[29] In grappling with the polarities of racialization and assimilation as impossible choices, the everyday rituals of *Itsuka* and *Tea* model performances of community that seek a dialectical "third way."

Salvaging the Unsalvageable

A sequel to Joy Kogawa's acclaimed 1981 novel *Obasan*, *Itsuka* focuses like its predecessor on the internment and dispersal of Japanese Canadians during and after World War II. It continues the story, however, by tracing in detail the Japanese Canadian movement for redress, which was most vigorous in the period between the publications of the two novels. Almost instantly canonized, *Obasan* was a critical success as well as a best seller and is credited with stimulating popular support for the redress movement in Canada. The first part of *Itsuka*, like *Obasan*, is fragmentary in style and moves fluidly between times, suggesting the immersion of the narrator, Naomi Nakane, in her memories of the internment and the dispersal. In the second half of the novel, however, the initially reluctant and skeptical Naomi becomes increasingly committed to the redress movement, and Kogawa depicts its struggles and accomplishments in a chronological, almost documentary fashion. Through Naomi's transformation and a concomitant shift in style, *Itsuka* rejects a purely instrumental assessment of the movement's value. It shows that in addition to bringing about an official apology and monetary compensation, the struggle for redress enabled performances of community that countered decades of silence and isolation. The internment and the dispersal deprived Japanese Canadians of multiple manifestations of "home," not only discouraging affiliations with both Japan and Canada, but also severing familial and communal ties. In the novel, the ritualization of mundane acts is integral to the rearticulation of these broken connections.

After the bombing of Pearl Harbor by Japan on December 7, 1941, those of Japanese descent residing near the western coasts of Canada and the United States were subject to progressively harsher civil restrictions, eventually leading to their relocation and internment. When World War II began, over 95 percent of Japanese Canadians, a population of approximately twenty-two thousand, lived in the province of British Columbia. Stirring (and stirred by) existing anti-Asian sentiments, fears of Japanese

Canadian treachery led to curfews, interrogations, confiscations, and mandatory registrations. In 1942, Order in Council PC 365 decreed the removal of male Japanese nationals from a stretch of British Columbia's coast thought to be vulnerable to attack. Soon after, Order in Council PC 1486 legislated the relocation of all people of Japanese descent from this "protected" zone. The British Columbia Security Commission, which was in charge of managing the removal of Japanese Canadians, distributed them among various prisoner-of-war camps, provisional internment centers, and ghost towns. Families found themselves broken apart as a result of the fitful expansion of the internment, the assignment of men to work camps, and the separation of genders in detention centers. The government later exploited the desire to maintain family units by allowing those who volunteered to work on Canadian beet farms to stay together. Meanwhile, the Security Commission seized and sold the property of the internees, and then used a portion of the proceeds to pay for their relocation and imprisonment.

Although the Canadian and U.S. internments were congruous in many respects, the U.S. government neither confiscated property nor separated families. Perhaps the most striking difference, however, was in the governments' postinternment policies. While the approximately 120,000 interned Japanese Americans were released from the camps and allowed to return to their homes on the west coast as the war came to a close, Japanese Canadians had to choose between dispersal to areas east of the Rockies or "repatriation" to Japan. Masquerading exile as return, the government's claim to "repatriate" Japanese Canadians to a nation many did not consider their home affirmed the suspicions of entrenched racial allegiances that had helped justify the internment. Forced either to corroborate accusations of disloyalty or to dissolve all ethnic and communal associations, Japanese Canadians had no choice but to uphold the border between "Japanese" and "Canadian" that made an interstitial or coincident identity untenable.

The dispersal policy expedited the push toward assimilation that became the modus operandi of wary Japanese Canadians during the postwar decades. Although the internment and the dispersal might seem to reflect opposing directives, one concentrating a population and the other scattering it, they collaboratively worked to compel the "choice" of disappearance. Pamela Sugiman succinctly describes, "Many social bonds were severed and ethnic identities and loyalties were denied, as Japanese Canadians sought assimilation as a strategy to protect themselves from the harsh racism that they had experienced in Canada."[30] Sugiman suggests that the internment of Japanese Canadians encouraged their compliance with the goals of the dispersal policy by instilling in them a fear of being seen as different. Dissolving any possible links to Japan included not only rejecting certain cultural and linguistic practices, but also limiting associations with other Japanese Canadians, as such affiliations might draw attention and censure as racial self-segregation. The rootlessness that resulted from the uncertainty of ties to Canada and the necessary denial of ties to Japan constituted just one facet of a comprehensive social fracturing brought about by the internment and the dispersal, which splintered familial, communal, and national bonds.

In *Itsuka*, Naomi's separation from her parents and itinerant childhood and adolescence emblematize the severing of familial and communal ties effected by government policies during and after World War II. Naomi recounts,

> Not long after [Mother and Grandma disappeared], the whole world fell apart as, day after day, people disappeared. In our family, father's brother went first. Then Father was gone. Aunt Emily and Grandpa also vanished. And suddenly one day, Obasan, my brother and I were in the middle of a black-haired throng, milling about a train station in a ghost town called Slocan. We were separated, and we were concentrated. The displaced Canadians.
>
> In Slocan, we survived. Men built flumes for water from the hills. People planted gardens, built bathhouses and a school. But three years later, and just as suddenly again, we were on trains once more, headed for sugar-beet farms, fruit farms, sawmills—as laborers, servants and factory workers across the country. The government's "Dispersal Policy," Aunt Emily says, was a "smashing success."[31]

Short, punctuated sentences capture the erratic yet continual disappearances and relocations that pervade Naomi's childhood. She loses both of her parents when her father passes away during the internment, and her mother is unable to return from a trip to Japan after the attack on

Pearl Harbor (in *Obasan*, her disfigurement and eventual death from the Nagasaki atomic bomb are kept from Naomi for many years). In addition, the multiple, abrupt migrations Naomi must undertake with her aunt Obasan and her brother Stephen, from their beloved home in Vancouver to the ghost town of Slocan to the beet fields of Granton, discourage attachments to place and people. In noting, "We were separated, and we were concentrated," Naomi tersely highlights the government's paradoxical treatment of Japanese Canadians: while geographic concentration made the racial difference of a "black-haired throng" more sharply visible, the separation of families and communities, which was exacerbated by the dispersal policy, pushed for their dissolution.

The novel emphasizes that the cumulative effect of these seemingly inconsistent directives was the internalization of the drive to eradicate difference (whether associated with ethnic communities or racialized bodies), and it is in this context that the significance of ritualizing the mundane becomes intelligible. When Naomi's friend and eventual lover Cedric asks her opinion of the Japanese Canadians' fight for redress, her response highlights the dispersal policy's "smashing success" in dissipating any inclination toward communal affiliations: "I stare at the floor. 'I'm not really part of the community,' I say hesitantly. It's my guess that we don't really have a community at all. After all, as Aunt Emily puts it, we were all 'deformed by the Dispersal Policy' and grew up striving to be 'the only Jap in town.' 'No, I don't speak Japanese,' we'd say proudly" (126). Naomi suggests that Japanese Canadians are isolated by their common impulse to reject those who are similarly racialized: the collectivity implied by the "we" in Naomi's rumination is therefore characterized by a drive to disintegrate itself.

Bodily malaise—simultaneously shared and personal—accompanies the disavowal of communal affiliations. According to Emily, Naomi's aunt and a spirited activist for the redress movement, Japanese Canadians subconsciously continue to follow the government's injunction to erase themselves:

Japanese Canadians, [Aunt Emily] says, are an endangered species. Some study she read somewhere shows that more niseis [second-generation Japanese Canadians] are dying of stress diseases than any other group. . . . She says a study should be done on the many older nisei like herself who never married. It would show how deeply they've obeyed the order to disappear.

We've had a cultural lobotomy, she says, and have lost the ancient ways. There's a button in the brain that signals when to die and there's a universal law—if you honor your mothers and fathers, the button stays on hold. (138)

As an orphan, Naomi literally embodies the split from a generative history that Emily sees as afflicting Japanese Canadians more generally. As I mentioned above, the vilification of Japan during World War II exerted pressure on Japanese Canadians to reject any connection to Japan (as Naomi's brother Stephen often vehemently does), yet their internment simultaneously rejected their claims to a Canadian identity. Cut off from a viable relationship to a Japanese or a Canadian heritage, Japanese Canadians, Emily suggests, are also cutting themselves off from the future. She posits that they are subconsciously but faithfully fulfilling the Canadian government's order to disappear by erasing their bodies from the nation. In particular, the stress disease—a distinctly psychosomatic illness—points to the intersection of physical and emotional strains that continue to carry out the policy of dispersal long after it is no longer officially in effect.

Naomi's life of solitude and physical ailments, while particularly acute, manifest the homesickness of the larger Japanese Canadian population. Quiet and aloof, Naomi also suffers from a general sickliness and reacts uneasily to touch. Although Kogawa implies in *Obasan* that these physical ailments are related to a neighbor's molestation of Naomi during her childhood, she shifts the emphasis in *Itsuka* to other potential factors and focuses on the fragmentation of Naomi's family. Naomi contemplates, "Who knows what the psychogenesis of an illness may be? There are so many mysteries in the past—so many unknowns and forbidden rooms. According to Aunt Emily, I was fat and funny and healthy and never cried as a baby. I have no memory of that. She says I became sickly after Mother disappeared" (134). Naomi here speculates that the severing of maternal ties may have had long-term physical consequences. Describing her search for the reason behind her illness as an exploration of an inhospitable house full of "forbidden rooms," Naomi suggests that it reflects a distinct "homesickness" born of the strange disappearances and separations that marked her childhood.

In a rebuttal of Prime Minister King's declaration that "the sound policy and the best policy" for Japanese Canadians is dispersal, *Itsuka* repeatedly insists on its damaging effects and the necessity of forming and maintaining both familial and communal ties. The novel highlights, for example, the efforts of Naomi's aunt Emily, who assiduously works to reforge broken connections by sharing memories with her family and distributing community news to Japanese Canadians. Naomi describes, "The *Nisei News* was one of Aunt Emily's many efforts to keep people in touch after the war when our community was scattered across the country. In those anxious and lonely times, Aunt Emily's mimeographed letter carried news to her hundreds of isolated friends—one here, one there, in hamlets, cities and farms" (4). The accelerated rhythm that accompanies the description of the *Nisei News*'s circulation, "one here, one there, in hamlets, cities and farms," captures both the initial challenge of reaching people in distant, remote locations and the proliferation of contact sparked by Emily's work. In addition, as the storyteller of the family, Emily continuously reminds Naomi of a childhood she only hazily recalls. Naomi insinuates that these stories help to ease her sense of rootlessness: "Aunt Emily's stories are pebbles skipping over my quiet sea. Each one of her stones helps to build the ground on which I seek to stand" (74). Portraying her consciousness as a "quiet sea," Naomi emphasizes that she lacks a binding attachment to place. In contrast, Aunt Emily's stories, while small "pebbles" disturbing her peaceful isolation, form the foundation that connects Naomi to the places and peoples of her past. While Naomi's own memories are full of "unknowns and forbidden rooms," Emily's recollections serve as grounding narratives that prevent her from drifting in the still waters of silence and loss.

Itsuka emphasizes, however, that while Emily's stories form vital connections, counteracting the profound disaffection of Japanese Canadians requires situated and *embodied* performances of these connections. Naomi explains, "In the end, [Aunt Emily] says, home is where our stories are, and that's not just a question of ethnicity or even country, though she passionately loves Canada. Home for her is where the struggle for justice takes place, and because that is happening in our backyard she has returned with a will" (192). By claiming that home is "where our stories are," Emily stresses that narratives connect the displaced to place. Yet the relationship between stories and home is not simply an abstract or imaginative one: the emphasis on "where" the stories are highlights the importance of physical situatedness, of materially inhabiting the space to which one is connected through narrative. Furthermore, Naomi notes that Emily's story is the "struggle for justice," connecting story to practice. The novel thus suggests that rebuilding "home" in its various manifestations necessitates embodied as well as verbal connections, performances as well as narratives. As homesickness finds both physical and psychological symptoms, it is only fitting that its remedy should require both embodiment and narrative.

The ritualized mundane enters here as a response to the effects of dispersal. The novel is replete with images of everyday activities, some closer to habit and others closer to formal rituals, which become a means of grappling with the contradictory demands of concentration and separation, racialization and assimilation. When I speak of these practices as "ritualized," I am not assuming an intention to create ritual, but rather emphasizing a style and a significance that become discernible through Naomi's narration: namely, they are explicitly symbolic and repeatedly enacted, and they dynamically configure and reconfigure communal relationships.

While Naomi's other aunt Obasan does not engage, like Emily, in overt community-making efforts like distributing newsletters, her tender routines anchor their family to the most desolate of sites. Her continuation of the family's custom of taking Sunday afternoon tea exemplifies a practice whose symbolic value and social effects acquire a notable density and urgency when carried out through their various dislocations. Naomi relates,

Obasan clung to memories of Miss Best and happy days in Vancouver. In the beet fields of Alberta, she made pancakes and we'd sit in the dirt and the heat with thermos bottles and pancake "biscuits" and have our Sunday afternoon tea.

When my brother and I were teenagers, we moved from farm shack to town shack. Gone were the long rides in the yellow school bus. We bought a coal stove and lo!—real biscuits on Sundays once more. (10–11)

Fondly remembering their Sunday custom of taking tea and biscuits, Obasan insists on retaining a version of this activity even in "the dirt and the heat" of the beet fields. Seemingly quaint and trivial, Obasan's "Sunday afternoon tea" is a ritualized routine with deep symbolic significance: not only is it a physical reenactment of their memories of a happier past, it is also an effort to materialize a home while in a displaced, itinerant state. Underlining the efficacy of rituals in creating place, Grimes argues, "Not only is space founded to become ritual place, but actors themselves become grounded by acting in it. We hide, display, and boundary-mark ourselves by the way we transform space into place."[32] Although their family is forced to move "from farm shack to town shack," Obasan nevertheless attempts to found a home for Naomi and Stephen in the bleakest environments. She performs a rootedness to Canada by repeating a practice that links them to their happier days in Vancouver as well as to the nation's historical and cultural ties to England. Obasan thus draws attention to what Rita Felski describes as the less remarked attributes of habit, namely "the ways routines may strengthen, comfort, and provide meaning."[33] The family's afternoon tea, however, does not simply re-create their pleasant Vancouver residence or insist on a shared Anglo-Canadian identity; the practice also makes explicit their displacement through the incongruity between the rough surroundings and the dainty custom. It is thus an ambivalent performance that traces a fraught line between the English traditions adopted as Canadian and Japanese Canadians who continue those traditions after the state has banished them.

The reenactment of Sunday afternoon tea with "thermos bottles and pancake 'biscuits'" in the beet fields is but one example of the recycling characteristic of Obasan. At a fundamental level, her tendency to re-create activities and reuse objects in different contexts reflects the material exigencies of the internment, the confiscation of their property, and the postwar dispersal. Yet the novel, through Naomi's accounts of the past, also imbues Obasan's habits with heightened symbolic value and stresses their critical effect of maintaining family and home; in other words, ritualization here is a narrative strategy that, in depicting everyday activities as kinds of rituals, makes legible those aspects of the practices that exceed their obvious functions.

Obasan's death and the destruction of their shack in Granton compel Naomi's recognition that her aunt's recycling had turned their otherwise unattractive abode into a place with which she had forged visceral connections. She recalls that Obasan always took great care in transforming apparently disposable household items into useful ones: "Obasan is salvaging the unsalvageable. Nothing is ever to be discarded. Plastic bleach bottles are wastepaper baskets and plant trays. Mandarin orange boxes are covered stools. . . . Unlike Pastor Jim, she does not divide the world into the saved and the lost" (79). By comparing Obasan to Pastor Jim, Naomi not only lends Obasan's recycling a spiritual significance that elevates it from the quotidian activity of reusing disposable items, but also underscores an important difference in belief between the two characters.

The full significance of Obasan's recycling strikes Naomi as she discards her aunt's "saved" treasures after her death:

I alternate between frenzied packing, discarding and fits of weeping. Obasan has spent her lifetime treasuring these things that I am now throwing away. . . . I'm an undertaker disemboweling and embalming a still breathing body, removing heart, limbs, lifeblood, all the arteries, memories that keep one connected to the world, transforming this comatose little family into a corpse. . . . When the garbage collector carts away the mound of black bags, I can feel the muscles and bones, the last connective tissues, strain and snap. The new owners bulldoze it. Our shack of memories disappears. (84)

Obasan's engagement with "unsalvageable" objects has made them the "heart, limbs, lifeblood . . . arteries" of their home and family, the embodiments of "memories that keep one connected to the world." For Obasan, collection and recollection are intertwined pursuits, and her work materializes familial connections by fusing objects and memories. In Naomi's account, the salvaged objects are the organs that keep alive their "shack of memories," and the metaphors that weave together objects, memories, and bodies simulate the deep and intricate connections among them forged by Obasan's loving recycling. Recalling Leistle's observations on rituals, Obasan's seemingly unremarkable "handling of objects," her recurrent engagement with unsalvageable items, is what "creates cultural meaning,"[34] animating ostensibly useless junk and making it a conduit for the memories that link Naomi to the shack and to her family. In addition, much like the family's Sunday afternoon tea, Obasan's recycling is a practice that highlights the conflicted situation of Japanese Canadians. Making trash constitutive of home, her recycling both acknowledges and counters the rejection of undesired excess by recuperating it. As Naomi observes, Obasan does not "divide the world into the saved and the lost" (79), but rather finds value in traversing such lines.

Understanding Obasan's routine activities as ritualized allows questions of intentionality to recede and instead draws attention to the wider communal effects of her practices, particularly as they circulate through Naomi as participant, witness, and narrator. Bell suggests that the full creative force of ritualization is not always self-evident: "[Ritualization] is a way of acting that sees itself as *responding* to a place, event, force, problem, or tradition. It tends to see itself as the natural or appropriate thing to do in the circumstances. Ritualization does not see how it actively creates place, force, event, and tradition, how it redefines or generates the circumstances to which it is responding. It does not see how its own actions reorder and reinterpret the circumstances so as to afford the sense of a fit among the main spheres of experience—body, community, and cosmos."[35] Bell stresses that ritualization does not merely respond to social conditions but actively sustains and reshapes them, even if, as Naomi realizes, this generative quality is not immediately obvious. Responding to the displacements effected by the Canadian government, Obasan also redefines, reorders, and reinterprets her family's circumstances. She engages in the kind of "bricolage" described by Michel de Certeau, "making do" not only by using thermos bottles in the place of teacups and recycling orange boxes as stools, but also by involving her family in acts of homemaking while in exile.[36] In emphasizing Obasan's "bricolage," I do not intend to downplay the material constraints to which she is clearly responding, namely the limited resources available to her family after the government confiscated their property. Yet in the novel, these quotidian acts of survival are inextricable from their production of relationships among "body, community, and cosmos."

Obasan's careful recycling and continuation of Sunday afternoon tea implicate those around her, as they must constantly interact with the transformed objects in their new function as containers, furniture, and teacups. Serving as a foil to Obasan, Naomi's brother Stephen engages in similar activities of repetition and preservation, but with the opposing effect of isolating himself. Naomi recalls, "Stephen remains in the rubble. He is quick to anger. He catalogues, categorizes, and tries to control the debris. He puts precise labels on every book and photograph. He preserves Father's music on cardboard. His notes are meticulous and detailed" (22). Like Obasan, Stephen is fastidious in the routines that recall better times. Stephen, however, "remains in the rubble," stuck in the past and unable to find a way to ground himself in Slocan and Granton. He inclines toward control and stasis—the containment of "debris" rather than its reuse. Whereas Obasan's tea taking and recycling have a radiating force, drawing the other family members into practicing the custom or using her refashioned objects, Stephen's cataloguing seems only to draw him further into himself. Years later, Naomi watches Stephen, now a famous violinist, on television, and observes that her brother has adopted displacement as a fundamental mode of existence: "He's turned himself into one of those unreal TV people. There he was, like so many of them, wearing a decapitated rose on the lapel of his jacket. No stem. No thorn. No roots" (292). Pristine in his isolation, Stephen has severed all messy ties to the unpleasant past, their broken family, and other Japanese Canadians.

In setting Stephen's tendencies against those of Obasan, the novel suggests that repeated, quotidian efforts to connect to a preinternment life are not inherently recuperative. Such practices are, however, everyday acts of survival, seemingly minor efforts to grapple with the pressures of internment and dispersal. For Naomi, Obasan's tender routines, with their distinctly collective inclinations, demonstrate the potential for displaced customs and modest habits to sustain, manage, and reshape the relations between peoples and places undermined by exile.

The Tasks of Redress

Naomi's accounts of Obasan's routines reveal how such activities exceed their obvious practical functions by managing the contradictory pressures placed on Japanese Canadians and encouraging the enactment of rejected communal ties. Obasan's persistent recycling and reinstatement of Sunday afternoon tea require those around her to perform their bonds, however fraught, to one another and to their various Canadian homes. Ritualized routines, specifically those tied to political mobilization, are also prominent in the second half of *Itsuka*, which offers a detailed portrayal of the Japanese Canadian redress movement. Following Naomi's transformation from a figure of isolation and a skeptic of the movement to a dedicated proponent of redress, the novel tracks the gradual, tentative process by which her participation *realizes* rather than follows her political beliefs. It shows that adequate reparation for the internment and the dispersal required more than the apology and monetary compensation that the government ultimately offered. While charting the movement's official accomplishments, *Itsuka* calls attention to the ritualizing by-products of routine organizational tasks, which not only serve practical purposes, but also materialize, through repeated enactments, the connections made untenable by the dispersal. Through her participation in the movement's day-to-day undertakings, Naomi comes to embody—in its full corporeal and visceral sense—the community that it seeks to represent.

In contrast to its depiction of the internment and dispersal, which is fragmentary and dense with imagery, *Itsuka* narrates the Japanese Canadian redress movement in a largely linear, documentary fashion. The movement achieved its explicit goals on September 22, 1988, when Canadian Prime Minister Brian Mulroney formally apologized for the internment and offered both individual and community reparations before the House of Commons. The government's settlement with the National Association of Japanese Canadians, however, was reached only after five years of fraught negotiations and decades of silence. In 1947, soon after the internment, the government assigned Justice Henry Bird to lead a commission to reimburse Japanese Canadians for property losses. The Bird Commission eventually distributed $1.2 million based on very limited criteria for calculating damages and stipulated that recipients waive all future claims for compensation. With its meager offering, the commission refused to acknowledge the extent of the losses suffered by Japanese Canadians, and stifled further efforts to hold the government accountable. Nonetheless, in the late 1970s and early 1980s, the release of classified wartime records, the 1977 commemoration of the one hundredth anniversary of Japanese immigration to Canada, and the establishment of the U.S. Commission on Wartime Relocation and Internment of Civilians helped invigorate the movement for redress in Canada. The National Association of Japanese Canadians led these efforts, but when its National Redress Committee began negotiations with the government in 1983, an internal struggle ensued between George Imai, the chair of the committee, and NAJC members who advocated for wider participation in determining the terms of the settlement. For several years, the NAJC grappled with both the government's conditions for offering reparations and arguments among Japanese Canadians concerning appropriate procedures. In 1988, however, a successful rally for redress in Ottawa and the signing of the Civil Liberties Act in the United States, which offered compensation to Japanese Americans, helped bring about the long-anticipated "Settlement Day."

Although Kogawa changes the names of the groups and individuals involved in the redress movement, she otherwise offers a meticulous account of its development. The leadership struggles, thorny negotiations, and milestones find close parallels in *Itsuka*.[37] Yet Naomi, as the first-person narrator, specifically recounts these events from the perspective of someone who is initially skeptical of the movement and the need to build a Japanese Canadian community. Roped into participating by Emily, Naomi confesses, "I wouldn't dare admit it right now, but I'm not a true believer in redress. I'm not a true believer in anything much" (185). Her account of the movement therefore tracks not only its history, but also her gradual transformation into a "true believer." The novel begins in September 1983, after Naomi has fled from the affectionate touch of her friend Cedric, who, like Emily, encourages her to become more involved in the movement. Eventually returning to this opening moment after taking many winding detours into the past, the novel explicitly marks this point as transformational: Naomi relates, "I'm sick of my safe old dead-end tale. Give me a crossroads where the beginning of an altogether new story touches a turning point in the old" (165). Frightened and inspired by her budding romantic relationship with Cedric, Naomi seeks a different narrative in which to belong. At this self-declared "crossroads," the novel matches Naomi's change in outlook with a change in style, leaving behind the fragmentary structure and lyrical language of *Obasan* to move forward chronologically with an account of the redress movement. Despite Cedric's importance in bringing about this transformation, the "new story" that Naomi comes to inhabit is the tale of the movement for redress, rather than a love story.[38]

While the second half of the novel unfolds in a markedly different style from the first, quotidian activities continue to play a critical role in animating communal bonds. Through the day-to-day activities of the movement, Naomi comes to embody the beliefs that her involvement ostensibly precedes and brings into being the community that she is supposed to represent. In other words, Naomi helps to perform a Japanese Canadian community in the dual sense of presenting and achieving. In the following passage, for example, the task of putting together a mailing list takes on a symbolic, performative significance in excess of its explicit practical value:

> I was going through the Anglican church directory and finding a few names of kids I knew in Slocan. . . . It was like the day when I first came to Anna's house and raindrops were plopping onto my face. Something wet and unexpected was seeping up out of childhood and tingling through the dry rootlets of my memories. . . . The niseis seem to be innately organized. In the midst of the paper chaos, they understand what needs to be done—the cross-checking for duplication, the alphabetical ordering, the phoning to get apartment numbers and to check ambiguous names. . . . I could feel the passion beneath the banter. It was contagious. Each name mattered. Each life. (191–92)

Naomi takes on basic organizational duties with the practical goal of easing political mobilization by creating a database of contacts. The passage indicates, however, that these highly organized, repetitive acts have a ritualistic as well as instrumental function. Regardless of how the group actually uses the completed list, Naomi's execution of the routine tasks involved in its creation already begins to materialize the goals of the movement. Stimulating her dry and dying "rootlets," it connects Naomi to the people and places of her past, as well as to the other volunteers. The "contagious" banter of those around her implicates her in their passion and rouses a visceral engagement with their political commitments. An admitted nonbeliever, Naomi nevertheless comes to perform community through the rather prosaic activity of making a mailing list. The novel thus suggests that attending only to the most instrumental effects of the movement's activities obscures the ritual elements that realize political beliefs and communal bonds.

The novel's preoccupation with the routine processes of political mobilization complements the position it takes with respect to the actual debates that emerged among Japanese Canadians during the redress movement. As I mentioned above, a disagreement transpired within the NAJC between George Imai and members who wanted wider participation in negotiating a settlement with the government. Kogawa depicts a parallel situation in *Itsuka*, in which the character Nikki Kagame seeks to expedite the redress process by carrying out talks with the government without conferring with the larger community. Narrated from Naomi's perspective, the novel is unabashedly skeptical of Nikki's approach. In a crucial moment of the narrative, delegates representing the various branches of the National Japanese Canadian League (the NAJC's fictional counterpart) vote to implement structural changes to expand involvement and thus reject Nikki's proposals. Attending this decisive meeting, Naomi enthuses, "I drink in the excited faces around me. We all know that something significant has just happened. A tiny green political shoot has nudged its way through a long winter's sleep. And in the wall of our community's long silence, a faint crack has appeared. A thin spear of light leaps toward us" (199–200). Recalling the depiction of Naomi's reawakening as she helps organize addresses, this passage extends the metaphor of a plant stirring back to life with the imagery of Naomi's "dry rootlets" growing into a "tiny green political shoot." Much like the contagious "passion beneath the banter," the "excited faces" of her fellow attendees leave a decidedly physical impression on Naomi. Characterizing Naomi's response as a "drinking" of ecstatic visages, Kogawa conflates two understandings of partaking: the vitality afforded by consumption is inseparable from participation, as Naomi is nourished by her involvement in the activities of the NJCL. Furthermore, the metaphor suggests both an upward and a downward growth: Naomi and the other members are revived to the extent that they are rooted, and thus to the extent that they are able to ground themselves on the land from which they have repeatedly been displaced.

Like the gathering of names, the vote to change the group's structure has specific practical, organizational effects, yet it also synchronically performs and brings into being the community that it projects into the past (the community that was dissipated) and the future (the community that will be forged through redress). The "excess" effects of these routine procedures highlight the limitations of Nikki's plan to attain redress as quickly as possible. Although her plan would accomplish the instrumental objectives of the movement, it also disregards the significance of the "ritualizing" energies of the mundane, which symbolically and physically join Japanese Canadians in collective practices that materialize ties across time and space.

In returning to the imagery of the reanimated plant, the passage noticeably widens the scope of the metaphor's tenor to encompass the revitalization of Japanese Canadians at large. At this point in the novel, Naomi's "I" becomes increasingly subsumed by a "we" designating a robust Japanese Canadian community, not one inclined toward self-disintegration. Naomi's increasing use of the plural "we" actualizes the community it denotes; as Connerton argues, to assert the pronoun is to constitute its referent: "The community is initiated when pronouns of solidarity are repeatedly pronounced. In pronouncing the 'we' the participants meet not only in an externally definable space but in a kind of ideal space determined by their speech acts. Their speech does not describe what such a community might look like, nor does it express a community constituted before and apart from it; performative utterances are as it were the place in which the community is constituted and recalls to itself the fact of its constitution."[39] Reiterations of "we," like the mundane rituals described in the novel, perform community, bringing it into being through the continual rearticulation of bonds in an embodied present. Although Kogawa's depiction of Naomi's increasing involvement in the movement through organizational activities remains in the realm of narrative description, its intersection with a distinct turn to performative utterances of "we" also suggests an extra-diegetic ambition to constitute community in the spatial and temporal present of the reader.

Yet despite continual pronouncements of "we" from this point in the novel until its last passages,[40] Kogawa maintains a tension between Naomi's articulations of a singular and a plural voice. Naomi explicates,

Although, as we all know, we must speak with one voice, there is more than one view. From within the turmoil, it's commitment that's being formed. We're no longer on the sidelines watching others. Japanese Canadians are in the spotlight's glare.

Government's intention is that we should harmonize in perfect Government-approved song. But no matter how ardently the choirmaster flails his arms, we sing out of tune. It's a cacophonous choir, howling its way through the redress blues. I expect that any moment the curtain will thud at our feet. But some people having discovered their voices, will no longer be still. (240)

The passage highlights Naomi's increasing identification with the movement for redress, as she speaks primarily as part of a collectivity. Yet the "we" that constitutes this collectivity—and becomes the voice of the novel—is hardly uniform. The pronoun's referent is not always clear, variously gesturing to the larger Japanese Canadian population, those directly advocating for redress, and the smaller community with which Naomi works most closely. Furthermore, Naomi emphasizes that disagreements and turmoil are what forge commitment, rather than jeopardize it. Although the government demands that calls for redress be channeled into a single voice (preferably that of Nikki), Naomi suggests that for the choir to continue singing, it must sing "out of tune." The image of the "cacophonous choir" captures the movement's struggle to speak as a unified community while allowing divergent voices to emerge.[41] Given that essentialist notions of race and accusations of self-segregation were used to justify the internment and the dispersal, cacophony is perhaps the only viable way to articulate a productive dissonance that simultaneously rejects gross characterizations of Japanese Canadians and affirms communal ties as necessary to defying the mandate to disappear.

Naomi describes the community's rowdy "song" as the "redress blues," drawing a parallel between their experiences of internment and dispersal with the oppression of African Americans in the United States. Ralph Ellison, in his essay "Richard Wright's Blues," suggests that the blues offers the possibility of surviving and overcoming tragedy by delving deep into one's sorrow: "The blues is an impulse to keep the painful details and episodes of a brutal experience alive in one's aching consciousness, to finger its jagged grain, and to transcend it, not by the consolation of philosophy, but by squeezing from it a near-tragic, near-comic lyricism. As a form, the blues is an autobiographical chronicle of personal catastrophe expressed lyrically."[42] Ellison's emphasis on the evocative function of the blues, its continuous reanimation of suffering in musical form, elucidates why it resonates with the redress movement. Given the wide-ranging repression of wartime and postwar injustices, by both the government and those dispersed, the "redress blues" serves as a delayed effort to keep alive "the painful details and episodes of a brutal experience." Moreover, the image of blues sung not by an individual but by a choir underscores the importance of expressing "personal catastrophe" as part of an inharmonious collective.

Through its depiction of Naomi's fitful inching toward belief in the struggle for redress, *Itsuka* stresses that communal affiliations are not the inevitable or inherent result of a shared ethnic identity. In her sociological study of how nisei women remember the internment, Sugiman observes that it was necessary for Japanese Canadians to develop a sense of collective memory from individual recollections of the internment in order to make a case for redress; she adds, "In future years, community bonds may paradoxically rest not on 'racial blood' but rather on shared memories and a place in this nation's political history."[43] Kogawa's novel proposes that the narration and politicization of these memories must also be accompanied by their literal incorporation as part of embodied practices. Melding the organizational with the restorative, Naomi contemplates, "And within our cocoons, new life is being formed. One by one, we are coming forth with dewy fresh wings. The more meetings we attend, the more we need to attend. We're learning how to fly by stuffing envelopes" (243). Naomi explicitly connects the proliferation of banal activities with the emergence, from dispersed and cloistered "cocoons," of a vibrant movement and community. To the extent that Naomi's participation in such tasks *precedes* her pronouncements of a collective identity, the performativity of her discordant "we," its actualization of community, is inseparable from the collection of addresses, the attendance of meetings, and the stuffing of envelopes. Such activities resonate beyond the practical to give a flexible body and rhythm to the "cacophonous choir," holding it together in the face of internal and external pressures to disband.

The Curious Case of the Disappearing "War Brides"

Although the Canadian and U.S. governments largely carried out their respective internments as separate if parallel projects,[44] the fates of Japanese Americans and Japanese Canadians were closely intertwined, both during the war and long after its conclusion when the two redress movements flourished. With decorated veterans and elected officials among the former Japanese American internees advocating for redress, the movement in the United States helped propel similar efforts in Canada, where the dispersal policies and a smaller Japanese Canadian population made the fight for recognition more difficult. By the 1980s, Japanese Americans had also been designated by various media reports and politicians as a "model minority" whose educational and economic achievements apparently exceeded those of the white majority. Capping a narrative of triumph from adversity, the U.S. government's offer of an apology and reparations in 1988 reflected the political changes enabled by the civil rights movement *and* the growing backlash against its gains. As Chapters 3 and 4 elaborate, critics of the model minority myth have called attention not only to its elision of significant disparities between and within racialized groups, but also to its deployment in efforts to dismantle affirmative action and other programs intended to alleviate race- and class-based inequities.[45]

Narrating the transformation of Japanese Americans from enemy aliens to ideal citizens, however, required glossing over the immediate postwar era. Tetsuden Kashima observes that studies of Japanese Americans during this so-called period of transition are sparse, and contests the notion that it was characterized by steady advancement. Instead, he asserts that this period was marked by crisis and social amnesia.[46] Building on Dorothy Swaine Thomas's extensive study in *The Salvage* of the voluntary dispersal program that relocated Japanese Americans from internment camps to white, middle-class communities,[47] Caroline C. Simpson also emphasizes the disappointments that prevailed in the years following World War II. Remarking on the volunteers' struggles to adapt to their new homes and abide by pressures to avoid ethnic affiliations, Simpson notes, "The resettled population's inclusion as 'loyal' Americans was ultimately purchased at the price of their alienation from *both* the white and Japanese American communities."[48] In her analysis of the decade following World War II, Simpson argues that it was the Japanese wives of U.S. soldiers, rather than Japanese Americans returning from internment, who functioned as precursors to the Japanese American model minority myth inaugurated in the 1960s.

Various factors in the postwar period helped bring about the immigration of Japanese "war brides" to the United States: a shift in U.S. relations with Japan from antagonistic to paternalistic, the attenuation of race-based restrictions on immigration, and the beginnings of a decisive reckoning with Jim Crow. The U.S. military's central role in the postwar reconstruction of Japan facilitated contact between American soldiers and Japanese women, while legislation allowing the wives of servicemen to immigrate despite racial quotas and the gradual elimination of the quotas themselves enabled couples to marry and move to the United States.[49] Tracing a shift in popular representations of "war brides" from predictions of failure to fulsome accounts of success, Simpson contends that these women came to serve as exemplars of American cultural pluralism and harbingers of successful integration. She argues that they made more appealing candidates for this role than either African Americans, who were haunted by a long history of slavery and struggling with the persistence of Jim Crow laws, or Japanese Americans, who had just emerged from internment and were struggling with the disappointments of the resettlement policies.[50]

The *Saturday Evening Post* article by William L. Worden that begins this chapter participates in the elevation of Japanese "war brides" as embodiments of successful racial integration. The story moreover repeatedly implies that racial discrimination is no longer a problem, or at the very least, it has not impinged on the brides' ability to assimilate. Worden raises the possibility that racial prejudice might persist only when he discusses the hostility directed at the women by "the Japanese who were here earlier than the brides"—that is, by those similarly racialized.[51] He quotes a second-generation Japanese American social worker as saying, "The existing Japanese community just doesn't accept the brides."[52] Although the social worker points to differences in class and education as the reason behind this rejection, Worden insinuates that his remarks reveal lingering *racial* intolerance by offering them as the potential counterargument to another interviewee's theory that "apparently we Americans are losing our race prejudice."[53] Worden therefore makes the perplexing suggestion that racial discrimination against the "war brides," if it exists at all, comes from Japanese Americans. He then proceeds to dismiss these Japanese Americans from his story by declaring, "At any rate, few of the brides cling to Oriental communities."[54] Worden thus sets recently immigrated Japanese "war brides," whom he characterizes as paragons of American pluralism, against recently released Japanese Americans, who insist on racial differentiation by staying within ethnic communities. Even as the government was on the verge of enforcing desegregation and still in the process of lifting prohibitions on miscegenation and Asian immigration, the article maintains that successful assimilation is the result of individual choice and sheer determination.[55]

Yet in its praise of the women's disappearance, the article paradoxically makes their difference all the more visible. It begins by setting up a presumably familiar scene:

> The house is large, two-storied and almost precisely like its neighbors in Seattle's slightly academic university district. Children's swings in the yard duplicate equipment up and down the street, and in the living room a visitor is likely to be shown school reports—two children doing very well—before the children's short and smiling mother will talk about anything else. . . .
>
> Perhaps this is nothing unusual: a mother-in-law proud of her daughter-in-law, Mrs. Conrad Cotter. The unusual aspect is that Mrs. Frederick Cotter is a tall and graying Caucasian; her son, Conrad Cotter, is a Cornell University graduate student studying governmental economics. The daughter-in-law Michiko, and her two children are Japanese.[56]

Opening with a description of a house that *seems* to resemble those that surround it, Worden reveals rather dramatically that the daughter-in-law in question and her children (from a previous marriage) are Japanese. Worden therefore materializes the ostensibly disappearing "war bride," and makes her closeness to American norms ("almost precisely like") remarkable rather than banal. She is visible in her invisibility, peculiar in her familiarity.

Worden's study of these women began several years earlier, with an article he cowrote with Janet Wentworth Smith titled "They're Bringing Home Japanese Wives," which was published in the January 19, 1952, edition of the *Saturday Evening Post*. A story to which Worden's 1954 article could serve as a sequel, it reports on the immigration of Japanese "war brides" and describes their enrollment in schools established by the Red Cross to help prepare them for life in the United States. The sub-headline proclaims, "Six thousand Americans in Japan have taken Japanese brides since 1945, and all the little Madam Butterflys [*sic*] are studying hamburgers, Hollywood and home on the range, before coming to live in the U.S.A."[57] Intended to instill the women with the values and domestic skills of middle-class American housewives, the bride schools, which began in 1951, adopted and transmitted a limited notion of proper American behavior.[58] Although the article can only speculate about the outcome of these efforts to "Americanize" the "Madam Butterflys" before their arrival in the United States, it assumes that they desire and greatly need this training. Smith and Worden recount,

> Country girls not only are innocent of slip technique but imagine that they are being American by having their sleek black hair frizzled into dulled mops in "Hollywood" beauty salons on Japanese side streets. They mix unbelievable hues in their outer clothing and have no idea of what to do with a girdle, although they buy them, thus annoying the life out of slightly spreading American women who find the PX never has the right size at the right time because some Japanese bride just bought it, perhaps to hang on the wall of her home as a decoration.[59]

As in Worden's article on the disappearing brides, the apparent aspiration of these women to be more "American" only brings into relief their difference. Elena Tajima Creef, whose mother was one of the subjects of this article, observes, "The Japanese women are disciplined and trained by the brides' schools to imitate domestic American culture and style yet at the same time are subjected to the *Post*'s ridicule for presuming such an affectation."[60] Although the two stories are dissimilar in tone, the earlier one tending to mock the brides and the later one largely praising them, they jointly articulate the contradictory logic of the racial mundane: they insist that the women should (and should want to) seek assimilation, yet their very movement toward this elusive horizon—tracked by their enactment of quotidian domestic tasks—comes to serve as a persistent measure of their difference.

Moreover, while assimilation receded as a constantly deferred and interrupted possibility, the "war brides" were propelled to its promise by the disintegration of social ties. Numerous factors coalesced to isolate these women: the disapproval of miscegenation in Japan and the United States; the defamation of these women as opportunists, "Japs," and prostitutes (despite the rigorous examinations to which they were subject before the military would approve their marriage);[61] the breaking of bonds with family and friends in Japan, whether as a result of geography or social censure; and the dispersal of the women in scattered locations throughout the United States (mostly army bases or their spouses' hometowns), where they were largely dependent on their husbands and their husbands' family.

In contrast to Worden's implicit censure of any inclination to "cling to Oriental communities," Velina Hasu Houston's drama *Tea* insists that the discrepancy between the promises of "Americanization" and its frustrations makes the development of a community among "war brides" both difficult and imperative. First produced in 1987 at the Manhattan Theatre Club, *Tea* is the third installment in a trilogy inspired by the experiences of Houston's mother, who immigrated to the United States from Japan after marrying an American soldier. *Asa Ga Kimashita* (1981) introduces Setsuko Shimada and Creed Banks, the characters based on Houston's parents. *American Dreams* (1984) then follows the couple to New York to meet Creed's family. In the course of this play, they learn that the army intends to send Creed to a base in Kansas. In contrast to *Tea*, which employs role-doubling and a fluid temporal structural, these earlier plays follow a more straightforward realist style, and everyday behaviors primarily convey the characters' attachments to Japanese or American conventions. In *Asa Ga Kimashita*, for example, the mundane helps to dramatize growing tensions in Japan after World War II between those, like Setsuko's father Kiheida, who resist the changes that accompany the American occupation, and those, like Setsuko's cousin Fumiko, who embrace them. Thus, Fumiko's insistence on hugging Setsuko draws her uncle's reprimand that it is a sign of "Western indulgence."[62] While this initial chastisement suggests a gruff affection for his niece, he later explicitly prevents the two from embracing in a gesture that connects hugging to a more serious offense. Kiheida berates Fumiko for her friendly relationships with Americans and argues with her about the transformations they are effecting in Japan. When he then stands in Fumiko's way as she reaches for Setsuko, the thwarted hug symbolizes his refusal to let what he regards as damaging Western and American influences touch his family.

When Fumiko and Setsuko reunite in New York in *American Dreams*, hugging returns to provide a measure of the different paces at which they adjust to American life. The stage directions instruct, "The women laugh joyously and bow. They then embrace, a move which appears awkward for Setsuko but she tries all the same."[63] The awkwardness that Setsuko should exhibit while hugging indicates her lingering resistance to adopting, as her cousin swiftly does, a different set of cultural norms. Setsuko moreover persists in bowing to people as is customary in Japan. Bowing, rather than hugging, is a more significant point of contention in this play, a difference that highlights the change in setting as Creed tries to persuade Setsuko to stop the practice once they arrive in the United States. When Setsuko declares in the play's final scenes that she will stop bowing, she makes it clear to Creed that her decision reflects not accommodation, but critique: "And I am not going to bow. Americans do not understand the honor of a bow."[64] Whereas hugging in *Asa Ga Kimashita* expresses a rupture in Japanese society and emphasizes Kiheida's destructive rejection of all challenges to the status quo, Setsuko's eventual refusal to bow in *American Dreams* tenders a bodily critique of postwar American society, where segregation continues, anti-Japanese sentiments linger, and interracial couples are marginalized.

In *Tea*, the mundane retains its metonymic function, reflecting the characters' relationships to one another and to Japan and the United States. Yet *Tea*'s more experimental, ritualized style also intensifies the mundane's performative force. It is not that everyday behaviors are no longer symbolic in *Tea*, but that these representational aspects lend texture to performances that above all facilitate community building across difference. Whereas gestures such as hugging and bowing add to *Asa Ga Kimashita* and *American Dreams* but are not entirely necessary to our understanding or experience of the play, the enactment, transmission, and transformation of the mundane are critical to the rituals choreographed by *Tea*.

Tea picks up Setsuko's story several years after the end of *American Dreams*. Creed has passed away, leaving Setsuko in Kansas to raise their two daughters. Although Setsuko remains a central character, *Tea* disperses its attention among five "war brides." The play opens with the suicide of one of these women, an event that brings the others to her home to clean and take tea. The sharing of tea, which frames the women's conversations and the flashbacks that make up a substantial portion of the drama, notably occupies a middle ground between ritual and routine. As Houston explains in an interview with Roberta Uno, "This is not tea in the Japanese ceremonial sense, but the ritual of everyday life."[65] Gathering to observe an acquaintance's passing but not participating in a formal ceremony, the women's tea drinking on this occasion reflects— and ultimately reshapes—how they share tea on a more quotidian basis. As in *Itsuka*, the ritualization of the mundane plays an integral role in forging a community among the women in the midst of numerous pressures and inclinations to maintain their solitude. *Tea*, however, specifically explores the productive "liminality" of ritual—what Victor Turner theorizes as its characteristic ambiguity—as it materializes in casual, day-to-day activities. In the play, these "rituals of everyday life" are the means through which the women come to perform community as the continuous reenactment and *renegotiation* of their relationships with one another.

Set in 1968 in Junction City, Kansas, the play begins with the suicide of Himiko Hamilton, a woman whose loneliness was exceptional even among the fragmented group of "war brides" residing near the Fort Riley army base. Living by herself after the deaths of both her abusive husband Billy, whom she shot in an apparent act of self-defense, and her daughter Mieko, who was raped and murdered after running away, Himiko had few friends. A "dance hall girl" from a poor family when she met her husband in Japan, she was shunned by other women for her suspected improprieties and eccentric behavior. Four of them nevertheless gather at her home to take tea after her death: Setsuko Banks and Chizuye "Chiz" Juarez, the two women who attempted to befriend Himiko while she was alive; Atsuko Yamamoto, who scorned Himiko but comes out of duty and curiosity; and meek Teruko MacKenzie, whom Atsuko treats as a sidekick. As the women prepare and take tea together, the performance moves between present and past, offering glimpses of their lives in Japan and early experiences in the United States, as well as scenes involving their husbands and daughters. During the performance, Himiko's ghost remains onstage, speaking to the audience and frequently interjecting her own thoughts into their discussions.

A recurring theme in the women's conversations is their relationships (or lack of relationships) with one another. A tendency to reject their shared identification as "war brides"—because of its denigration, class differences, or pressures to assimilate—reinforces the women's solitude. When Chiz expresses surprise that so many people were interested in joining for tea after Himiko's death, Setsuko admonishes her and explains, "After all, this is a difficult occasion for us: the first time a member of our Japanese community has passed on." Chiz counters, "What 'community'?" and Himiko concurs with her skepticism, explaining to the audience, "Yes, what community? We knew each other, but not really. . . . We didn't care enough to know."[66] Like *Itsuka*, the drama highlights its central characters' ambivalent feelings about forming a community around a denigrated identity. While Setsuko suggests that this community already exists by virtue of their shared ethnicity and history, Chiz and Himiko express doubts about its existence and its desirability.

As the women debate the status of a Japanese "war bride" community, the sharing of tea simultaneously manifests differences and forges connections. In her introduction to *Tea* in the anthology *Unbroken Thread*, Uno underlines the dual function of this everyday ritual: "The ritual of drinking tea becomes a device that draws [the characters] together, forcing them to examine their common experiences and the essence of what being Japanese means. Houston illustrates the women's differences through the very manner in which they take tea."[67] Uno's observation that tea both brings the characters together and illuminates their differences points to a central tension in the play between claims about essential Japanese qualities and reiterations of fundamental differences between the women. The drama stresses each woman's distinct personality, and tea-drinking preferences help establish the characters as representatives of specific types. For example, the energetic and humorous Chiz, who is the most overtly "Americanized," explains as the women introduce themselves to the audience that she takes her tea "Very hot. In a simple cup" (164), and later asks for coffee instead. In contrast, Atsuko, the snobby wife of a Japanese American nisei, prefers fancy cups and her own special tea. Meanwhile, mild-mannered Teruko likes her tea "cool" in any cup.

This emphasis on typical differences among the women, however, is set against references to a quintessential "Japaneseness." Chiz remarks, "Ever since [Himiko] shot her husband two years ago, she's kind of haunted me. It made me remember that underneath my comfortable American clothes, I am, after all, Japanese. (*a quick smile*) But don't tell anybody" (170). Suggesting a Japanese core masked only by her American clothes, Chiz's unexpected comment is one of several made by characters that imply inherent ethnic qualities. These claims, however, often lead to disputes about who is more or less Japanese. Thus, rather than reveal a consensus about what constitutes a Japanese "essence," they manifest efforts by the women to articulate their relationships to one another. The following dialogue typifies these discussions:

> CHIZ: [Himiko] was *not* crazy.
> TERUKO: It is the Japanese way to carry everything inside.
> HIMIKO: Yes. And that is where I hid myself.
> ATSUKO: [Himiko] came from Japan, but the way she dressed, the way she walked. Mah, I remember the district church meeting. She came in a low-cut dress and that yellow-haired wig, (*mocks how she thinks a Korean walks*) walking like a Korean.
> SETSUKO: Atsuko-san, ne, we have something in common with all the Oriental women here, even the Vietnamese. We all left behind our countries to come and live here with the men we loved. (172)

As descriptive claims, Teruko's assertion that silence and suppression are the "Japanese way" and Himiko's confirmation of this view assume an essential Japanese quality; considered in terms of their broader perlocutionary intent,[68] however, these statements reflect an impulse to connect Himiko to a Japanese identity and an imagined community by associating her with the qualities assumed to be typical of it. Setsuko similarly refers to their common background to insist on their ties and responsibilities to one another. She reminds the women, "we are all army wives—and we are all Japanese" (171), and suggests, "But we're here today because we're Japanese" (171). Yet despite the importance she places on being Japanese, Setsuko extends the basis for identification in the dialogue above by pointing to a history shared with "all Oriental women" who came to the United States as "war brides."

In contrast, Atsuko makes references to an essential Japanese character in order to establish differences and implement a hierarchy. Responding to Teruko's comment that Himiko behaved in a "Japanese way," Atsuko is quick to point out that Himiko, despite coming from Japan, did not act like a proper Japanese woman. She later criticizes Chiz in the same manner, remarking snidely, "I don't expect Chizuye to understand the importance of being Japanese" (188). In making a distinction between coming from Japan and exhibiting the behaviors and beliefs appropriate to that heritage, Atsuko assumes the role of standard-bearer and distances herself from Himiko and Chiz.

In their variety, these declarations of being more or less Japanese, similar or different, work strategically and performatively. "Japanese" becomes a dynamic point of reference through which the women build and break ties, and calibrate their proximity to Americanness.[69] Yet it is also haunted by the potential to slip, truncated, into a racial epithet, as in Teruko's husband's offhand remark, "Kinda like shooting at Japs again" (190), while on a hunting trip. Such derogatory associations shadow the positive pitch of Atsuko and Setsuko's claims about Japanese identity and cast doubt on its use as a basis for affiliation. Here, as in *Itsuka*, the notion of a community based on a shared history of migration and racialization is fraught: the scorn directed at both "Japs" and "war brides" competes with the need to offset the accompanying alienation by connecting with those who made similar choices to marry and leave Japan.

Despite occasional attempts by Setsuko to invoke Japanese identity as a unifying force, such verbal declarations alone prove to be infelicitous, as J. L. Austin designates unsuccessful performative utterances. The other women, particularly Atsuko and Chiz, largely qualify, dismiss, or reject such claims. Instead, *Tea* emphasizes the significance of everyday rituals in allowing the women to enact a community, one that reveals relationships of both incongruity and affinity, and mediates between the siren calls of disappearance and the derisive calls of racism.

The play namely explores the productive intersection of ritual's "liminality" with the mundane rhythms of everyday life. Victor Turner's seminal work on rituals drew attention to the generative possibilities of hybrid, ambiguous identities. Turner's theories are particularly instructive here, however, for thinking about how ritual as a *process* functions within the play. Inspired by Arnold van Gennep's identification of the three phases of rites of passage as separation, *limen* (margin or threshold), and aggregation, Turner seizes on the middle, "liminal" phase as crucial to rituals and offers a particularly evocative description of this state:

> The attributes of liminality or of liminal *personae* ("threshold people") are necessarily ambiguous, since this condition and these persons elude or slip through the network of classifications that normally locate states and positions in cultural space. Liminal entities are neither here nor there; they are betwixt and between the positions assigned and arrayed by law, custom, convention, and ceremonial. As such, their ambiguous and indeterminate attributes are expressed by a rich variety of symbols in the many societies that ritualize social and cultural transitions. Thus, liminality is frequently likened to death, to being in the womb, to invisibility, to darkness, to bisexuality, to the wilderness, and to an eclipse of the sun or moon.[70]

Liminality is a condition of suspension between established social positions. Occupying an interstitial, undecided space, liminal *personae* are marked by ambiguity. They moreover manifest a society's ambivalence, the uncertainties and contradictions within its accepted "network of classification." This "betwixt and between" state, however, does not imply a paralyzing indeterminacy. Instead, ritualization exploits the dynamic potential of liminality's ambiguity. Turner argues, "The liminal phase is the essential, *anti*-secular component in ritual *per se*, whether it be labeled 'religious' or 'magical.' Ceremony indicates, ritual *transforms*."[71] Through ritual, liminality acquires a transformative force.

This does not mean, however, that liminality (or ritual) is inherently subversive or radical. The debates in ritual studies that I described above highlight ritual's conservative effects as well as its oppositional possibilities, and the ambiguity of ritual is often part of larger practices that consolidate and maintain established social orders. Jon McKenzie's critique of the "liminal-norm" in performance studies, "where the valorization of liminal transgression or resistance itself becomes normative,"[72] cautions against ignoring liminality's more conventional inclinations, which Turner himself recognized. Hardly a naïve celebration of liminality, *Tea* stresses the burdens placed on "liminal personae" to sustain existing social distinctions, and imagines mundane rituals as practices of surviving, rather than subverting, their ambiguous positions. The *passage* supposedly afforded by liminality (and thus its efficacy) is, moreover, complicated in the play by its attachment to the everyday.

Liminality is in many ways the predominant mode and preoccupation of *Tea*. In presenting the women as participants in a ritualized routine, the performance also takes on the structure, trajectory, and rhythms of a ritual, with a particular focus on its liminal attributes. Fittingly set in Junction City, Kansas, it situates itself between life and death, the United States and Japan, and the past and the present. Himiko explains to the audience, "I am suspended between two worlds. There is no harmony here (*indicates the women in the tatami room*) nor here (*indicates her soul*)" (167). Himiko's gesture suggests that the other women are also in a limbic state, even if they are not trapped, as she is, in a more literal purgatory. The music that begins the play further emphasizes that the characters occupy the uncomfortable interstices between "Japanese" and "American": the stage directions stipulate, "In the darkness, an unaccented, female American voice belts out 'The Star Spangled Banner.' A traditional Japanese melody—perhaps 'Sakura'—cuts into the song's end as lights fade slowly half to suggest a netherworld" (162–63). The intermixing of two culturally emblematic songs immediately locates the characters in an ambiguous space between nations, which the dim lighting then infuses with further uncertainty by overlaying it with the "netherworld."

Tea's temporal structure and its use of role-doubling further heighten its liminal quality. Kimberly Jew suggests that these devices manifest a shift from the "real world," where Himiko is ridiculed for occasionally donning a blond wig and otherwise "acting out of character," to an explicitly theatrical world in which such behavior is no longer aberrant: "In the real world, Himiko's attempts to escape her identity were painfully unsuccessful, interpreted as signs of her mental instability. But in the unreal world of her interiority (i.e., the theatrical performance of *Tea*), her transformative acts are no longer unnatural."[73] The fluid movements between times, places, and characters establish role-playing and ambiguous identities as the conventions and norms of the performance and the world it represents, and thus situate the play in Himiko's limbo.

In terms of its temporal structure, the performance continuously vacillates between the present, in which the women are taking tea, and various moments of the past, such as the women's difficult lives in Japan immediately after World War II, their encounters with U.S. soldiers, and their first experiences in Kansas. In these shifts between past and present, the drama weaves the five women's stories in alternating patterns of likeness and difference. Bickering with Atsuko, who is protesting that she is not a "war bride" since she did not marry the war, Chiz remarks, "And then we came here—to Kansas. Not quite the fairy tale ending you ordered, eh, Ats?" (185). Chiz's remark then seems to trigger a "flashback" to their arrival in the United States, with each of the women recalling her difficulty adjusting to the move: Atsuko reenacts her efforts to find a Japanese restaurant, while Setsuko re-creates her indignation at discovering that she and her husband cannot stay at a hotel because they are an interracial couple. As the women then list Japanese foods that they miss, the dialogue takes on a repetitive, incantatory style:

> ATSUKO: Sasa-dango.
> TERUKO: Kushi-dango.
> CHIZ: Hot oden.
> SETSUKO: Kaki. There's nothing like Japanese persimmons.
> ATSUKO: He never told me there would be no Japanese food.
> SETSUKO: He never told me about "we reserve the right."
> CHIZ: I never thought he would die and leave me here to be an American without him.
> TERUKO: I never thought they would be scared of us, too.
> *The shrill whistle of a tea kettle blasts through the air, bringing the women back to the tatami room . . .*
> TERUKO: More tea.
> HIMIKO: (*to audience*) Yes. Please. They *must* keep drinking. (186)

Framed by Chiz's provocative statement and the piercing call of the tea kettle, the scene draws attention to each of the characters' distinct personalities and experiences even while progressively highlighting parallels with recurring words and sentence structures that recall the highly stylized, conventional speeches of formal rituals. The repetitions of "He never told me" and "I never thought," for example, establish analogies between their respective disillusionments. Although the women are ostensibly not doing much more than talking and sipping tea, the play infuses their recollections with a ritual style that underscores the dynamic adjustment and readjustment of their relationships. Despite the antagonism between Chiz and Atsuko, Chiz's bitter remark points to their common disappointments, which are remembered in a chant of missed foods and unpleasant revelations.

The five actors, however, must play not only the women in the "present" and their younger selves, but their husbands and children as well. The scenes in which they take on these different roles are introduced with appropriate remarks during the conversation and initially suggest a reenactment of the women's memories much like their remembrances of arriving in Kansas. The actor playing Setsuko begins the role-doubling by performing her husband's reaction to her first, failed attempt to use a washing machine: "Uh, Baby-san, why are you staring at the washing machine? . . . Yes, I promised it's all automatic. But honey, even when it's automatic, you have to push the button to turn it on" (188). Re-creating an interaction between wife and husband, the scene seems to be presenting the latter as the former remembers him (thus, as mediated by her perspective in the aftermath of Himiko's death). As the role-doubling continues, however, it begins to include situations in which the women would not have been present, such as their husbands' hunting trip and their daughters' sleepover. In these later scenes, the actors seem to play these characters as roles distinct from the "war brides" and their memories, although the three characters taken on by an actor remain linked by familial bonds. The performance therefore makes it difficult to determine if the reenactments of other family members represent the women's memories or projections, or mark a more complete shift to other roles.

This ambiguous layering of roles underscores the liminality that persists in theater in the nebulous relationships it makes possible between actors and characters. Moving from a "war bride" to her husband or her daughter, the actor carries traces of each role into the others. Marvin Carlson argues that actors are not transparent vehicles for characters but are instead haunted by previous performances.[74] In *Tea*, the assignment of several roles to one actor in a single production makes the haunting more acute.

While the uncertainty of the relationship between the minor roles and the primary characters adds to the liminal quality of the performance, the device also highlights the wider social networks in which each woman is situated—networks that become discernible through the changes in minute behaviors that accompany the actors' passages between roles. The doubling (or more precisely, the tripling) of roles joins the characters of one family together and makes the boundaries between them more permeable, but it also brings into relief the gulfs and differences between them by staging the actor's shifts from one character to the next, and thus the *work* required by such a passage. This work takes place largely through the mundane—that is, through the adoption of alternate mannerisms, accents, and other behavioral tendencies, as well as through repeated commentary on the quotidian disorientations of the "war brides."

The secondary characters of husbands and daughters explicitly verbalize their difference from the "war bride" characters performed by the same actor through remarks that stress the latter's apparent peculiarities, particularly those that seem to reflect their distance from normative American behaviors. Setsuko's husband thus explains to her that she must turn on the washing machine, while her daughter recounts to her friends, "Mom's so funny. We were separated in a store and, over the intercom, I heard: 'Japanese mother lost in dry goods. Will her daughter please claim her?'" (196). Such anecdotes would fit neatly into Smith and Worden's article on the Red Cross schools intended to "Americanize" Japanese women married to U.S. servicemen. The women's lack of proficiency in carrying out domestic tasks such as washing clothing and buying groceries becomes the sign of their difference and further accentuates the disparities between characters by highlighting their varying degrees of ease with everyday American living.

These accounts of quotidian behaviors that seem to set the women apart, however, are complicated by the shifts in minute bodily expressions that must accompany the leaps between characters. In moving from one character to the next, the actors must simulate the behavioral transformations demanded of the "war brides" by becoming their "more American" husbands and children. The switching of roles, while clarified and emphasized by the ensuing dialogue, must initially be indicated by a change in comportment: when the women first play their husbands, "they appear rigid, stoic with the carriage of men" (188). As the actors adopt corporeal expressions of masculinity and military training, their bodies become sites of incomplete transformations. Haunted by their previous enactments of the "war brides" as well as physical attributes and habits that exceed their performance in the play, they materialize both the possibility *and* the impossibility of becoming another. The daughters' sleepover captures an even more complicated dynamic: during this scene, several of the teenagers mockingly imitate their mothers' accents as they share stories of the latter's eccentricities. As the same actors who play the mothers also play the daughters *mimicking* the mothers, verbal inflections must embody subtle degrees of proximity and distance. When imitating their mothers, the daughters must suggest their familiarity with their parents' verbal tendencies, even as their accents must be distinguishable from the actors' *direct* performances of the mothers, which would not be channeled through the daughters' voices and bodies. As the three roles assumed by each actor reflect on and interact with one another, they manifest each character as the *incongruent* coalescence of family relationships.[75]

By assigning actors multiple roles, each accompanied by specific temporal and spatial shifts, the play locates each "war bride" in a constellation of sociohistorical exigencies and familial bonds, which, when juxtaposed, situates them in an increasingly complicated matrix of social relations.[76] This interplay of difference and affinity, enacted through the mundane and patterned by the stylized repetitions and heightened liminality of ritual, propels the performance as the women continue to talk and take tea, and constitutes the flexible, provisional community they form by its conclusion. The last scene connects an explicitly religious ritual with the more quotidian sharing of tea among friends, thus emphasizing the productive joining of the sacred and the mundane. The scene begins with the women doing a Buddhist chant to call Himiko to join them for tea. Chiz then sets down a fifth cup for Himiko: "The women sit for a last drink of tea. Himiko joins them. They lift their cups simultaneously and slightly bow their heads to one another. Himiko forms a cup with her hands and drinks from it in unison with the others. She looks happier" (200). If, as Turner argues, ritual *trans-*

forms, the primary transformations traced by the play are the passage of Himiko's spirit from limbo to the afterworld and the development of a community among all of the women. Or more precisely, Himiko is able to find peace through the women's ritualized performance of community, which transforms their limbic state "between two worlds" from a condition of solitude to a site of generative bonds.

As significant as rituals are to the play, however, it is their ongoing engagements with the mundane that promise to sustain the characters' dynamic ties to one another. As the women leave Himiko's home, Chiz seems to confirm the ritual's success by declaring, "I am glad I came here today. Somehow, I feel at home with you women, you Japanese women. (*smiles*) Today" (200). Chiz's statement suggests an affirmation of their solidarity, but it also leaves some uncertainty as to whether or not the community they perform is sustainable. By claiming that she feels at home with "you Japanese women," Chiz simultaneously identifies with them and sets herself apart. Furthermore, she punctuates her remark with "Today," suggesting their friendship may be transient. The ambiguity of Chiz's statements thus suggests that the women must continually perform and re-perform their fragile community, materializing it in the repetition of distinctly *everyday* rituals—those that are not framed and rarefied as special if regularly repeated events, but are instead integrated into the restless, uneven currents of daily life.

Ritual at the Limits of Form

The publication and production records of *Itsuka* and *Tea*, respectively, suggest broad cultural dispersals that aptly flout the pressures to disappear exposed in each work. *Itsuka*, while not matching *Obasan's* popularity or reputation, was nevertheless a best seller in Canada. *Tea* is Houston's most frequently performed work and one of the most staged plays by an Asian American writer, with over fifty productions in a range of cities in the United States, as well as in Japan, Taiwan, and Singapore. The recipient of numerous awards, *Tea* has been continuously produced since its world premiere in 1987. These public disseminations, however, have also been accompanied by strikingly parallel criticisms of the novel and the play as excessively documentary and political, alternately too prosaic or ornate, and insufficiently novelistic or dramatic.

These reviews, like any other, reflect particular assumptions about eval-
uative criteria and the proper relationship between politics and art, as
well as the critics' own social positions and aesthetic preferences. Yet
the discomfort elicited by the two works' interest in the ritualized mundane also sheds light on the inevitable limits of demonstrating, through
literary and dramatic representation, the significance of practices that
require continuous, communal enactments. In other words, the play
and the novel must paradoxically stay *unconsummated* efforts to convey
the generative force of the "rituals of everyday life" precisely in order to
remain consistent with the importance they place on sustained, collective participation in quotidian acts.

Tea's numerous performances suggest its effectiveness as a medium
for sharing what Houston describes in her dramatist's notes as "the vir-
tually undocumented historical fact of communities of Japanese 'war
brides' who have lived in Kansas over the last twenty to forty years" (162).
Lukewarm reviews of the drama in mainstream publications, however,
seem to stand in contrast to its frequent and widespread production. I
am not implying here that there should be a direct correlation between
critical reception and popularity, but contradictory patterns in critical
and popular responses can help illuminate a work's complex engagements with its audiences. In the case of *Tea*, I find reviews of the play
instructive not so much for cataloguing its weaknesses, but for register-
ing the entirely apposite limits of its attempt to straddle the gap between
conventional theater and mundane ritual.

The *New York Times* review of the Pan Asian Repertory's 2007 production of *Tea* illustrates the kind of dubious reaction that, I suggest,
must be considered in relation to the drama's preoccupation with "the
ritual of everyday life." The article is one of several that criticize the play
as insufficiently theatrical and too documentary, prone to stereotypes,
clichés, and melodramatic language, or simply tedious.[77] The writer,
Anne Midgette remarks, "Since the plot calls for a climactic catharsis,
one almost forgets to notice that the characters' actions don't actually
seem enough to trigger it."[78] Midgette thus criticizes the unmotivated
nature of the change that the characters undergo. Yet as a performance
of the ritualized mundane, the play depends on a different logic of causality and efficacy. Grimes argues, "Ritualizing requires meandering; it
is not reducible to causal, narrative, or rational sequences. This drifti-

ness of logic and storyline is undramatic, even though ritualized events may be thick with theatrical elements."[79] Grimes likens the cadence of ritualization to a distracted tapping rather than a carefully developed crescendo.

Furthermore, in a ritual, transformation depends on participation and execution as much as conflict and resolution. Although the climactic moment in which Atsuko threatens to leave and then decides to stay may seem insufficient to reviewers as the trigger for catharsis, the effectiveness of everyday rituals is intrinsically tied to the collective execution of mundane activities. Feeling insulted one too many times by Chiz, Atsuko rises to leave and demands that Teruko follow. The usually compliant Teruko, however, insists on staying:

> To [Atsuko's] shock, Teruko even more firmly turns away. Devastated, Atsuko moves toward the door and then, defeated, falls to her knees; Himiko immediately comes to her side.
> HIMIKO: Atsuko-san, stay. If you leave now, no one will rest.
> Himiko stands in front of Atsuko and, without touching her, helps her to stand and balance using her hands as delicate guides. Atsuko fights with herself and then turns back to the women. She bows in apology to Teruko who bows back. She turns toward the door again, but Setsuko bows to her. Feeling much better, Atsuko returns the bow. Still uncomfortable, Atsuko glances at Chiz who motions kindly for her to sit down. (195–96)

This scene (and, ultimately, the play) turns on Teruko and Atsuko's decision to remain until the women have finished taking tea together. Teruko's tendency to defer to Atsuko and Atsuko's tendency to belittle the other women make both of their decisions not to leave a significant departure from their preceding behaviors. Himiko's plea for Atsuko to stay, or "no one will rest," raises the stakes of the choice. Although nothing particularly distinctive occurs before or after the women decide to stay, they tacitly affirm the necessity of developing their nascent community. Culminating not in a dramatic revelation but in the women's resolution to keep sharing tea, the play advances participation as the crucial undertaking that enables transformation. Teruko and Atsuko's continued involvement allows the tea taking to "meander" and "drift" along to its completion in a rhythm characteristic not only of ritual, but also of the everyday.

The play's investment in collective undertakings extends to the relationship it strives to develop with the audience, which it occasionally invokes as ritual participants as opposed to theater spectators. According to Richard Schechner, "The move from theater to ritual happens when the audience is transformed from a collection of separate individuals into a group or congregation of participants."[80] By setting Himiko as an intermediary not only between life and death, but also between the audience and the stage, the performance cultivates a more participatory relationship with the audience. In the opening scenes, as the women prepare to gather for tea, Himiko "holds out her arms in welcome to the audience as the other women exit," and ostensibly invites the audience to join the gathering: "Come, . . . it is time for tea" (165). This gesture insinuates the audience's involvement in the ritual about to unfold. By aligning spectators with Himiko, it situates them in a murky, limbic space between silent witness and active participant. Himiko continues to address the audience throughout the play, but the script calls for her to speak "as if she is on trial and offering a matter-of-fact defense" (165). She therefore implicates the audience as her interlocutor yet assumes that they, like the other "war brides," view her life critically. In the final scene, however, the performance presents the possibility of a different relationship between Himiko and the audience, one that replicates the community instantiated among the women: "Himiko kneels downstage center. Holding the cup outward, she bows gracefully to the audience and then drinks the tea with extreme thirst that appears to be satisfied from the drink. She sets the cup down in front of her and smiles a half-smile, perhaps like that of Mona Lisa, to the audience. She bows low, all the way to the floor" (200). When Himiko turns to the audience at the play's end, taking her final sip with them after the women leave, she asks those in attendance to see themselves not as spectators, but as participants in a ritual of continuous community making.

In addition, other conventions employed by the play, such as the assignment of multiple roles to one actor, highlight the liminal aspects that endure even in dramatic productions that enforce a segregation of audience and actor, or emphasize (theatrical) entertainment over (ritual) efficacy.[81] Repeatedly blurring the lines between spectator and participant, between actor and role, and between the doubled roles, the performance prompts the audience to manage their indeterminate boundaries. In other words, it accentuates the audience's active engagement in the processes of theater making as they accommodate the passages that an actor makes between her multiple roles.

Despite these gestures toward turning actors and audiences alike into Schechner's "congregation of participants," *Tea* ultimately remains a theatrical representation of ritualized practices. As I argued above, the play's particular rhythm, logic of causality, and arrangement of typical (or stereotypical) differences become comprehensible when viewed as a reflection of its investment in mundane rituals. Yet this very emphasis on ritualization and the everyday strains against its concurrent enforcement of a now more conventional divide between actors and spectators. If, as *Tea* suggests, cultivating a community that can flexibly negotiate the dual pressures of racialization and assimilation requires repeated, collective, and quotidian practices, audience members as witnesses who ultimately remain on one side of the stage/seat divide must drift, like Himiko in the play's beginning, at the edges of its ritualizing force, where the productiveness of liminality remains only a potential.

Reviews of *Itsuka* even more explicitly point to what I characterize as the novel's ritualization of the mundane as its major weakness. In a review that Kogawa cites as having eroded her confidence as a writer,[82] Stan Persky simultaneously praises *Obasan* and lambasts *Itsuka*. Denouncing the second half of the novel for subsuming aesthetics to politics, he declares that "scenes that unfolded like the paper birds of origami in the earlier novel give way to a clunky succession of public meetings, demonstrations, and office-bound strategy sessions," and later adds, "The rhetoric of Community Studies 101 is laid on with a trowel in Kogawa's earnest, well-meaning, ultimately lifeless documentary-a-clef."[83] Comparing *Obasan*'s aesthetic merits to the elegance of origami, Persky's review characterizes *Itsuka*'s interest in the mundane details of political mobilization as an unfortunate deviation from the poetic sensibilities of the first novel.[84] Like Persky, Mary di Michele in the *Toronto Star* hones in on what they both regard as Kogawa's excessive chronicling of the redress movement's organizational activities. She claims, "Through too much of the novel the reader is lost at the back of the room in meetings where characters are not people but a show of hands," and muses, "Kogawa appears to be overwhelmed by the aesthetic problems of depicting the workings of a bureaucracy."[85] Di Michele supports the latter criticism with a passage from the novel that I quoted above: "The more meetings we attend, the more we need to attend. We're learning how to fly by stuffing envelopes" (243). For di Michele, these lines exemplify the difficult marriage of figurative language and bureaucratic minutiae. Transforming characters into votes and envelopes into wings, Kogawa (these reviews claim) has turned her novel into an uneven work of historical or political—but not literary—interest.

Emphasizing a clash between the novel's more documentary accounts of political mobilization and its more expressive accounts of Naomi's personal development, these reviews illustrate their awkward merging by highlighting the passages that depict the ritualization of mundane behaviors. Di Michele thus turns to the scene of stuffing envelopes to demonstrate the strain between politics and aesthetics, or between a bureaucratic "show of hands" and an inspired portrayal of a character's blossoming. Like Midgette, di Michele seems puzzled by the significance bestowed upon banal occurrences by aesthetic effects, such as the assumption of dramatic catharsis or elaborate metaphors.

What I have argued in this chapter, however, is that in Kogawa's novel and Houston's drama, these quotidian activities are efficacious for those who practice them precisely *because* they seem unremarkable and routine. The symbolic links they construct between bodies and stories are cemented by being interwoven with the familiar textures of the participants' everyday motions. Furthermore, they achieve their full effect (namely, the performance of community) only through repeated enactments. The uneasiness generated by the novel and the play's efforts to incorporate the "I" into the "we," or to join metaphors of healing with an ardently political rejection of disappearance exposes, then, a gap between reading or seeing their performances of community and materializing community as an everyday performance. The limits reached by the novel and the play in conveying the significance of such practices therefore aptly, if somewhat paradoxically, make the case that scrupulous documentation, dense imagery, and even staged representations can only partially capture the force of the ritualized mundane.

With respect to *Tea*, however, extending the boundaries of analysis to include the processes leading up to its productions unveils other sites that might more fully realize its conception of everyday rituals. Schechner contends that "the workshop-rehearsal process and the ritual process are analogous,"[86] and emphasizes that the former is "'betwixt and between' the fixed world from which material is extracted and the fixed score of the performance text."[87] In her study of the 1993 performance of *Tea* by the Horizons Theatre in Washington, D.C., Susan Haedicke describes these preproduction processes and highlights their consistency with the drama's themes. She argues, "This intercultural exploration [of the 'between-world' condition] turned out to be conducted more in the process of mounting the play than in the actual production."[88] She then describes how the rehearsals included the sharing of stories and food, replicating the exchanges that take place in the play. During these gatherings, one of the actors recounted her mother's experiences as a "war bride," while the director, who is Jewish American, initiated a discussion of ethnicity by describing her experiences confronting prejudice after moving from New York to the Midwest.[89] In this instance of life imitating art, *Tea*'s ritual potential was realized not in the execution of the final performance, but in its participants' collective involvement in the routine processes of theater making.

While some form of ritual possibility might inhere in the rehearsal process itself, the specific models of interaction (exchanging food and stories) as well as the subjects of discussion (social alienation, lineage, and geographic displacement) were directly informed by Houston's script. The concerns of the drama and the modes of performance that it presents are thus not insignificant to what the rehearsals accomplished, and how. Although the audience members of an already rehearsed performance might be the assumed addressees of a dramatic script, at least one intended for production, the cast and crew that stage a play are, necessarily, its first audience, and the one that accompanies it from the initial readings to the final performances. When Himiko therefore begins the play by "hold[ing] out her arms in welcome to the audience," and bidding them, "Come, . . . it is time for tea" (165), her invitation extends to the audience of actors, directors, and stage crews already charged with turning these words into a live performance. By writing her mother's story as theater, Houston etches into the script the promise that communities will come together to take tea and share stories and, through everyday practices on and off the stage, continuously forge new constellations of affinity and difference.

*   *   *

In 1988, the Nikkei International Marriage Society, headed by Kazuko Stout, held the first convention for Japanese American "war brides," which brought together over three hundred participants. International conventions followed in Hawaii in 1994 and in Japan in 1997, and the latter became the first visit back to Japan for several attendees, who had been reluctant to return earlier due to lingering feelings of shame.[90] According to Regina Lark, Stout chose to use the term "international bride" for the convention because of the negative connotations still carried by the term "war bride." Lark relates, "Stout aims to change the sobriquet 'war bride' [to] mean courageous and strong, rather than passive and dependent. The annual meetings help to see her goals to fruition."[91] A tireless organizer who strives to build and maintain connections among the women, Stout is reminiscent of *Itsuka*'s Aunt Emily. Her desire to redefine a "war bride" identity indeed resonates with the climactic moment of Kogawa's novel, when the prime minister offers an official apology. Naomi recounts, "Aunt Emily and I look at each other and smile. We've all said it over the years. 'No, no, I'm Canadian. I'm a Canadian. A Canadian.' Sometimes it's been a defiant statement, a demand, a proclamation of a right. And today, finally, finally, though we can hardly believe it, to be Canadian means what it hasn't meant before. Reconciliation. Liberation. Belongingness. Home" (328). For Emily and Naomi, the success of the redress movement transforms what it means to claim a Canadian identity. Once fraught with a history of rejection and mistreatment, it comes to mark the homecoming of Japanese Canadians on their own terms—that is, not through dispersal and disappearance, but through the struggle for redress.

In their influential work *Racial Formation in the United States*, Michael Omi and Howard Winant stress that the rearticulation of identity is crucial to social movements and political change: "Social movements create collective identity by offering their adherents a different view of themselves and their world; different, that is, from the worldview and self-concepts offered by the established social order. They do this by the process of *rearticulation*, which produces new subjectivity by making use of information and knowledge already present in the subject's mind. They take elements and themes of her/his culture and traditions and infuse them with new meaning."[92] Rearticulation imbues existing "elements and themes" with a different significance and force. It is made possible by social movements, but also shapes their course and effects. Omi and Winant argue, for example, that the "rearticulation of black collective subjectivity" from one of survival to struggle was vital to shifting the civil rights movement in a more radical direction.[93]

The cultivation of new views, self-concepts, and knowledge, however, always occurs alongside and in tension with quotidian practices and habitual behaviors. *Itsuka* and *Tea* make the case that the collective, repeated embodiments that constitute everyday rituals are integral to materializing and sustaining such rearticulations. Combining the transformative liminality of ritual with the subtle authority of the mundane, such performances charge shared identifications and realize declared affiliations. The point is not that political battles are won and lost in the field of the mundane, but rather that an engagement with the everyday is critical, as well as inevitable.

3

Making Change

Interracial Conflict, Cross-Racial Performance

Offering an image as startling as the meeting of an operating table, a sewing machine, and an umbrella made famous by the surrealists,[1] Allen Cooper, a former gang member and an activist for gang reconciliation, recounts seeing an unsettling juxtaposition of a pistol and a bubble gum machine:

> I was at one of these swap meets
> and a bubble gum machine man pulled a gun out.
> Now what a bubble gum machine man doin' with a pistol?
> Who wanna rob a bubble gum machine?
> Because we live here, the conditions are so
> enormous and so dangerous,
> that they have to be qualified to carry a firearm.[2]

For Cooper, the pairing of gum and gun, innocence and violence, is both remarkable and ordinary. The mystery he initially presents ("what a bubble gum machine man doin' with a pistol?") is explained by "the conditions," the everyday circumstances that are themselves "so/enormous and so dangerous" that they render the collocation of pistol and bubble gum machine necessary and common. If, as Ben Highmore describes, surrealism "is about an effort, an energy, to find the marvellous [*sic*] in the everyday, to recognize the everyday as a dynamic montage of elements, to make it strange so that its strangeness can be recognized,"[3] the image that Cooper provides similarly brings into relief the strangeness of the everyday, but highlights what is horrifying rather than what is marvelous.

The lines above come from Cooper's conversation with performance artist Anna Deavere Smith. After interviewing approximately two hundred people about the 1992 social upheaval most commonly known as the Los Angeles riots, Smith reenacted their responses in a performance titled *Twilight: Los Angeles, 1992*. In the excerpt that Smith later published, Cooper insists that the very designation of certain behaviors and incidents as mundane or spectacular, ordinary or strange, has important repercussions for how people live and what they find credible. Ruminating on the uprising, Cooper explains,

> But we're not basin' our life on Reginald Denny;
> neither are we basin' our lives on Rodney King.
> Only thing we're expressing through the Rodney King—
> through Reginald Denny beating—
> it shows how
> a black person gets treated in his community.
> And it was once brought to light
> and shown
> and then we still . . . we see no belief,
> because they never handled, from the top of the level, the way it
> should have been handled,
> because they handled it like a soap opera . . .
> If you put twenty hidden cameras
> in the country jail system
> you got people beat worse than that
> point blank. (100)

According to Cooper, the widely broadcast beatings of Rodney King and Reginald Denny, which came to emblematize the Los Angeles riots, simultaneously made visible *and* obscured everyday conditions of physical threat ("how / a black person gets treated in his community"). Cooper argues that although the recording of four Los Angeles police officers beating King, an unarmed African American man, brought attention to issues of racism and police brutality, depictions of this act of violence and the upheaval that followed it as a "soap opera" by the media asserted their exceptional nature, and thus did little to increase public "belief" in quotidian experiences of discrimination and violence, the everyday strangeness of the gun next to the bubble gum machine. Meanwhile, the spotlight put on the beating of white trucker Reginald

Denny shifted attention from the violence inflicted on King to the violence inflicted by African American men.

Like Anna Deavere Smith, Elizabeth Wong explored the relationship between the everyday and the spectacular and its influence on interracial relations in her drama *Kimchee and Chitlins* (1990). The play depicts tensions between black customers and Korean American merchants in New York City and had a staged reading at the Mark Taper Forum in Los Angeles several months after the uprising. It follows the efforts of a reporter, Suzie Seeto, to cover a protest that closely resembles the 1990 boycott of two stores in Flatbush, Brooklyn. Near the end of the drama, after failing to discover the truth about the altercation that triggered the boycott, Suzie remarks, "I still don't know what happened in the store, and whatever *did* happen isn't as important as what *has* happened. How did such a trivial event cause all *this*—boycott, court injunction, pain, suffering."[4] Reverend Carter, an African American activist who takes leadership of the boycott, responds, "History, Suzie, has often been triggered by such trivial events. Someone in Montgomery, Alabama, orders a black woman to give up a seat on a bus. Mahatma Gandhi created a free India all because he got thrown off a train" (441). For Suzie, her search for an accurate account of the instigating dispute has led her not to the truth, as she had anticipated, but to the limits of her reporting. As Reverend Carter reminds her, however, the everyday interactions that she finds both elusive and trivial can give rise to large movements of resistance, producing history from routine.

Delving into the connections between the crises in Los Angeles and New York and daily encounters in inner-city neighborhoods, *Twilight* and *Kimchee and Chitlins* draw attention to the representational practices that constrain the possibilities for effectively addressing tensions. The semantic overlap between the "mediation" of representation and the "mediation" of arbitration is particularly appropriate here, as it points to a correlation between the medium through which such events are portrayed, and its impact on efforts at reconciliation. Accounts of antagonistic relations between black customers and Korean American merchants that proliferated during and after the 1990 boycott and the 1992 uprising evinced a recurrent interest in the role that the conduct of store owners and employees may have played in aggravating the communities in which their businesses were located. Reporters, community and government representatives, and affected individuals all stressed a link between the conflicts in New York and Los Angeles and seemingly trivial behaviors such as making eye contact or giving change, and raised the question of how modifying such mannerisms might prevent future disputes. These deliberations on the habits of interaction between merchants and customers, however, tended to presume and affirm broad notions of racial difference, evading biological essentialism only through generalizations about clashing cultures. Exemplifying the contradictions of the racial mundane, everyday behaviors came to embody both intractable differences and their potential attenuation through the retraining of individual conduct.

Kimchee and Chitlins and *Twilight* draw attention to the limitations of media representations of the boycott and the uprising to suggest the possibility of reconfiguring habits of perception and interaction through a different kind of "mediation," namely that of performing the mundane *across* the social divides intensified by the conflicts. Exploring the effects of assuming the gestures, mannerisms, and speech of others, these performances grapple with the dangers of such reenactments even as they demonstrate that traversing racial boundaries and mixing theatrical and journalistic conventions can expose the multiple, unremarked exchanges that trigger and exacerbate antagonistic encounters. The two works moreover supplement theories of theater that emphasize its ability to offer a distanced, critical view of established social relations with models of cross-racial performance that materialize the productive *entanglement* of bodies at the moment of sight and speech. They therefore investigate theater's potential to reconceive the messy intersections of habitual behaviors and habituated perceptions that make representing and ameliorating interracial conflicts so risky and difficult.

The "Black-Korean Conflict"

On January 18, 1990, an argument between Bong Ok Jang, the manager of the Family Red Apple Grocery in Flatbush, Brooklyn, and Giselaine Felissaint, a customer of the store, led to allegations by Felissaint that Jang physically attacked her after accusing her of shoplifting. Jang meanwhile insisted that Felissaint became angry after a dispute over the bill and began throwing produce at him. The difficulty of verifying either of these accounts left the truth of what happened between Felissaint and Jang unclear. This incident precipitated a months-long boycott of the Family Red Apple Grocery and a nearby store that was also owned by Korean Americans. These demonstrations were among a series of boycotts in New York in the 1980s and 1990s that set Korean American store owners and employees against black protestors, who declared that the merchants treated customers with disrespect and contributed to the economic depression of the neighborhoods in which they ran their stores.

Similar tensions between merchants and customers came to the fore in Los Angeles on March 16, 1991, when liquor store owner Soon Ja Du shot and killed teenager Latasha Harlins. Du apparently saw Harlins place a carton of orange juice in her backpack and grabbed the bag as Harlins approached the counter to pay, mistaking her actions as an attempt to shoplift. Harlins then punched Du, who threw a stool at the teenager and shot her as she turned to exit the store. Captured by security cameras, this confrontation occurred just thirteen days after another violent encounter recorded on video: the beating of Rodney King by four Los Angeles police officers. Through the repeated juxtaposition of the two videos, these incidents became intertwined as confirmations of a persisting disregard for the lives of black Americans. The results of the two trials further aggravated tensions. A jury convicted Du of voluntary manslaughter and recommended sixteen years in jail, but the presiding judge sentenced her to five years of probation instead. Several months later, on April 29, 1992, a mainly white jury in the suburb of Simi Valley charged officer Laurence Powell with one count of excessive force in the King beating but otherwise acquitted the officers of all charges. The verdict sparked a multiday uprising in Los Angeles during which a clip of several African American men beating white trucker Reginald Denny joined the constellation of videos that came to epitomize the riots. Over fifty people, most of them black and Latino men, died in the upheaval, and large parts of the city were destroyed, with Korean American–owned businesses constituting a majority of those burned and looted.

The New York boycott and the Los Angeles uprising exposed the untenable intersection of various economic and social pressures in neglected urban areas. In the 1980s, cuts in federal funding for social programs and the shipping of jobs to other countries, including South Korea, increased the economic depression of inner-city neighborhoods. Meanwhile, close economic and political relationships between the United States and South Korea created conditions that encouraged South Korean immigration to the United States. Ivan Light and Edna Bonacich argue that the rapid growth of an export-based economy, a repressive government, and relatively depressed wages in South Korea were among the factors that, combined with the easing of U.S. immigration restrictions, prompted many in the South Korean urban middle class to emigrate.[5] Arriving in the United States with some capital and access to community "money clubs" (the *ggeh*), which allowed for the pooling of resources, Korean immigrants were able to establish stores in neighborhoods where the flight of capital made such businesses profitable and affordable—although not affordable enough for residents who were consistently denied bank loans.

Relations between Korean American merchants and black customers were only a part of the complex multiracial and multiethnic topography of the affected neighborhoods. In Los Angeles, increasing numbers of Latino and Asian immigrants moved into these areas through the 1980s as residents and business owners, respectively, while the number of African Americans gradually declined. Peter Morrison and Ira Lowry's study of the demographics of the Los Angeles uprising includes revealing maps of the residential patterns of different racial groups immediately before the riots. These maps show a concentration of African Americans living in the center of the city, overlapping with neighborhoods in which Latino communities resided; Asian Americans primarily lived at the edge of these areas, and the outer zones were made up of mostly white residents.[6] Despite common depictions of the uprising as a black-white or black-Asian conflict, the Los Angeles Latino community suffered a significant portion of the murders, arrests, and property damages. Similar characterizations of the New York boycott in broad racial terms obscured the impact of immigration from both Korea and the Caribbean on Brooklyn neighborhoods like Flatbush. For example, Philip Kasinitz stresses that complicated relationships of both solidarity and antagonism exist in these communities between recent Afro-Caribbean immigrants such as Felissaint and African Americans whose lineage in the United States stretches back multiple generations.[7]

The prevailing idiom through which the public came to understand interactions between black customers and Korean American merchants tended to elide these complexities and accordingly limited the possibilities for mediation and change. Namely, discussions of potential causes and solutions frequently pointed to "cultural differences" as an instigating factor and focused on the everyday behaviors that seemed to reflect these differences. In her study of the Los Angeles riots and the so-called Black-Korean conflict, Regina Freer notes that although many African Americans and Korean Americans expressed an awareness of the economic circumstances contributing to tensions, they also stressed the significance of a "culture clash": "Echoing concerns about 'disrespectful' merchants, individuals on both sides of the conflict pointed to ignorance of 'American customs' on the part of the first generation Korean Americans as being a crucial piece of the conflict puzzle."[8] Among the behaviors of Korean American merchants repeatedly cited as causing friction were the tendencies to avoid eye contact, drop change on the counter, and watch shoppers with suspicion, as well as a general lack of effort to treat customers with respect. The mundane, as what presumably embodied "cultural differences," became a central concern in debates about the "Black-Korean conflict."

Despite varying assessments of the importance of these behaviors in relation to socioeconomic issues, the habits of interaction between merchants and customers received much attention across the nation as a critical factor in understanding and ameliorating the crises in Los Angeles and New York. For example, in August 1990, in the midst of the Brooklyn boycott, a conference on "Human Relations: Racial and Cultural Diversity" attended by those of African, Caribbean, and Korean descent included a discussion of Korean customs that might aggravate the clientele of Korean American businesses.[9] The numerous stories on the "Black-Korean conflict" that appeared after the riots reiterated this interest in "cultural differences." In a passage that encapsulates a refrain common in these articles, Rhonda Richards of USA Today relates, "Many blacks and Koreans just don't seem to understand each other, experts say. There are language barriers, racial stereotypes and cultural differences. Many Koreans avoid eye contact with customers, which they say shows respect. But that infuriates many blacks, used to being shunned at store counters by white clerks."[10] Kathryn Tolbert in the Boston Globe similarly emphasizes a disjuncture between how customers and merchants perceive the latter's conduct: "Koreans explain the problem between shopkeepers and customers as stemming from cultural differences, such as their reluctance to make physical contact when passing change across the counter—a familiarity that in Korea is inappropriate between businessman and customer—to limited English that inhibits friendly small talk. Customers, meanwhile, view the Koreans as sullen, unfriendly, and racist."[11] In both articles, a single, seemingly minor behavioral tendency—the avoidance of eye or physical contact—comes to exemplify the opposing perspectives and conventions that collide in these encounters. Although both customers and merchants imply that the latter are conducting "business as usual," the merchants, who are largely recent immigrants, claim that they are running their businesses as they would in Korea, while their customers see their behavior as continuing a long tradition of racial discrimination.

Public interest in these everyday exchanges gave aggrieved residents an opportunity to voice their anger at the behavior of merchants, and store owners an opportunity to suggest that a cultural gap, as opposed to an intent to offend, explained their conduct. Yet the emphasis on "cultural differences" tended to reinforce racial divisions and overshadow the historical and economic circumstances that affected relations between merchants and customers. Kyeyoung Park argues that "the media-led discourse portrays black-Korean conflict as a racial confrontation yet describes the details largely in terms of cultural differences, seldom mentioning the lack of public policy to deal with urban problems such as racism and poverty."[12] Nancy Abelmann and John Lie further stress that popular accounts of hostilities reified "essentialized views of the two ethnic groups,"[13] not only obscuring material factors but also encouraging ahistorical notions of difference. The reference to "culture" allowed for an evasion of biological essentialism, yet perpetuated ideas of fundamental racial dissimilarities that obscured, for example, class disparities among Korean Americans and ethnic heterogeneity in black communities. Heon Cheol Lee suggests that these discussions about cultural differences contributed to the tensions that they purportedly explained: "Instead of the conflict being generated by the cultural differences, the conflict itself seems to generate ethnic myths about both Koreans and blacks in America."[14] Arguing that repeated accounts of a culture clash propagated racial divisions, Lee points to the performative nature of this discourse: reiterations of cultural difference, retroactively instituted as the primary cause of conflict, manifested the apparent "truth" of racial difference, and diverted attention away from the historical and structural conditions shaping merchant-customer interactions.

Attempts by government and community organizations to ease tensions by retraining the behavior of merchants, however, only validated sketchy assessments of a fundamental culture clash and encouraged merchants to adopt "nicer" manners that would effectively sustain rather than change the socioeconomic makeup of these neighborhoods. Given that parties offered differing interpretations of the same behaviors, the act or mannerism itself would seem less important than the particular historical or social frame with which various individuals understood such conduct. Nevertheless, changing the behaviors themselves became a crucial component of efforts to ameliorate relations. For example, a committee appointed by the mayor after the New York boycott recommended "cultural exchange programs or sensitivity training" for Korean American merchants.[15] Meanwhile, Korean American community organizations ran advertisements in Korean-language newspapers and cable channels to encourage different business practices, and conducted seminars to teach merchants to smile, place change directly into customers' hands, and offer a thank-you.[16] By habituating recent immigrants to the "proper" way to run an American business, these programs for Korean American merchants merely trained them to conform to these norms. Abelmann and Lie point out that "smiling Korean American merchants and understanding African American customers leave both groups in the same place they were in to begin with."[17] Even if such efforts could change everyday interactions between merchants and customers, they would help maintain rather than alter aggravating economic and social conditions.

By focusing exclusively on the relationship between residents and shopkeepers, programs to reduce cultural misunderstandings moreover obscured the role of parties not visibly implicated in the "Black-Korean conflict." The uprising and the boycott were as much the result of what was and continues to be absent in inner-city neighborhoods (e.g., employment opportunities, public funding for schools and recreational spaces, and a variety of options for purchasing food and other goods), as they were the result of unhappy relationships between the individuals living and working there. Yet in contrast to the hypervisibility of the Korean American "middleman minority,"[18] the economic and political influences that determined the terms in which these interactions took place remained largely invisible. For example, corporations profited from the goods sold in the markets, but did not have to bear the brunt of anger at the continuous flow of money out of these neighborhoods. Freer observes, "Because they so often represent the only economic activity in the black community, and are thus held up as examples of success by larger society, Korean merchants come to represent the economic exploitation felt by South Central Los Angeles residents."[19] Eclipsing less provocative factors, the issue of "cultural differences" obscured the responsibility of the government, corporations, and other institutions whose imprints were mediated through the surrogacy of the middleman minority, or felt in the absence of public support and financial investments.[20]

I am not arguing, however, that everyday interactions between merchants and customers were insignificant, or only significant as a smokescreen for economic factors. The perception of business owners as rude or residents as threatening, for example, had clear consequences. The violent altercation between Du and Harlins and the dispute between Felissaint and Jang are inseparable from the accumulation of everyday tensions and sedimentation of stereotypes. In both cases, persistent, reciprocal suspicions provoked aggressive behaviors that seemed to confirm the perception of hostility. During the riots, the quality of daily relationships between merchants and customers affected the fates of some businesses. Ella Stewart recounts that in one neighborhood, residents protected a store run by a reportedly pleasant Korean American couple, whereas another business nearby was destroyed.[21]

I therefore direct my critique not at the interest in everyday encounters per se, but rather the propensity in depictions of the "Black-Korean conflict" to detach the mundane from other considerations. Insofar as media reports and responses by government and community organizations emphasized an inherently cultural conflict between African Americans and Korean Americans, they not only reinforced notions of intractable racial difference, but also simplified the historical pressures and material constraints that shape habits of behavior and perception *and* inform how such habits interact.[22]

As Bourdieu stresses in his elaboration of the habitus, perceptual and behavioral tendencies are always developed within sociohistorical relationships that they also perpetuate. He argues, "The *habitus*, a product of history, produces individual and collective practices—more history—in accordance with the schemes generated by history. It ensures the active presence of past experiences, which, deposited in each organism in the form of schemes of perception, thought and action, tend to guarantee the 'correctness' of practices and their constancy over time, more reliably than all formal rules and explicit norms."[23] The habitus consists of the quotidian, ostensibly unremarkable ways of seeing and behaving that are all the more influential for their apparent triviality in shaping and transmitting social practices. For Bourdieu, the tacit acquisition and enactment of these conventions reflect *and* reproduce established relations of difference and inequity, lending existing social conditions their concreteness as well as an inevitable quality.

The grievances that culminated in the boycott and the uprising, however, point to the necessity of complicating Bourdieu's analysis with a consideration of the interface between habitus developed within markedly differing sociohistorical circumstances. According to Bourdieu, the habitus is rarely questioned because those with similar proclivities tend to congregate: "The *habitus* tends to protect itself from crises and critical challenges by providing itself with a milieu to which it is as pre-adapted as possible, that is, a relatively constant universe of situations tending to reinforce its dispositions by offering the market most favourable to its products."[24] Yet in neighborhoods like those at the center of the boycott and the uprising, rapid demographic changes and distinct financial constraints bring together minority residents and recent immigrants of various, unequal socioeconomic backgrounds, and complicate the construction of a "constant universe of situations."[25] Interactions between merchants and customers of differing habitus would presumably disrupt and alter the effects and meanings of everyday behaviors.[26] The apparent reluctance of merchants to make physical contact, for example, might stem from any combination of social conventions and exigencies, but its enactment before customers with their own habits of behavior and perception would determine whether it materializes racism, cultural difference, or class disparity. The significance of these seemingly routine encounters thus lies in both their historical density *and* their intricate chemistry.

Although Heon Cheol Lee's analysis of the boycotted stores is not explicitly in conversation with Bourdieu's theories, his attempt to link the quotidian interactions between merchants and customers to an overdetermined complex of economic and historical circumstances helps elucidate the connections articulated by the habitus. Lee's study highlights the various structural features of the stores that might contribute to merchant-customer tensions, such as their size (between mom-and-pop stores and supermarkets), lack of formalized customer service, and long hours of business. In addition, he takes into account the impact of a long history of racialization, noting, "Self-consciousness of their minority status and a constant fear of being treated differently are strong currents among both Korean merchants and black customers."[27] When a reliance on human observation to monitor stores converges with the historical criminalization and surveillance of black communities, interactions between merchants and customers are likely to affirm mutual suspicions. Similarly, the economically inflected racialization of Asians as greedy and unscrupulous, and African Americans as delinquent and insolvent facilitates the interpretation of conduct born of specific material constraints as performances of racial difference. Thus, in these encounters between merchants and customers, behaviors informed by a combination of economic necessities, social conventions, and patterns of migration and racialization come to confirm the reality of racial divisions.

The boycott and the uprising moreover illustrate that the very "crises and critical challenges" presumably avoided by the habitus can affirm governing social institutions and relations. On the one hand, the boycott and the uprising announced a rejection of existing conditions, and led those affected by the dramatic protests to question both accepted patterns of behavior and established institutions, including the government, the media, and law enforcement. On the other hand, the absorption of everyday tensions into broad characterizations of a "Black-Korean conflict" encouraged notions of inherent differences, and the targeting of Asian American–owned businesses during the uprising marked an intensification of racial divisions. The link between the mundane and the historical, articulated by the concept of the habitus, remained obfuscated, even (or perhaps especially) by programs that focused on quotidian interactions as a site for alleviating tensions and transforming social relations. As I mentioned above, these programs substituted "nicer" manners for substantial changes.

If both small- and large-scale challenges to the habitus do not necessarily alter the sociohistorical circumstances they embody and perpetuate, what kind of change, if any, is possible through the scrutiny and adjustment of naturalized behaviors? This question, so urgently raised by the uprising and the boycott, has been critical to the development of modern and contemporary theatrical practices and theories. Most famously elaborated by Bertolt Brecht, the argument that theater can affect how we view naturalized behaviors and potentially reflect back on and reshape their constitutive social conditions has been seminal to explorations of the political efficacy of theater. In Elin Diamond's succinct and commonly quoted formulation, "Performance . . . is precisely the site in which concealed or dissimulated conventions might be investigated."[28] While conventions may go unremarked in the everyday, their reenactment in theatrical performance makes it possible to examine their relationship to social and political concerns. This perspective finds an offhand echo in Bourdieu's work when he suggests that the distanced observation of established behaviors can lead to a questioning of their purpose and significance: "One only has to suspend the commitment to the game that is implied in the feel for the game in order to reduce the world, and the actions performed in it, to absurdity, and to bring up questions about the meaning of the world and existence which people never ask when they are caught up in the game—the questions of an aesthete trapped in the instant, or an idle spectator."[29] Although for Brecht the ideal spectator is not so much idle as critical, he similarly theorizes that in order to encourage the audience to interrogate (and change) the social conditions represented on the stage, the actor must produce an "alienation effect" that emphasizes a distance from her or his role and detaches "socially-conditioned phenomena from that stamp of familiarity which protects them against our grasp."[30]

Exploring the relationships between habitual behaviors and social conflicts, Elizabeth Wong's *Kimchee and Chitlins* and Anna Deavere Smith's *Twilight: Los Angeles, 1992* exemplify the kind of theatrical performance in which "concealed or dissimulated conventions might be investigated." In confronting the distinct representational problems posed by the "Black-Korean conflict," these works further suggest that the potential of theatrical performance to mediate tensions rests not just in the critical *distance* it can provide, but also in the messy entanglements of actors, roles, and audiences that materialize complex networks of influence and association, as well as their gaps. Stressing the potential hazards of exposing the interactions between merchants and customers to the public, these performances caution against assuming that increased attention to and detached depictions of these daily exchanges will lead to a questioning of the untenable conditions they enact and manifest. They suggest that in offering up the behaviors of inner-city residents and merchants for scrutiny, mainstream media accounts only reinforced divisions between these groups while further disengaging those who encounter one another in depressed neighborhoods from those whose invisibility obscures their involvement.[31]

Explicitly confronting the limitations of media coverage decried by those most involved in and affected by the boycott and the uprising, *Kimchee and Chitlins* and *Twilight* propose an alternative model of representing the conflict, one that involves simultaneously observing and embodying others across racial lines. From the minstrel shows of the nineteenth century to recent controversies over casting (such as the debate over *Miss Saigon* discussed in Chapter 2), cross-racial performance in the United States has historically been dominated by white actors playing other racial and ethnic groups. Although such enactments may manifest contradictory identifications (a dynamic evident, for example, in productions of *The Yellow Jacket*), Angela Pao argues that they are inextricably tied to the privilege of "white neutrality or invisibility."[32] Pao further notes that only in the past few decades has casting white actors in Asian or Latino roles followed blackface performances in becoming an objectionable practice.[33] At the same time, nontraditional casting practices have become more common, with some performances opening up previously unavailable roles to minority actors and others purposefully emphasizing the gap between actor and character to put pressure on established theatrical and social conventions.[34]

Kimchee and Chitlins and *Twilight* directly engage with both the troubling history of cross-racial performance in the United States and its more hopeful possibilities. In excavating the nebulous borders between caricature, appropriation, identification, and empathy through reenactments of the mundane, they grapple with the risks of playing those regarded as racial others. Yet they also illuminate the potential of such performances to reveal unrecognized connections—both those that sustain social divisions and those that offer channels for new affiliations. Traversing theatrical and journalistic conventions as well as racial delineations, they suggest the need to complicate and expand Brechtian models of political theater to account for the complex enmeshments of bodies, habits, and perceptions that make reconciling interracial conflicts a particularly challenging task. *Kimchee and Chitlins* and *Twilight* accordingly test not only the possibilities of performance suggested by Brecht and Diamond, but also Bourdieu's argument that "one cannot really *live* the belief associated with profoundly different conditions of existence, that is, with other games and other stakes, still less give others the means of reliving it by the sheer power of discourse."[35] In staging various attempts to embody the beliefs of others through their habitual behaviors, rather than through "the sheer power of discourse," these works ask if such performances can have any effect on our respective conditions of existence.

Playing across the Picket Line

Elizabeth Wong's *Kimchee and Chitlins* premiered at the Victory Gardens Theater in Chicago in 1993. A production by the West Coast Ensemble in Los Angeles followed in 1994 and received the NAACP Theatre Award for best production. Written during the Brooklyn boycott, the drama's timeliness became all too evident with the 1992 Los Angeles uprising. The play traces the efforts of Suzie Seeto, a Japanese American television news reporter, to cover the boycott of a Korean American–owned grocery store. By focusing on how Suzie reports on the boycott, it explicitly questions media accounts, which, under the guise of objectivity, mask the contingencies and uneven distributions of power that inform how a story is told. While drawing attention to problems in press coverage of the boycott, however, the play also asks whether presenting more information and perspectives can lead to truth, empathy, or reconciliation. Stressing instead the mediation of discourse through the body, the play explores how understandings of what happened change when those involved must not only hear another's perspective, but embody it as well—through the accents, gestures, and habits that materialize their formative histories.

The boycott at the center of the play is fueled by a dispute and alleged physical altercation between a customer, Matilda Duvet, and the store's owner and employees: Grocer Key Chun Mak, his nephew Willie, and his niece Soomi. Among those protesting the market are residents Nurse Ruth Betty and Barber James Brown, as well as Reverend Lonnie Carter, a political figure of some celebrity who becomes a spokesperson for the boycott. Assigned to cover the protest months after it begins, Suzie works to untangle the competing claims of those involved, while also negotiating the romantic advances and editorial demands of her news director Mark Thompson, and attempts to sabotage her career by news anchor Tara Sullivan.

Throughout the performance, characters spend much time discussing the economic, historical, and social circumstances surrounding the boycott. Wong undercuts the play's documentary elements, however, with a comic, exaggerated style and a nonlinear structure that jumps between times and places. In the stage directions, Wong stipulates, "The world of the play must be symbolic and not literal. It must reflect the humor of the play, or be humorous in some way" (396). Conventions such as Black and Korean Choruses, the miming of props, and the doubling of roles further reinforce the play's emphatically nonrealistic style. A journalist herself before becoming a playwright, Wong highlights a tension between the necessity of examining economic and social issues raised by the boycott, and the unavoidable mediation and refraction of information by representational practices.

Moving between the newsroom and the field, the performance underscores the various factors that influence how the boycott reaches the public. When Suzie first approaches the Black Chorus to get an interview, they ask, "Who do you talk to? How do you choose? Do you pick them? Or, do they pick you?" (401). The Black Chorus immediately emphasizes the process of selection that will shape how Suzie tells her story. The play then undermines the homogeneity implied by the Chorus by suggesting that the choice of interview subject is to an extent predetermined by the differential social positions of those participating in the protest. Although Nurse Ruth Betty volunteers to speak for what she calls a "grassroots movement," she is interrupted by the appearance of

Reverend Carter. Carter, as Betty notes, is not from the neighborhood, yet Suzie immediately selects him as a spokesperson, telling the audience, "At last! The leader of the pack" (403). Carter's notoriety makes him the "natural" choice for a reporter looking to draw attention to her story and quickly settles the question of "do you pick them" or "do they pick you," as he and Suzie mutually profit from picking each other.

The performance also repeatedly draws attention to the contingencies and imperatives that impact the selection and editing of these interviews for broadcast. Accidental damage to a recording of an interview with the Maks and rivalry between Suzie and Tara lead to a report that includes only the boycotters' perspective. Mark also occasionally makes unilateral decisions to exclude stories that provide economic and historical context if he deems them uninteresting. Those that do not make the cut include a Korean Church Woman's explanation of the money-lending system among Korean immigrants that allows them to avoid going through banks, and Ruth Betty's account of how she rejected the name of her ancestor's master by taking two first names. The Chorus explains, "As news director, Mark Thompson has the final say. He always has the final word. He decides what you see on teevee, and . . . what you don't" (445). The drama makes clear that decisions about what counts as newsworthy are inseparable from the hierarchies of the newsroom, as well as mishaps and editorial constraints.

By dramatizing the process of news making, *Kimchee and Chitlins* is able to include exactly those debates, perspectives, and issues that do not make the final cut, while simultaneously critiquing their exclusion. When Suzie selects portions of her interview with Nurse Ruth Betty for broadcast, the play stages a struggle between journalist and subject over what should be included. Although Suzie initially seems to be listening to a recording of an earlier interview with Ruth Betty, the nurse begins to interject in the "present" of the scene with her opinions on Suzie's editing:

NURSE RUTH BETTY: I been asking the bank for three years now. I
    need a loan so I can start my own shop in my own neighborhood.
    I want to get out of working for other people, start working for
    myself . . .
SUZIE SEETO: Yeah, yeah, yeah . . . let's skip that.

NURSE RUTH BETTY: [*Insistently.*] They say I'm a bad risk. They say, you don't have the proper collateral. I've been trying to get a loan, but no one will give me one . . .

SUZIE SEETO: It's really a side issue.

BLACK CHORUS: It's the central issue. Put Ruth Betty back in.

NURSE RUTH BETTY: Why are you cutting me out?

SUZIE SEETO: I'm slotted for a one minute-fifteen package. This is no time for an economics lesson.

BLACK CHORUS: But she's telling it like it is. She's giving the story balance, context, motive. (426)

Despite Suzie's reluctance to spend precious seconds on an "economics lesson," Ruth Betty and the Black Chorus insist that the boycott is inextricably tied to racist banking practices, and the spatial and temporal flexibility of the stage allows the performance to place them directly in the cutting room to argue their point. Without the comfortable distance between newsroom and field, Suzie must interrupt and silence Ruth Betty as a physical presence with the ability to question her choices directly, as opposed to a recording that she can cut and edit at will. Emphasizing the often arbitrary choices that make up the final broadcast story, the play envisions an alternative editorial process in which decisions about what is or is not relevant are made with, rather than for, the interview subject.

Such strategic placements of actors also help materialize those influences that, despite affecting the news *and* the events it reports, remain largely hidden. Wong's stage directions specify, "All characters, *including* Mark *and* Tara, must be on stage to witness the action at all times" (396). As the performance begins, the Chorus introduces Mark by telling the audience, "That's him. Over there. Behind the headlines" (400). By placing Mark on the stage but making explicit his place "behind the headlines," the play draws attention to his influence while also recognizing that it tends to go unnoticed. It thus counters the invisibility of Mark's authority, which relies on what Peggy Phelan describes as the "real power in remaining unmarked" (*Unmarked*, 6). In addition, by requiring that Mark and Tara be constant witnesses to the action, the play implicates them in the stories they report and underscores the consequences of how they relay the conflict to the public. The news team's coverage leads to an exacerbation of tensions and phone calls to the station denigrating both African Americans and Koreans. Undermining Suzie's insistence that she is an objective outsider merely reporting on but not participating in what is happening in Brooklyn, the performance makes clear that the news team's decisions tangibly affect outcomes, bringing more or less support for the boycott and even leading to violence.

Despite its interest in decrying the unacknowledged contingencies, constraints, and power dynamics that lead to biases and exclusions in the news, the play suggests a profound skepticism about the transformatory potential of simply rectifying omissions. As the performance progresses, Suzie becomes increasingly less certain that her investigation will uncover the truth or lead to a resolution. Early in the narrative, she declares, "That's right. I believe in facts. Gather up enough facts, and they add up to a decision, an action, even a revelation. I'm not in this business for the glamour or the money" (417). By the end of the performance, however, she admits to Reverend Carter, "I still don't know what happened in the store" (441). Suzie comes to realize that the accumulation of more information, an expressly quantitative endeavor to gather "enough" facts, is not necessarily efficacious or revelatory. The sincerity of her claim that she is only collecting facts with no selfish motives is also belied by choices she makes throughout the play that seem largely motivated by ambition or expedience. Yet even Suzie's effort to cover both sides of the dispute comes to demonstrate only its intractability:

The Street. Suzie conducts interviews—Ping-pong style.
BLACK CHORUS: We want Koreans to put their money in black-owned banks.
SUZIE SEETO: Black-owned banks?
KOREAN CHORUS: We did that. We got no service.
SUZIE SEETO: You got no service?
BLACK CHORUS: We want Koreans to hire blacks to work in their stores.
SUZIE SEETO: Blacks working in Korean stores?
KOREAN CHORUS: We did that. They stole from us.
SUZIE SEETO: They stole from you?
BLACK CHORUS: You paid them slave wages.

SUZIE SEETO: They did?

GROCER MAK: We paid them more than we paid ourselves. (436)

The "ping-pong style" of the interviews suggests a continuous and competitive exchange with no evident conclusion. Placing Suzie between the Black and Korean Choruses with the other characters as distant witnesses, the play dramatizes Freer's observation that "these two relatively resource-poor groups are being asked to develop the solution to the inevitable conflict, a problem which does not begin with them."[36] The dialogue above emphasizes the irreconcilability of interests when the differential distribution of capital and opportunities imposes distinct limitations on how the disputing parties alone might remedy inequities.

Furthermore, Suzie's attempt to reach a revelation or a reconciliation by fact-finding alone is complicated by the networks of *embodied* relationships through which understandings of "what happened" emerge, clash, and take effect. During the performance, characters echo the debates about the conduct of Korean American store owners that surfaced in media coverage of the Brooklyn boycott. Referring to Grocer Mak, Nurse Ruth Betty complains, "I've been putting money into that Korean man's pocket for five years, and he can't even look me in the eye when I open my purse. Once, I held out my five dollars, good honest money, and he refused to take it from my black hand. Do I look like I have a social disease?" (409). Ruth Betty thus denounces Mak's avoidance of eye and physical contact, recalling the complaints of customers interviewed during and after the boycott and the uprising. In response, Mak reiterates that "cultural differences" have led to a misunderstanding of his behavior: "Plenty of respect. I don't look in their eyes. I don't touch them in false sign of friendly greeting. This is our way. This is the Korean way" (422). The financial transactions between Ruth Betty and Mak not only result in the transfer of money, but also generate a sense of racial difference: Ruth Betty becomes conscious of her "black hand" when Mak refuses to touch her while taking her money, and criticism of his ostensibly rude behavior forces Mak to insist on an essentially "Korean" way of showing respect.

In staging these disagreements over Grocer Mak's manners, the play literally if somewhat ambivalently applauds the limited "solution" proffered in response to the 1990 boycott by programs aimed at retraining immigrant business owners. Although Mak is initially reluctant to attend sessions organized by his church to help "Korean businessmen . . . get along with American people" (442), he eventually agrees to "Americanize" the way he interacts with customers and practices his new approach on Suzie:

> WILLIE MAK: Practice. Be nice. Make change.
> GROCER MAK: [*Gruffly.*] Your change.
> SOOMI MAK: Put the change in her hand. Look her in eyeballs . . .
> GROCER MAK: Please, thank you. Come again! [*All applaud, including Black Chorus. Grocer Mak grumbles.*] Only children and Chinese say, "Please, thank you." Now buy something, or get out of my store. If you can't help us, then leave, please, thank you. (443)

Willie and Soomi suggest that altering the way in which Grocer Mak makes change can actually "make change" in a broader sense by reshaping relationships between merchants and residents. The repetition of "change" and scripting of applause after Mak rehearses polite greetings mark his unenthusiastic effort as a significant accomplishment. Mak's grouchy remarks immediately after the applause, however, attenuate the celebratory response and point to the limitations of such behavioral training. Disparaging the manners he agrees to adopt, Mak emphasizes the disparity between his understanding of such conduct and the perception of his customers. For Mak, "cultural difference" becomes a justification for leaving both of their assumptions and expectations unquestioned, and his willingness to change his comportment reflects only a desire to maintain his business.

However, Grocer Mak's training in politesse is not the only model of trying on unfamiliar behaviors—and thus taking advantage of the mundane's ambiguous relationship to the body—presented in the play. For Suzie, the central question to pursue in her investigation is what exactly happened in the store between Matilda Duvet and Grocer Mak. When she asks those involved to recount the incident, each Chorus presents her with a reenactment while decrying the other side's version as false with the exclamation, "That's not what happened at all" (415). The characters only ever act out what happened the day of the altercation, and what routinely happens in the store, as imaginative simulations. By having the Black and Korean Choruses perform both themselves and the "other" in these reenactments, the play situates their bodies emphatically within their respective retellings of the story—a sharp contrast to Suzie and Mark's distanced reporting and editing. The performance therefore emphasizes the mediatedness of every attempt to represent these interactions, and never offers a definitive portrayal of what occurred. Yet these reenactments also seem to ask, if the respective choruses embodied the habitus of those with whom they are in conflict—if their performances were informed by the pressures shaping the behaviors of those they play—could they begin to "make change" in a substantive way?

Initially, each Chorus's dramatization makes its biases evident through the sympathetic contextualization of their respective members' behaviors. As the Black Chorus prepares for their reenactment, Reverend Carter tells Barber Brown, "You are Matilda Duvet. You are going home after a long day sweeping and cleaning for some uptown peoples" (413). As Matilda, Brown laments that her sister's husband in Haiti has disappeared, a likely victim of the repressive regime's secret police (the *ton ton macoute* or bogeymen). Carter and Brown thus help explain Matilda's mood and conduct by underlining her difficult work and concern for family members in Haiti. In contrast, when Carter introduces himself as Grocer Mak, he assumes an exaggerated "Korean" accent and a stereotypical persona: "I Key Chun Mak, store owner. Two time alleady today, I catch shopliftahs. Stupid things—candy, potato chips, cig-a-lettes. How come dey never steal tofu?" (414). The Korean Chorus then interjects, "Makie was a civil servant in his own country. Now he is stacking cans of soup. Vegetable soup. Tomato soup. Miso soup. Cup of Soup" (414). Offering its own contextualization, the Korean Chorus echoes Carter's enumeration of merchandise, but to capture the repetitive, manual tasks that engage Mak in his current occupation and to contrast it to his former career, rather than to set up a joke. Similarly, when Soomi plays Matilda in the Korean Chorus's version of events and yells impatiently at Willie, the Black Chorus informs the audience, "Matilda has had a long day. She is worried about her sister; her husband has disappeared" (419). Each Chorus thus insists on augmenting the reenactments with accounts of the larger social circumstances that inform the characters' conduct, even interrupting the other Chorus's dramatization when it does not seem to provide all of the information relevant to telling the story.

Yet the apparently strict division between the Choruses is not always upheld, as Carter nevertheless draws attention to the petty crimes that trouble Mak. As the reenactments progress, these lines break down further. When Ruth Betty introduces herself in the role of Soomi, she echoes the Korean Chorus's emphasis on the economic necessities and family hierarchies that determine how the Maks run the store: "I Soomi Mak and I am in high skoo. My uncle work me like a dog. I am behind da cash registah" (415). The exaggerated accent again implies caricature, but her acknowledgment of Soomi's difficult situation undermines the absolute bifurcation of potentially extenuating information along racial lines. A similar juxtaposition of stereotypical and sympathetic impersonations is evident in the Korean Chorus's simulation. As Soomi is about to enter the store as Matilda, she interrupts herself by noting, "No, first comes two customers. They are from a gang, you know. Lots of big muscles, and a bandana on his head. The other one, he wears big pants" (417). By prefacing Matilda's arrival with the entrance of these two customers, Soomi initially seems to be drawing attention to the harassment and threat of violence with which the Maks must grapple. Playing one of the customers, Willie even displays a gun kept in his coat. Yet instead of directing it at Soomi, he asserts, "Yeah, I'm not gonna go down, that's for sure. I'm gonna make it to my sixteenth birthday. Yeah. Brothers killing brothers, that's bullshit" (418), and declares before leaving, "You can't knock a man for trying to survive. Hear what I'm sayin'? [*Beat.*] Put that shit on my tab, Chinaman. Later" (418). Beginning with a stereotype of aggressive urban youths, Willie comes to underline the violence that burdens their everyday lives. He momentarily blurs the careful segregation of sympathies by the Choruses, even as he concludes by emphasizing the customer's failure to pay.

Often explicitly superfluous or improbable, these continuous asides do not pretend to be realistic representations of what any particular character might know. Perhaps best capturing the spirit of Brechtian practices in the play, they emphasize a critical distance from the reenacted behaviors and the need to supplement these reenactments with an understanding of the material limitations and demands informing the conduct of those involved. In addition, although the characters offer similar explanations throughout the play, here they must embody the link between everyday behavior and sociohistorical context as the intersection of their own habitus and that of the character they are playing. In other words, contextual details that might work to justify or explain *individual* actions elsewhere in the drama are situated here in a complicated overlapping of bodies and behaviors across racial lines. The reenactments therefore highlight the materialization of sociohistorical pressures through the mundane, as well as the complex dynamic *between* bodies that determines the performativity of the habitus.

These cross-Chorus performances make visible the production of racial difference at the interface of the characters' respective habits of sight and speech. Intricate relationships of identification and estrangement emerge in the space between actor and role, which characters variously emphasize or obscure. For example, when Reverend Carter, as Grocer Mak, watches Matilda and wonders, "Do I know her? Dey all rook arike to me. All those brack monkeys rook arike to me" (414), the evident affectedness of his performance stresses his distance from the role he plays. Yet this seemingly clear division between "actor" and "role" is inextricably tied to the murkier relationship between watching and being watched implied by Carter's performance. The reenactment of Mak watching Matilda simultaneously racializes the grocer's look as exemplifying Korean prejudice and racializes Matilda as indistinguishable from other black customers. The act of watching is thus both a racialized *and* a racializing gesture, establishing the Korean merchant as suspicious, racist, and greedy, and the black customer as delinquent, poor, and untrustworthy.

By assuming the role of Grocer Mak, Reverend Carter occupies the exact intersection of the dual implications of "looking alike"—appearing the same and seeing the same. His performance exemplifies the dynamic articulated in Du Boisian racial double consciousness, as both the racializing gaze of the other and its incorporation into one's self-awareness are materialized in the uneasy relationship between actor and character. Despite the emphatic distancing of self and role, black and Korean, Carter's impersonation of Mak underscores the mutual permeation of "passive" and "active" looks through which racial difference takes on a reality. The scene thus dramatizes the "exchange of gaze" elaborated in Phelan's reading of Lacan: "Unable to reverse her own gaze (the eyes obstinately look only *outside* the self), the subject is forced to detour through the other to see herself."[37] While embodying the grocer, the reverend also sees himself as the object of the grocer's scrutiny. Although "Mak" is ostensibly watching "Matilda," his stated inability to differentiate between black customers implicates the reverend as well. While the actor presumably animates the character, the latter in this case ("Mak") also infuses the corporeal awareness of the former (Carter), as the character's "look" racializes the actor.

These exchanges of looks are moreover accompanied by contests of tongue and ear in which adopting exaggerated accents becomes a way of conveying the depicted individual's otherness—in relation both to the one performing the accent and to normative American speech. Soomi as Matilda asks Willie, who plays himself, "How much are ze limes?" Willie responds by asking "What?" and then explains to Suzie, "I said. Just like that. The lady has very big accent" (418). As the scene continues, "Matilda" becomes frustrated by Willie's inability to understand her and demands, "Why don't you speak English? I've been here in dis countree tee years, and see how good my English is? Lime, lemon, how much?" (419). By emphasizing Matilda's Haitian accent, Soomi and Willie, who are also nonnative English speakers, position themselves as less foreign by comparison. The redundancy of Willie's comment that he spoke "Just like that" underlines the consistency of speech when he steps "out of character," while the obvious disjuncture between Soomi's usual way of speaking and her imitation of Matilda's accent stresses their dissimilarity. Racial difference materializes in the seams between Soomi's speech and her re-creation of Matilda's voice.

Yet however ironic "Matilda's" criticism of Willie's English given the Korean Chorus's caricature of her accent, the remark also posits incorrect *hearing* as a performance of foreignness and points to the constitution of difference in the exchange between verbal articulation and aural perception. "Matilda" interestingly denounces Willie's inability to *speak* English, although their miscommunication is presumably due to his inability to *hear* her English correctly. This slippage, much like Carter's performance of racializing "looks," suggests that the line between hearing and speaking is never absolutely clear—even when reciprocal accusations of stunted linguistic assimilation buttress racial divisions. The reenactments thus convey what Michel de Certeau describes as

the paradox of the frontier: "Created by contacts, the points of differentiation between two bodies are also their common points. Conjunction and disjunction are inseparable in them. Of two bodies in contact,
which one possesses the frontier that distinguishes them? Neither."[38]
The cross-Chorus reenactments bring to dramatic life the simultaneity
of "conjunction and disjunction," the materialization of racial difference
at the moment of contact.

Separated by picket lines and mutual animosities, the Black and Korean Choruses are able to explain to Suzie what happened in the store
only by representing those positioned as the enemy. As the reenactments
described above demonstrate, one of the effects of embodying the other
side of the dispute is to hold in suspense, on one body, the one who sees
and the one who is seen, the one who speaks and the one who hears.
In the course of the dramatizations, however, as the lines of sympathy
between Choruses become less distinct, the interstices between actor
and role—along which the performances materialize racial difference—
begin to dissolve as well. In the climax of each simulation, physical and
verbal outbursts mark a point when the imaginative reenactment of the
incident briefly threatens to turn into an actual altercation. The Black
Chorus's reenactment in particular leads to a moment of confused sympathies that almost ends in violence. Suspecting "Matilda" (played by
Barber Brown) of shoplifting, Reverend Carter confronts her as Grocer
Mak:

REVEREND CARTER: "Let me see inside your bag."
BARBER BROWN: "No, I tell you, no! Let go of my bag!" [*They have a*
tug of war with the shopping bag.]
REVEREND CARTER: "I'm sick and tired of peepole who talkin' too
fast. I'm sick and tired of working so hard. Five A.M. to one A.M.
[*sic*] I sick and tired of peepole yelring at me. Of peepole who do not
understand even when I speakin' Englrish. I sick and tired of being
sick and tired."
NURSE RUTH BETTY [AS SOOMI]: "Watch out! She's going to lrun!"
REVEREND CARTER: "No, you don't!" [*The Reverend pulls back his fist
to strike the Barber. The Korean Chorus gasps, as does Suzie.*]
BARBER BROWN: Rev. Hey, Rev! You can be yourself now. Rev? Hey!
Snap to. (415)

The characters' reenactment of this event suggests that caricature and empathetic identification are not mutually exclusive, as they can coexist as well as shift from one to the other in the course of an impersonation. Playing Mak with a stereotypical accent, Carter nevertheless articulates and, by the end, embodies the economic and linguistic constraints on the grocer's perception and conduct. The outcome of Carter's brief identification with Mak, however, is not reconciliation, but a threat of violence, followed by the return of animosities between the Choruses. The scene thus questions the value of "walking in another's shoes" as the reverend's angry reaction might justify or explain the grocer's alleged assault, but changes little. By so thoroughly inhabiting the pressures that shape Mak's interactions with his customers, the reverend loses any sense of critique or self-reflexivity, and his reenactment comes to assume a fatalistic view of the conflict. He loses the explicit tension between "self" and "other" apparent earlier in the simulation, when his performance maintained a critical distance between actor and role, yet highlighted their multiple entanglements. Thus, the simulations stage the risks of complete emotional immersion and identification, the theatrical propensities Brecht so distrusted, even as they complicate the practice of holding actor and role in critical suspense by emphasizing the messy, unavoidable intersection of behaviors and perceptions.

Although the play ultimately offers an ambivalent depiction of these reenactments, they nevertheless provide an alternate model of recounting what happened that brings into relief the limitations of media reports of the boycott. As I argued above, *Kimchee and Chitlins* repeatedly underlines the various obfuscated pressures that shape the news and its distribution of public sympathies. In contrast to Suzie's efforts to stand outside the story and accumulate facts "objectively," the Choruses' reenactments of the incident show their material implication in the stories they tell by requiring that they embody what they narrate.

The professional distance through which Suzie differentiates herself from the subjects of her reports finally collapses, however, when she tries to cover, at the height of tensions, the beating of a Vietnamese American boy by a group of African American children. She explains to Mark, "Standing there, watching those boys and that kid. I wasn't hating them. No, no . . . I was too busy, too preoccupied with disassociating myself from that squirming, weak, yellow boy on the ground. Coolly,

I hid behind my profession, thoroughly brainwashed by my complete-and-utter certainty that I could not and would not be hurt . . . because I was *not* like that kid. Those black boys with their baseball bat shattered my beautiful delusion once and forever. For if I wasn't yellow, then what color did I think I was?" (448). The divide between reporter and subject initially helps Suzie distance herself from the boy being beaten. Yet her reluctant recognition that the racialization of his body extends to her own undermines these dichotomies. The apparent targeting of the boy because of his "race" compels her to identify with him even as she attempts to assume a deracialized, disembodied position. In watching the boy, she is in some ways watching herself, and this confusion of "looks" makes it difficult for her to maintain her disinterest. Suzie's designation of both the boy and herself as "yellow" articulates a fraught identification with the abject that calls into question the possibility of choosing one's color.

In its critique of Suzie's journalistic detachment, the performance envisions a kind of reporting that might draw instead from the cross-Chorus reenactments. Specifically, it turns a theatrical device, the doubling of roles, into an imaginary journalistic device. According to the casting directions, the actors not only play one central character and serve as part of the Black or Korean Chorus, but also take on minor roles. One effect of this stipulation is that it troubles the apparent homogeneity of the Choruses. The play's script specifies that Barber Brown, for example, should also play a Haitian man. The doubling of a long-time resident of Brooklyn who would identify as African American with an Afro-Caribbean immigrant suggests the tendency to conflate them as part of a monolithic black community, while stressing the variations in speech, manner, and conduct that speak to their different, if at points overlapping, histories. Within the Korean Chorus, the actor who plays Grocer Mak also plays a Pakistani news vendor. Reflecting on the boy-cott, he remarks, "I been selling newspapers on the corner for a long time. Black people don't bother me. I am Pakistani. What is all the fuss? I guess black people don't know, Korean people are like that. They are rude to everybody" (445). Even as the news vendor differentiates himself from Grocer Mak, he also expresses an awareness of their shared position as immigrant businessmen in the same neighborhood. His dissociation from Grocer Mak, like Suzie's dissociation from the Vietnamese boy, seems inextricably intertwined with and compelled by a fear of being perceived as the same, a fear that is affirmed onstage by having the same actor play both roles, but is also undermined by his conspicuous shifts between characters.

Moving between multiple roles, the actors must make continual adjustments in how they manipulate their corporeal tendencies to match those of different characters. For example, Grocer Mak, Soomi, and Willie are all supposed to be immigrants from Korea with attendant linguistic preferences and limitations, yet these may or may not align with those of the actors, who are also asked to play other roles. Furthermore, what exactly their speech performs—the foreign or the familiar, a natural or an affected presentation, a caricature of "Asian" accents or an "authentic" reproduction of a particular dialect—depends on how the audience hears the dialogue, and whether or not they register a tension between the actor's speech and that of the character. Yet the audience's assumptions about the relationship between actor and character are also continuously destabilized by the role-doubling, which requires them to recalibrate their measurements of the gap between the performing body and enacted role. Finally, casting choices and audience conceptions of racial delineations at odds with those assumed by the script would complicate the effects and meanings generated by the role-doubling and the cross-Chorus reenactments. Whether Wong's directions are followed or deliberately flouted, the play's basic design forces productions to grapple with the challenge of presenting identities as settled one moment and variable the next, and to engage with the triangulated relationship between actor, character, and audience as a constantly moving target.

In contrast to the cross-Chorus reenactments, the script designates that most of the doubled roles do not traverse racial lines, broadly defined, with one exception: Wong stipulates that the actor who plays Suzie should also play Matilda. Despite Matilda's evasion of the press, Suzie is finally able to interview her, and in this scene, the same actor gives the interview as Matilda *and* retrospectively narrates the interview as Suzie:

SUZIE SEETO: (*as Matilda, Haitian Creole accent*) "Yes, I hope for a
    change. You see, I came from a poor, frightened, brutalized country.
    I came here of my own free will to make something of my life. I want
    to do it here in America. And this is the way I am greeted . . . poof,

I'm a teef. Poof, I'm no good. [*Laughs.*] Poof, I'm a celebrity, and everybody's wanting to know me business." [*As herself, Suzie.*] And then Matilda offers me tea, and I try to get her back to my questions. But she was one of those people, you know. She wasn't being dishonest, just difficult. I guess she didn't think my questions were very relevant. [*As Matilda.*] "I have more important tings to worry my mind. Don't you have more important tings?" (440)

By having Suzie reenact the interview as Matilda, the performance stresses the latter's elusiveness and underlines the mediatedness of her public representation, as she appears and speaks only through the actor who otherwise plays a news reporter. Yet in contrast to Suzie's other interviews, which the play dramatizes as dialogues, she recounts their conversation by assuming Matilda's voice and habits, just as the Choruses share their respective versions of the controversial incident by playing different characters. Suzie thus relinquishes the distanced objectivity of the journalist and draws attention to how she hears and sees Matilda in her "report." In other words, by embodying Matilda, Suzie implicates her own habits of perception and behavior in her representation, risking an inevitable gap in speech and manners as she attempts to re-create Matilda's demeanor or her Haitian Creole accent.[39]

Suzie's reenactment of Matilda's responses to her questions therefore offers a model of reporting on the boycott that counters the news practices critiqued in the play. While Mark and Tara watch the conflict from a distance, Suzie makes her involvement increasingly evident, and her interview with Matilda dramatizes the attenuation of her professional disengagement through her embodiment of Matilda's words. Blurring the distinctions between monologue and dialogue, past and present, actor and character, the interview between Suzie and Matilda brings together the conventions of the Choruses' reenactments (in which characters play one another) with those of the play's broader role-doubling (in which an actor plays multiple characters). Although the script gives a slight primacy to the role of Suzie (who plays both Matilda and "herself"), it does not make it entirely clear whether the audience should see the performance as the playing of two distinct characters (akin to the role-doubling) or the imitation of one character by another (akin to the reenactments). Furthermore, in contrast to other instances when actors and characters take on different roles, Suzie's interview with Matilda is characterized by fluid, rapid shifts between the two characters. The performance thus dwells here on the ambiguous, giving neither actor nor audience a clear sense of how to *distribute* the lines between actor and character, reporter and subject, black and Asian.

Together, the play's temporal and spatial manipulations, doubling of roles, and cross-racial reenactments capture the complex intersection of embodied histories and uneven social relations that shape interracial conflicts and their public narration. The behavioral and perceptual habits of customers and merchants materialize specific imperatives and limits—social, historical, economic—reflecting the impact of distinct patterns of immigration, segregation, and racialization. In these encounters, interactions between habitus dynamically and reciprocally realize difference and identity. Yet the presumed temporal and spatial discreteness of bodies masks these exchanges, while the hypervisibility of minority merchants and customers obfuscates the influence of institutions and peoples less visibly implicated in these conflicts. This division of those who encounter one another in the boycotted stores from those who profit from their transactions from afar, or those who seem merely to watch or report on their disputes, limits the prospects of "making change" by enabling the disavowal of shared interest and responsibility. *Kimchee and Chitlins* takes advantage of the possibilities of theatrical performance to evoke unrecognized relationships and to trouble facile explanations of the boycott as the result of "cultural differences."

At the conclusion of the play, Suzie ambivalently accepts a promotion made possible by her coverage of the boycott while Grocer Mak closes his store. Envisioning an alternate ending in which Mak and Brown become friends, Suzie comments on the bleak conclusion, "Just goes to show, the best stories are . . . the best stories are *invented*" (449). Although *Kimchee and Chitlins* self-consciously resists offering any solutions or resolutions, the imaginative reenactments it stages suggest ways of materializing connections that otherwise get erased in the lines drawn between bodies. Despite the risks of crossing those lines—the potential for caricature, appropriation, or exacerbated tensions—such performances may also bring to light their permeability, mutual constitution, and prospective reconfigurations.

Walking in the Speech of Another

In Wong's adamantly hyperbolic play, Suzie's interview with Matilda straddles fantasy and reality through the manipulation of theatrical devices, and the scene remains a hypothetical experiment in unconventional reportage. For her series *On the Road: A Search for American Character*, Anna Deavere Smith puts into practice the kind of theatricalized "reporting" imagined in *Kimchee and Chitlins* by Suzie's conversation with Matilda. In her performances, Smith reenacts people whom she has previously interviewed, closely re-creating their speech and behaviors. After the Los Angeles riots, the Mark Taper Forum, which also held a reading of *Kimchee and Chitlins* in May 1992, commissioned Smith to create a performance piece similar to *Fires in the Mirror* (1992), her treatment of interracial tensions in Crown Heights, Brooklyn. *Twilight: Los Angeles, 1992* opened in Los Angeles in June 1993, just over a year after the uprising.

Drawing from interviews with a range of subjects, from government officials and scholars to Los Angeles store owners and residents, Smith's "documentary theater" offers an alternative to the coverage provided by the mainstream media. Like Suzie's reenactment of her interview with Matilda, Smith's performance sits at the interface between the habitus of the actor and that of the character, and highlights the negotiations between speaking and hearing, and acting and seeing that become apparent in efforts to embody others. Yet if *Kimchee and Chitlins* repeatedly reminds the audience of its comic, *invented* elements, *Twilight* tempts the audience to refer continuously to the real in its portrayal of Smith's interviewees, especially those who are well-known public figures. Smith's work shares many characteristics with the solo performances of Danny Hoch and Sarah Jones, who also move between a diverse set of characters. Smith, however, emphasizes her interview process and her emulation of real individuals, whereas Hoch and Jones stress that they take inspiration from, rather than directly imitate, people whom they encounter. This explicit if complex attachment to the nonfictive has brought particular scrutiny on Smith's ability—or inability—to simulate her subjects accurately. The *incongruities* that emerge in Smith's attempts to capture her interviewees' mannerisms and accents, however, are precisely what make palpable both the historical and institutional pressures within which the mundane develops and the intersection of behavioral and perceptual tendencies through which identities take on substance and meaning.

Along with other performances in *On the Road*, *Twilight* has elicited divergent responses from audiences and critics, who variously characterize Smith's work as humanistic, poststructuralist, Brechtian, utopian, and/or stereotypical. The diversity of reactions is exemplified in scholarly analyses like that of Tania Modleski, who argues that critics who denounce the performances as caricature miss the "dynamism of Smith's portrayals,"[40] but admits that Smith's representation of white women made her feel uncomfortable.[41] Such conflicted evaluations reflect the challenge of neatly defining a performance that experiments with accepted conventions of representation and insists that attention be paid to the multiple layers of archive and repertoire that it brings together—the interview between Smith and her subject, the transcription of their conversation, the process by which she gets into character, the actual performance, audience reaction to the show, and so on.

The struggle to understand Smith's performances as journalistic or theatrical, modernist or postmodernist, subversive or stereotypical, which leaves critics embracing a "neither" and "both" approach to her work, seems particularly fitting given her expressed interest in capturing the "American character . . . alive inside of syntactical breaks."[42] In the introduction to the published version of *Fires in the Mirror*, Smith explains, "The break from the pattern is where character lives, and where dialogue, ironically begins, in the *uh*, in the pause, in the thought as captured for the first time in a moment of speech, rather than in the rehearsed, the proven."[43] The "uhs" and "ums" of critics and spectators trying to comprehend her performances in terms of an existing vocabulary similarly reflect an effort to articulate what has yet been codified. Positioned in the pause, Smith's performances are articulations that simultaneously verbalize and connect,[44] and not simply pluralistic or additive projects of making more bodies visible and heard (a reading of her work that has been accompanied by both praise and criticism).[45] Instead, her performances make legible revealing associations and tensions between the everyday and the historical, and between the corporeal and the discursive through the complex relationships they instantiate between reporter and subject, and actor and audience. At the crux of these performances is Smith's reenactment of the mundane, her careful re-creation of her subject/character's habits of behavior and speech.

In her performances, Smith emulates *how* her interview subjects speak, and not just what they say. She recounts the influence of her grandfather's assertion that "if you say a word often enough it becomes you,"[46] which inspired her to develop a technique of acting that moves away from the "self-oriented method" of psychological realism. Smith explains, "If we were to inhabit the speech pattern of another, and walk in the speech of another, we could find the individuality of the other and experience that individuality viscerally. I became increasingly convinced that the activity of reenactment could tell us as much, if not more, about another individual than the process of learning about the other by using the self as a frame of reference."[47] Stressing the limitations of dominant acting practices that encourage using the self to create the character, Smith argues for an "other-based" approach anchored in a distinctly corporeal understanding of the other. As she interviews her subjects, she notes their physical gestures as well as their verbal responses and prepares for her performances by frequently listening to and replicating their speech and comportment—or, by saying their words so often they become her. For Smith, speaking as the other does not mean psychologi-cally interpreting the other through one's own experiences, but physi-cally inhabiting or "walking" in their speech by re-creating the bodily habits and vocal inflections that carry their words.

Smith's performances have attracted critical interest for breaking with modern, "humanist" approaches to acting and their concomitant as-sumptions about identity. Referring in particular to Judith Butler's work on the performativity of gender, Debby Thompson argues, "While post-structuralist models of identity—notions of identity as 'performative'—have become almost dogma in current literary theory, acting practice in the U.S. has been slow to reflect this shift in models of identity, and is still very much based in liberal humanism."[48] Thompson elaborates that in contrast to a humanist approach that would assume a "you" preced-ing the words, Smith's method, as inspired by her grandfather, suggests that "if words become 'you,' then your 'you-ness,' your very self-hood, is made up of your interaction with words. Or, turned around, you be-come you by saying words."[49] Charles Lyons and James Lyons similarly observe that Smith's practices move away from prevailing "modernist" approaches derived from the Stanislavski method and influenced by Freudian psychology, which encourage "a spatial image of character that sees the outside of a dramatic figure—body, gesture, voice, overt action—as the refracted manifestation of an interior dynamic that must be discovered by the actor and revealed in performance as the energy that drives speech and action."[50] As opposed to this "inside-out" understanding of the subject, the reenactment of characters through the reiteration of their voices and behaviors underlines their interpellation as subjects within relations of power and inequity. Lyons and Lyons contend that in Smith's work, "the important alignment is between the actor and the conditions—the socio-economic dynamics—that make the other's statements necessary or, rather, the systems of power that position the speaker as the figure who can make those statements."[51] The character's speech, then, "represents the self-constitution of the speaker as a subject positioned by the degree of power or powerlessness they hold."[52] Lyons and Lyons emphasize that Smith's acting strategy conceives of the subject as a historical and institutional formation. The words her characters speak—and the manner in which they speak—not only manifest the particular limits and possibilities that inhere in their social position, but also materialize them as subjects (or, as Thompson describes, they become an "I" or "you" through such discursive and corporeal reiterations).

Both of these analyses associate Smith's work with that of Brecht, whose theories encourage acting practices that articulate a character's relationship to her or his socioeconomic conditions. The concept of the *gestus* is key to this project. Brecht explicates, "The realm of attitudes adopted by the characters towards one another is what we call the realm of gest. Physical attitude, tone of voice and facial expression are all determined by a social gest: the characters are cursing, flattering, instructing one another, and so on."[53] Expressed corporeally, the social gest is a position taken toward other characters that reflects their relationships to one another and to social conditions: "The social gest is the gest relevant to society, the gest that allows conclusions to be drawn about the social circumstances."[54] Using Bourdieu's terms, we might say that these theatrical enactments of social gest crystallize the habitus and frame it critically: the Brechtian actor draws attention to conventional behaviors that, when staged, come to typify the social relations that they usually embody implicitly. In their examinations of Smith's performances, Lyons, Lyons, and Thompson propose that her practices similarly reject the tendency of dominant acting methods to naturalize characters' actions and speech as expressions of an essential interiority, and instead accentuate the sociohistorical conditions that shape them.[55] Thus, Smith's performances make visible the relationship between an interview subject and a broader social context through specific configurations of body and voice that point out instead of in.

By asking her subjects to speak on the uprising, Smith indeed encourages them to consider issues of power and inequity raised by the conflict. By playing each of the characters herself and limiting her portrayals to short excerpts from her interviews, Smith highlights the idiosyncrasies of each speaker and the differences among them, instead of creating a sense of depth and coherence. In particular, she accentuates distinctive verbal and bodily tendencies to convey each character's relationship to the issues that they discuss.[56] These articulations of the sociohistorical through the mundane are particularly vivid in the moments of incongruity, the "breaks" not only in syntax, but also in comportment and *between* speech and comportment.

In Smith's portrayal of artist Rudy Salas,[57] an upright posture and raised head initially accompany his account of multiple experiences with police brutality. A carriage suggestive of masculine pride, however, is soon replaced by the thrust of his arms upward when he recalls advising his children to replicate the gesture for police officers to indicate that they are not armed. He then begins to slump in his seat and later struggles to speak while asking his wife Margaret about her encounter with the police: "Didn't they, / Margaret, / insult [our son] one time and they pulled you over . . . / the Alhambra cops, they pulled you over / and, aww, man . . . / My enemy" (7). The shift from a pose of defiance to one of submission and the subsequent inability to verbalize his frustration situate Salas at the intersection of multiple axes of power and powerlessness. Earlier in the interview, Salas explains that he enjoys seeing expressions of fear on white people when they encounter minorities: "It's a physical thing, / it's a mental, mental thing that they're [white people] physically afraid [of minorities]. / I, I can still see it, / I can still see it, / and, and, / and, uh-uh, / I love to see it" (5). Salas's remarks suggest that the visible trepidation of white people puts him in a position of power: their perception of minorities and his perception of their fear positions him as the one with the potential to intimidate. In contrast, raising his hands when confronted by the police demonstrates a reluctant compliance to authority and an expectation of mistreatment, a social gest that highlights the differential policing of racialized bodies. Thus, the racialization of Salas as a physical threat gives him a sense of power, yet it also makes him more susceptible to violence from those with greater institutional authority.

Smith emphasizes a similar disjuncture between assertions of masculine confidence and concurrent expressions of powerlessness in her depiction of Walter Park, a Korean American store owner shot during the uprising. In the published script, Smith prefaces his interview responses with an unusually full description of the subject:

Mr. Park speaks in the rhythm of a person who has full authority and ease, and a person who has all of the facts exactly straight. When he begins talking, his wife and son shake their heads to let me know that he doesn't know the answer to the question. He is sitting with his arms crossed and legs crossed, also in an easy but confident and authoritative position. From his body position and his rhythm you would think this was the most reasonable, sound response possible. It is, of course, emotionally sound, but there is a gap between the question and the answer. He is heavily sedated, and has been since he was shot. (142–43)

Smith stresses a gap between Park's physical comportment and manner of speaking, which suggest "authority and ease," and the content of his responses, which reflects the damage inflicted by what his stepson describes as an "execution-style" shot to the head. Park's disorientation becomes evident as he recounts his surprise at being informed that he had been hospitalized: "and one guy happened to tell me / 'Why you wanna go Korea / for? / You just came out of / hospital.' / You know, / that, / that makes me wonder too. So I came home and / I told her [his wife] about it / and / she didn't say nothing" (144). Here, the confusion expressed in his words belies the certainty with which he speaks them, and this inconsistency between his corporeal habits and verbal responses illuminates the seemingly divergent but inseparable positions he occupies as a successful businessman and a bewildered victim of violence stemming from economic and racial tensions.

In contrast to Salas and Park, whose postures of authority are set in tension with physical and verbal expressions of helplessness, Smith's performance of Sergeant Charles Duke, a "use-of-force expert" for the Los Angeles Police Department, suggests an eerily steady and largely seamless, if at times emphatic, discussion of physical force. A witness for the defense in the trial of the four officers who beat King, Duke explains, "If we had upper-body-control holds / involved in this, / this tape woulda never been on, / this incident woulda lasted about fifteen seconds. / The reason that we lost upper-body-control holds . . . / because we had something like seventeen to twenty deaths in a period of about 1975–76 to 1982" (62). In Smith's re-creation of Duke's response, he speaks calmly and forcefully with an easy confidence, which would seem unremarkable, were it not for the gravity of his statements. In other words, what is most notable about Duke is his apparent lack of discomfort or hesitation as he recounts the debates about using choke holds and batons to restrain people. His institutional authority is incarnated in his composed demeanor and speech, which in turn naturalizes his authority. Duke exemplifies what then-district attorney Gil Garcetti, in another interview with Smith, describes as the "magic" that seems to surround police officers, particularly in courtrooms:

> I mean, if a cop, for example, comes in with a raid jacket
> and guns bulging out
> he'll wipe himself out very quickly,
> because he'll look like he's a cowboy.
> But if you have a man coming in
> or a woman coming in—
> you know, professionally dressed,
> polite
> with everyone—
> the magic
> is there
> and it's a . . .
> it's an aura,

it's aye [*sic*] feeling
that is conveyed to the jury: "I am telling the truth
and I'm here to help you,
to protect you," and they want to believe that . . . (76)

According to Garcetti, the "magic" that authorizes police officers' testimony comes not from the ostentatious display of power, the "raid jacket / and guns bulging out," but from a polite manner that seems to affirm the truth of their words and the naturalness of their actions. Garcetti's remarks echo Bourdieu's analysis: "The purely social and quasi-magical process of socialization, which is inaugurated by the act of marking that institutes an individual as an eldest son, an heir, a successor, a Christian, or simply as a man (as opposed to a woman), with all the corresponding privileges and obligations, and which is prolonged, strengthened and confirmed by social treatments that tend to transform instituted difference into natural distinction, produces quite real effects, durably inscribed in the body and in belief."[58] To the extent that Smith's performance of Duke is remarkable for being so unremarkable, she captures and conveys some of the "magic" that makes certain identities and forms of authority seem natural, credible, and tangible. And as Garcetti and Bourdieu emphasize, this "quasi-magical process" has significant consequences.

Smith's reenactments of Duke and Garcetti suggest an effort to challenge the apparent soundness of Duke's authority through meaningful juxtapositions—of different interviews, of statements within an interview, and of words and behaviors. Wong similarly uses the flexibility of the stage in *Kimchee and Chitlins* to draw attention to Mark's unrecognized implication in the boycott. The format of Smith's performances, however, also lends them their own authoritative neutrality. Noting that she does not offer any added exposition on the interviews that she recreates, Lyons and Lyons argue, "These performances are polyphonic, both in the sense of representing multiple voices and in their refusal to synthesize differences in any intervening personal statement, any *authorial* commentary."[59] They contend that Smith allows her many interviewees to speak through her without interjecting her own perspective. Yet as other critics have noted, the absence of explicit commentary from Smith does not mean that her performances are free from other forms of editorializing.[60] Dorinne Kondo, for example, warns against missing "the degree to which there is a point of view expressed through the questions asked in the interviews, the selection and arrangement of material, the performance, and the production itself—lighting, sets, music, costumes, placement on the stage."[61] Kondo thus points to the kind of obscured editorial decisions critiqued in *Kimchee and Chitlins* as lending a false sense of objectivity to the news.

Smith's performances, however, do make explicit her *corporeal* mediation of the interviews. Even if Smith does not vacillate between "herself" and her "character" (thus explicitly foregrounding her choices as an interviewer, editor, and performer), her habitus is always in tension with that of the subject whom she plays, and the varying degrees of friction that become evident in the dramatizations call attention to her active struggle to manifest *and* bridge the gaps between the two. Neither a distanced report of her interviews nor an exact replication of them, Smith's reenactments repeatedly implicate her body in her representations of others. Her performances therefore do not simply materialize what she sees and hears, but *how* she sees and hears, and thus what she is able or unable to see, able or unable to hear, given her own social position and habits of body and perception. Recounting her efforts to develop an "other-oriented" method of acting, Smith reflects, "If I have an inhibition about *acting* like a man, it may also point to an inhibition I have about *seeing* a man or *hearing* a man. To develop a voice one must develop an ear. To complete an action, one must have a clear vision."[62] To the extent that Smith's dual roles as interviewer and interviewee are legible in her reenactments, her performances are not simply representations of the other, but expressions of how she sees and hears the other. For example, when Rodney King's aunt Angela King asks Smith in the middle of their interview, "You understand what I'm sayin' now? / You do?" (57), the reenactment of this moment explicitly positions Smith as both the observed and the observer, the speaker and the listener. Doubly mediated by her perception of individuals during these interviews and her subsequent embodiment of those perceptions, Smith's performances materialize the other at the intersection of voice and ear, action and vision.

When Smith reenacts Salas, Park, or Duke, her observations of these individuals are embodied in the choices she makes regarding intonation, gesture, posture, and so on. Even if these choices were consistently geared toward replicating her interviewee as accurately as possible, the act of hearing or seeing is already selective, already informed by the social and historical conditioning of her perceptions. As Phelan notes, "Taking the visual world in is a process of loss: learning to see is training in careful blindness. To apprehend and recognize the visible is to eliminate as well as absorb visual data."[63] The steady, unruffled quality of Duke's comportment, in contrast to Salas's assertive posture, speaks as much to what Smith sees or does not see, as it does to the men's actual attitudes. Yet to the extent that these are inseparable in the actual performances, Smith stages the difficulty, perhaps the impossibility, of ever making an absolute distinction. While the convergence of "actor" and "character" in her performances highlights the materialization of identity at their intersection, the disjuncture between them, which becomes more and less apparent at different points of the performance, reveals the distinct conditions that have shaped their respective bodies.

This disjuncture becomes especially evident in Smith's attempts to replicate accents and non-English languages. However often she repeats and mimics the speech of others, her tongue and ear cannot be reshaped to conform to an entirely different linguistic history. Her inability to capture the speech of nonnative English speakers with complete accuracy, however, has drawn criticism as an example of her performances' uncomfortable proximity to stereotypes. Smith recalls that Kondo, as a dramaturg for *Twilight*, informed her that some Asian Americans were disappointed with the performance because it did not "represent them adequately or with enough complexity."[64] While teaching *Twilight*, Sandra Kumamoto observed that her students were uneasy with Smith's depiction of Korean American characters. She relates their concern that in Smith's performance of Young-Soon Han, a liquor store owner who lost her business during the uprising, she "not only risks reifying cultural stereotypes, but, in imitating the voice of an immigrant, she risks caricaturing and offending Asian immigrants who often feel marginalized precisely because of their speech."[65] Smith's failure to close the gap between her speech and that of her characters threatens to turn her reenactments into performances of racial stereotypes.

The capacity for hearing and emulating another's speech, however, is already shaped by an existing history of caricaturing certain ways of speaking. In other words, these responses to Smith's reenactments implicate her audience's habits of hearing and speaking as much as her own. Caricature is no more an *inherent* feature of Smith's work than is utopian pluralism or poststructuralist performativity; instead, it emerges in relation to specific, historically situated audiences. I am not suggesting a radical relativity in which evaluations of representations as offensive are meaningless, but rather arguing for a consideration of the complex diachronic and synchronic relationships between bodies that inform such assessments. Describing the unsettling experience of watching Smith's performances, Modleski observes, "Just when people are presented as most like themselves, they suddenly seem like 'types,' our laughter as suddenly seems to border on ridicule, and we find ourselves confronting our own racism."[66] Modleski's account locates the moment when character becomes type between Smith's presentation and the audience's laughter, and her phrasing leaves ambiguous whether the presentation or the laughter is responsible for the shift to racial caricature. It accordingly situates the performance of racism at the point of contact between reenactment and reception. In setting the mannerisms of actor and character in tension, Smith elicits physical as well as verbal reactions (of pleasure, discomfort, anger, and ambivalence) from the audience that manifest the viewer's own social gest—a socially significant attitude that, in this case, points to the entrenched racialization of perception.

If theatrical performance in its most basic form is a meeting of audience and actor mediated through character, character in Smith's performances is an unstable center that amalgamates and refracts the interviewee's presentation of self before Smith, Smith's observation of the interviewee, her enactment of these observations, and the audience's interactions with her enactment. While it is possible to conceive of theatrical character more generally in similar terms, Smith simultaneously raises the stakes of distinguishing between the layers that constitute her performance and frustrates attempts to make such distinctions. In works such as *Fires in the Mirror* and *Twilight*, she delves into conflicts between differently racialized communities through a performance process that cannot help but provoke questions of authenticity and stereotyping. As her characters try to navigate the complexities of these conflicts, Smith's enactment of their gestures and accents implicates interviewee, actor, and audience in this project through the discomforts of the body: the body trying to articulate the contradictions of racialized inequity, the body trying to conform to another's habits of speaking and behaving, the body trying to decide when laughter is appropriate. Smith's performances draw all involved into a tight knot where, as in *Kimchee and Chitlins*, seeing and being seen, hearing and being heard become entangled processes.

Although the thematic concerns of *Twilight* invite the interview subjects and audience members to reflect on racial issues, if racial stereotyping also seems to happen *in* the performance, *where* it happens is not always clear. Today, cross-racial performances in the theater usually come with an explanation, such as a commitment to multicultural or color-blind casting, an intention to forward a social critique, or an acquiescence (sincere or not) to the demands of staging a production.[67] These explanations offer audiences a guideline for how to see (or how not to see) any apparent racial misalignments between character and actor, and thus provide some relief from having to maneuver these difficult gaps. For example, a white actor playing the biracial Engineer in *Miss Saigon* may cause controversy outside the theater, but spectators are asked to accept (with a little help of makeup) the character's racial identifications over those of the actor. By contrast, Smith's performances leave her and her audiences, like her characters, in the break between established patterns, caught between intimacy and distance, the promise of documentary faithfulness and the specter of racial caricature.

Smith's depiction of Young-Soon Han, as Kumamoto notes, has prompted especially uncomfortable responses, and I turn to this performance as a final example of how embodying the mundane of others might illuminate the reciprocal and interstitial constitution of difference. In her interview with Smith, Han stresses that while Korean American business owners remain devastated by damages incurred during the uprising, the African American community received the justice they sought with the guilty verdicts in the civil trials of the police officers. She explains, "Then a couple of months ago / I really realized that / Korean immigrants were left out / from this / society and we were nothing. / What is our right? / Is it because we are Korean? / Is it because we have no politicians? / Is it because we don't / speak good English? / Why? / Why do we have to be left out? / (*She is hitting her hand on the coffee table*)" (245). Emphasizing her inability to understand why Korean Americans remain marginalized, Han lists various possible explanations: racism, lack of representation, and linguistic difficulties. Through this seemingly random juxtaposition, Han expresses a suspicion that her habits of speech are linked not only to her racialization, but also to her prospect of being heard politically. She hints that having a specific kind of voice determines whether one has a voice at all. In contrast to the cool expositions of Duke and others interviewed by Smith, Han's ardent, drum-like banging during the interview conveys the frustrations of those whose improper speech positions them outside of proper citizenship.

Han's remark about linguistic capacity, however, stands out not only because of its specificity and ostensible triviality in comparison to being Korean or not having representative politicians, but also because of the particular attention that Smith received for her performance of Han's speech. As repeated by Smith, the question, "Is it because we don't speak good English?" may solicit assessments of Han's mastery of the language, but only as refracted through Smith's reenactment. Smith's performance consequently deflects the question from what it means to speak an "imperfect" or accented English, to what it means to imitate that speech imperfectly.

Yet the expectation that Smith either erase the inflections of Han's speech or replicate them with complete accuracy assumes the desirability—and the possibility—of assimilating others without grappling with the physical imprints of their formative histories. Replacing Smith's imperfect rendering of Han's speech with "normative" English would effectively obscure the demands placed on Han's body and behavior by migration, racialization, and the pressures of assimilation, as well as her struggle to articulate the relationship between the minor inflections of her voice and larger socioeconomic circumstances. On the other hand, the insistence that Smith provide an exact imitation of Han demands an implausible suturing of the fissures in speech and comportment that reflect the disparate social positions of Smith, Han, and, additionally, the audience. Even if Smith could mimic Han's accent with complete accuracy, such an imitation would not guarantee that the audience would *hear* the speech as authentic. Just as Smith's efforts to bridge "self" and "other" through her acting practice make tangible their distinct *and* mutual constitutions, uncomfortable "breaks" in the audience's engagement with her reenactments manifest the fraught convergence of various perceptual and bodily tendencies. My point, how-ever, is not that criticism of Smith's work as stereotypical is erroneous. Instead, like an interviewee's frustrated stammering or Smith's attempt to replicate it, visceral responses of amusement, anger, discomfort, or pity are iterations of the historical and social networks that appear—and disappear—at the interface of bodies.

Making Change, Breaking Bread

In the quotation from Allen Cooper with which I began the chapter, he decries the media's sensationalistic portrayal of the King and Denny beatings for further obfuscating the everyday violence with which residents of inner-city neighborhoods must live. He asserts, "You got to live here to express this point, you got to live / here to see what's goin' on. / You gotta look at history, baby, / you gotta look at history" (101). For Cooper, living in these neighborhoods is inextricably tied to looking at history: the history being made in Los Angeles, as well as the history that prompted the uprising. He suggests that those who watched the Los Angeles riots from a distance cannot fully comprehend the extent to which the uprising was not an exceptional outburst, a spectacular "soap opera" to appall viewers, but the manifestation of everyday tensions and entrenched inequities.

In his interview with Smith, Reginald Denny affirms Cooper's sense of a disjuncture between those for whom the uprising was inseparable from the mundane, and those for whom it ostensibly bore no immedi-ate relation to their daily existence: "I mean, / does anyone know / what a riot looks like? / I mean, I'm sure they do now. / I didn't have a clue of what one looked like / and / I didn't know that the verdict had come down. / I didn't pay any attention / to that, / because that / was some-body else's problem / I guess I thought / at the time. / It didn't have any-thing to do with me" (104). Denny acknowledges that he saw the King beating and trial as irrelevant to his life, as "somebody else's problem," until he suddenly found himself in the middle of a battleground. In her interview, Congresswoman Maxine Waters similarly characterizes the government as disconnected from the conditions that led to the upris-ing: "I mean, our leadership / is so far removed / from what really goes on in the world / they, um, / it's not enough to say they're insensitive /

or they don't care. / They really / don't / know. / I mean, they really don't see it, / they really don't understand it, / they really don't see their lives in / relationship to / solving these kinds of problems" (164). Waters's disconcerting observation suggests a deep-rooted obstacle to making policy changes that might effectively address the untenable conditions that led to the uprising. Both she and Denny stress a correlation between the possibilities of one's vision—of knowing "what a riot looks like" or seeing "what really goes on in the world"—and one's sense of connectedness to and responsibility for particular circumstances and events.

Twilight and *Kimchee and Chitlins* stage these profound chasms between those separated by geography, class, race, gender, and institutional position—divisions that shape and are shaped by everyday behaviors and habits of interaction. Both performances strive to articulate these divides, to suggest intricate and overlooked networks of influence by using theatrical conventions to cross established borders. In some productions of *Twilight*, Smith also explored the possibility of bringing her disparate characters into conversation by adding an imaginary dinner scene. Inspired by a discussion with chef Alice Waters, Smith explained, "I now have a scene with a group of people sitting around a dinner table, and I make the allusion that they are talking to each other. I put six characters in a fictitious setting and have them talking, with food as a meeting place—a civilized thing. Something I've always been interested in is finding ways to bring unlikely people together."[68] This dinner table scene, which is not included in either the published or the televised version, is the only segment of *Twilight* that is explicitly fictitious, although it is based on her interviews. It is also perhaps its most utopian moment, as Smith does not merely juxtapose diverse voices, but imagines them speaking to one another in a congenial, "civilized" context.

Challenging Suzie's observation at the end of *Kimchee and Chitlins* that "the best stories are *invented*" (449), Smith turned this hypothetical meeting into an actuality during the production of the film version of *Twilight* several years after the uprising. The film, which combines Smith's solo performances, videos from the uprising, and standard documentary-style (i.e., un-reenacted) interviews, also includes footage of a meal attended by, among others, Smith, former police commissioner Daryl Gates, academic Elaine Kim, journalist Ruben Martinez, and Paul Parker, chairperson of the Free the L.A. Four Defense Committee, which advocated on behalf of Denny's accused attackers. In the segment shown in the film, Parker begins to explain that unlike a revolution (his preferred term for the Los Angeles uprising), riots have "no political overtone." Gates then interrupts by asking if Parker himself participated in the uprising, and rather sarcastically inquires, "Do you steal when you're in a revolution?" As the two argue, Smith proposes that even as the diners talk, they should all "make sure [they're] listening" as well. Smith here echoes a recommendation that she makes in the introduction to *Fires in the Mirror*, where she suggests that one way to make the tensions between those in the center and those on the margins productive is to listen.[69] Yet if, as both *Twilight* and *Kimchee and Chitlins* emphasize, listening and looking do not involve just the reception of another's words and actions, but the intersection of distinct perceptual and bodily proclivities, Gates and Parker's capacities for hearing and seeing each other are already severely constrained and, to an extent, predetermined. Even as they face each other across a table, their bickering suggests that they lack a common vocabulary—discursive and corporeal—with which to turn physical proximity into an understanding of how their "profoundly different conditions of existence,"[70] as Bourdieu puts it, are inextricably linked.

These are, of course, exactly the divides that Smith attempts to overcome for herself through her acting process. By "walk[ing] in the speech of another," by repeatedly simulating verbal and physical expressions, she listens to the other by speaking as the other, and sees the other by inhabiting her or his behaviors. Her suggestion, then, that the individuals she brought together for a meal simply *listen* to one another seems strangely incomplete. Instead, the kind of listening that she may have hoped to generate is more evident in the hushed theaters where she gives her performances. Watching Smith at the Berkeley Repertory Theatre in *Let Me Down Easy*, her recent work on illness, death, and health care, I found myself a captive listener, riveted by the stories she told by intertwining her voice and body with those of her characters. I wondered, however, whether I would listen as carefully if I encountered her subjects outside the theater. Would I be patient enough to wait, like Smith, for interviews that must certainly be at times dull, rambling, confused, or even distasteful to reach their moments of shattering insight, eloquence, and poetry? In her analysis of *Twilight*, Cherise Smith points out that by reenacting interview subjects as they are speaking to her, she positions viewers in her place and compels them to identify with her.[71] Furthermore, the larger dynamics of the performance—a gifted storyteller speaking to an engrossed audience in a formal theater space—encourage viewers to listen as attentively as Smith must have to her subjects/characters. Set in relation to—not in contrast with—her performances, Smith's request that those present at the contentious meal listen to one another gestures toward the different forms of listening that are possible over dinner, in the theater, and through such frequent repetitions of another's words that they become you.

Smith's process of learning how to "walk in the speech of another" suggests the possibilities of putting into practice the kind of reenactments imagined by *Kimchee and Chitlins*'s cross-Chorus dramatizations, where the disputing characters enact others while simulating a controversial event. The explicit fictitiousness of Wong's play allows it to set these cross-racial performances next to Suzie's interview with Matilda (the scene most reminiscent of Smith's *On the Road* performances) and her customary news reports. It thus models and compares three different attempts to mediate the conflict, drawing out their respective limitations as well as the potential value of mixing theatrical and journalistic forms. Yet even as Wong's drama asks what difference it might make if those involved in the boycott could only narrate and understand what happened by inhabiting conflicting social positions, it stops short of envisioning that such performances might make substantial change. Instead, it highlights the apparent irreconcilability of perspectives informed by opposing material exigencies, as well as the difficulty of manifesting connections to distanced witnesses like Mark and Tara, who ostensibly remain untouched by and unconcerned with the boycott beyond their professional interest. Furthermore, Suzie's declaration at the play's conclusion that the best stories are "invented" institutes a divide between the possibilities of the real and the fictive—a gap that Smith repeatedly excavates and complicates in *Twilight*.

Aptly, these points of difference between *Twilight* and *Kimchee and Chitlins* may be the openings for further explorations of the potential for cross-racial performances to mediate interracial conflicts. Given the ongoing difficulty of responding verbally and practically to interracial tensions, the unlikely possibilities offered by invention and embodiment across conventions of journalistic inquiry and theatrical participation, as well as racial identification, might well be worth continued examination. The perils of cross-racial performance are evident in a long history of caricatures that reinforce stereotypes and direct ridicule at their subjects, as well as in recent struggles over casting in which claims of following "color-blind" practices can justify opening *or* closing opportunities to minority actors. Yet Smith and Wong's works suggest that cross-racial performances also hold the promise of articulating overlooked relations of affiliation, influence, and accountability. When Bourdieu argues that the "body believes in what it plays at,"[72] he distinguishes between the involuntary mimetic transmission of the habitus, which is what he is explicating, and the conscious imitation of an actor. *Twilight* and *Kimchee and Chitlins* tentatively propose, however, that attempting to play the mundane of others may lead the body to believe differently.

4

Homework Becomes You

The Model Minority and Its Doubles

The controversial memoir *Battle Hymn of the Tiger Mother* opens with a list of activities forbidden to the author's children: "attend a sleepover, have a playdate, be in a school play, complain about not being in a school play, watch TV or play computer games, choose their own extracurricular activities, get any grade less than an A, not be the No. 1 student in every subject except gym and drama, play any instrument other than the piano or violin, not play the piano or violin."[1] These lines provocatively set the banal quality of the restricted activities against the exceptional behaviors that were to be the norm. Author Amy Chua explains that these regulations were part of her efforts to raise her American daughters in what she calls "the Chinese way," that is, with a firm hand (or, some would say, an iron grip) and an eye toward Carnegie Hall and the Ivy League.

When the *Wall Street Journal* published a preview excerpt of Chua's book as "Why Chinese Mothers Are Superior," it triggered hundreds of angry comments from readers.[2] I focus here on just two strands of this criticism, which help elucidate Asian American racial formation's tendency to generate and close divides, to produce—as this chapter will elaborate—doubles as others and others as doubles. First, Chua's implicit embrace of the model minority myth jarred with long-standing attempts to dislodge the perception that Asian Americans have triumphed over obstacles—racial or otherwise—through good values and hard work. Since the 1970s, scholars, community advocates, and artists have denounced the model minority stereotype, pointing to its damaging psychological and social effects. It has been linked to mental health issues among Asian American students, to political justifications for cutting welfare and affirmative action programs, and to increased tensions between minority groups, such as those explored in Chapter

3. In rejecting the stereotype, critics have emphasized socioeconomic differences among Asian Americans and drawn attention to communities whose struggles might be overlooked or discounted because of this racial preconception.

These communities constitute what one article calls "the other half"[3] of the Asian American picture. "Asian-Americans: A 'Model Minority,'" a story in *Newsweek* published in 1982, opens by establishing a clear dichotomy: "In this centennial year of the Chinese Exclusion Act of 1882, the assimilated anchorwoman and the unskilled member of an obscure Indochinese minority embody the extremes of the fastest-growing segment of the nation's population."[4] In emphasizing a gap between the most successful Asian Americans and those who are at the very edges of American society, the article seems to ask whether the former are actually representative of Asian Americans in general. Yet insofar as the model minority myth promises that the latter can *become* just as successful, the persistence of struggling communities does not necessarily refute the stereotype; it can instead offer a useful image of what comes "before." By always projecting ahead (from hardship to triumph), the model minority myth makes efforts to repudiate it a Sisyphean task.

Furthermore, as Susan Koshy and erin Khuê Ninh point out, not all who might identify as Asian American oppose their designation as the model minority.[5] Some, such as Chua, regard it as a point of pride or a standard to emulate. From this perspective, examples of Asian Americans who do not fit the paradigm serve less to undermine the model minority myth than to drive it. In her memoir, Chua explains that in order to motivate her children, she invoked the experiences of first-generation immigrants, those who came with little money and never quite lost their outsider status. Revealing the class bias that informs the entire book, she limits her sample of first-generation immigrants to skilled workers and graduate students (20–21). Chua nonetheless recounts that she required her children to learn classical music because of her fear that they would exhibit signs of "third-generation decline" (i.e., "laziness, vulgarity, and spoiledness" [22]): "I knew that I couldn't artificially make them feel like poor immigrant kids. There was no getting around the fact that we lived in a large old house, owned two decent cars, and stayed in nice hotels when we vacationed" (22). The everyday realities of the upper-middle-class family might embody the model minority as fait accompli, but do not offer the more grueling experiences of first- and second-generation immigrants, which ostensibly propel their hard work. Chua insists that hardship must precede success, and that the model minority cannot do without its others.

When these others actually appear in Chua's book, however, their presence disrupts rather than facilitates her attempt to draw a line from her life to theirs. In her critique of Chua's idealization of the economic limitations and social alienation of immigrants, Grace Wang argues, "To celebrate immigrant toughness as a privilege, cultural exclusion as a form of capital, and institutionalized racism and downward mobility as a personal challenge to succeed, allows us to turn racism into individual failure."[6] Wang points out that despite romanticizing these figures, "when Chua finds herself face-to-face with her fetishized immigrant subjects, she feels distance rather than affinity."[7] She cites Chua's account of taking one of her daughters to audition for Juilliard: "In the waiting area, we saw Asian parents everywhere, pacing back and forth, grim-faced and single-minded. They seem so unsubtle, I thought to myself, can they possibly love music? Then it hit me that almost all the other parents were foreigners or immigrants and that music was a ticket for them, and I thought, I'm not like them. I don't have what it takes" (142).

This moment, when Chua encounters those whom she had been seeking to emulate, evinces a contradictory mix of identification and dissociation. The distance that Wang observes is clear in Chua's portrayal of the other parents as a crude Asian mass. Aesthetic appreciation seems impossible; music for them, Chua believes, is a financial investment. Yet what initially seems like a dismissal of the other parents becomes something else with the thought, "I don't have what it takes." Wistfulness suddenly exposes itself alongside condescension. If the difference Chua first describes is one that sets her above the other parents, their positions are soon reversed in her mind. According to her logic, because she is not a foreigner or a recent immigrant, she simply cannot compete with their determination. Chua reveals that for all her claims to be a "tiger mother" (and her dislike of drama as an extracurricular activity for her children), she is playing a role that she has studied and carefully put into practice. What forces a crisis in this performance is an encounter with her doubles: the "real" tiger parents.

Yet how does Chua determine that the other parents are the real thing? The pacing and grim faces might be suggestive, but certainly not enough to discern that they are "foreigners or immigrants." Chua identifies something un-American or not-yet-American about the others, as well as something that reveals their need for a ticket, a meal ticket or a ticket to a better social status. One can only guess that Chua was assessing the other parents' ways of speaking, behaving, and interacting, and finding them incongruous with her own. These differences presumably reflected back the inadequacy of her performance as a "Chinese mother," even as they indicated to Chua the other parents' inadequate performances of a particular cultural and social status that she might claim. The question nevertheless remains, how precisely do the textures of the mundane connect to actual material circumstances? And while Chua clearly sees herself as separate from the others, do they see her in the same way? If Chua had hoped to simulate the experiences of "foreigners and immigrants" while remaining distinct from them, their meeting forces a confrontation with an *unverifiable* difference, and a similarity that she both rejects and desires.

This brief scene in Chua's memoir exemplifies a distinct form of Asian American doubling, one that also energizes director Justin Lin's film *Better Luck Tomorrow* (2002) and Lauren Yee's play *Ching Chong Chinaman* (first produced in 2008). An unlikely trio, these cultural productions all highlight the contradictory identifications prompted by the model minority stereotype. The model minority rarely goes without its "other half," whether manifest as the yellow peril perpetually threatening the West, or as figures of economic and cultural alienation who seem to contradict the stereotype (or, according to Chua, to hold the secret to its perpetuation). If Asian American racial formation maintains a dichotomy between "good" and "bad" Asians, "good" and "bad" minorities, the double lives and alter egos that gradually take over *Better Luck Tomorrow* and *Ching Chong Chinaman* illuminate how this split can serve as a provocation to be *like* the other, and expose the complex system of incentives that compel such appropriations.

The film and the play, as well as a significant portion of Chua's book, focus on Asian American teenagers who seem to typify the model minority. Like the accounts of Chinese immigrant laborers, Japanese "war brides," and Korean American merchants examined in previous chapters, contemporary depictions of Asian American youths evince a fascination with the racial mundane—that is, with habitual, quotidian behaviors that come to exemplify the possibility and the limits of crossing racial boundaries. Since the 1980s, the apparent academic achievements of Asian American students have drawn attention to their daily practices as the potential source of their success. With an opening parallel to that of *Battle Hymn of the Tiger Mother*, a *New York Times* article published in 1986 claimed to examine why, as the title observed, "Asians Are Going to the Head of the Class."[8] It begins, "Le Thi Ngoc, a 32-year-old computer technician in Fremont, Calif., follows a set schedule when she comes home from work. After preparing dinner, she spends the next two hours helping her 10-year-old son, Alan, with his homework. Alan is not allowed to watch television on weeknights, and if he plays with his G.I. Joe toys when he is supposed to be doing his schoolwork, his mother throws them away."[9] Like Chua, the writer stresses the regular schedules, dedicated hours, and restrictions on play that organize Alan's days. Yet while this sketch of mother and son launches a story on the lack of consensus about why Asian American students are ostensibly doing so well—and then presents everything from genes to Confucian values to the background of the parents as potential explanations—*Battle Hymn* proposes that a strictly enforced routine of study and practice is the key.

The second, predominant strand of criticism directed at Chua focused on her defense of these parenting methods. Responding to the furor, Chua informed an interviewer that some readers found the book comforting: "Everybody wants to know why so many Asian kids are good at math and achieve so much, and many readers said, 'This is such a relief: it's not genetic, it's not in the rice! It's about hard work, so we can do this!'"[10] The memoir, in Chua's view, rejects the idea that achievement is the result of racial differences owing to genes or culinary preferences, and instead posits that success is the result of hard work, as embodied in everyday practices such as playing the piano for hours and doing extra exercises for school.

In narrating her readers' steps toward revelation, Chua moves from genes to rice to work. Rice, as discussed in Chapter 1, became the focus of anti-immigration polemics, which claimed that it endangered the very substance of the nation: as a cheap alternative to meat, it fed (cheap) Chinese labor and threatened American vigor. Placed between genes and work in Chua's account, rice bridges what seems purely bodily with what seems purely behavioral. It thus mediates the shift from race (Chinese mothers are superior) to practice (anyone can be a Chinese mother). While Chua celebrates the possibility of cultivating successful children through a change in habits,[11] an anxiety not unlike the one that fed early efforts to restrict Chinese immigration pervaded conversations about her book. *Time* magazine succinctly put it, "Though Chua was born and raised in the U.S., her invocation of what she describes as traditional 'Chinese parenting' has hit hard at a national sore spot: our fears about losing ground to China and other rising powers and about adequately preparing our children to survive in the global economy."[12] Other publications captured these trepidations with titles such as "Tiger Cubs v. Precious Lambs."[13] Such responses, however, are hardly unique to Chua's book. Earlier accounts of the achievements of Asian American students also characterized them as Asia's challenge to American and Western dominance. The aforementioned 1986 *New York Times* article, for example, claimed, "suddenly they [successful Asian American students] seem to be everywhere," and described, "they are surging into the nation's best colleges like a tidal wave."[14] These images of startling growth and ubiquity imply a dangerous propagation through seemingly praiseworthy stories about Asian American youth.[15] It is in this context that the title of the Pew Center's 2012 report, "The Rise of Asian Americans," takes on a more ominous tone.

In these depictions, long-standing fears of Asian masses (the yellow peril) converge with tales of unlikely success (the model minority).[16] Koshy contends that while the model minority myth was initially engaged to counter demands, originating from the civil rights era, for domestic policies to address racial inequality, it has more recently come to express global economic concerns.[17] She observes, "The model minority has become an anxious figure of the prized human capital needed to navigate the insecurities and volatility of the global knowledge economy."[18] In the slippage between "Asian" and "Asian American," which Chua's loose use of the term "Asian" perpetuates, the "tiger cub" comes to embody concerns that the United States will soon lose its economic edge to Asian countries. As both ideal and threat, the product of tiger parenting unites the model minority and the yellow peril. Arguing that these two figures, "although at apparent disjunction, form a seamless continuum,"[19] Gary Okihiro points out that they can look more like twins than antitheses: "'Model' Asians exhibit the same singleness of purpose, patience and endurance, cunning, fanaticism, and group loyalty characteristic of Marco Polo's Mongol soldiers, and Asian workers and students, maintaining themselves at little expense and almost robot-like, labor and study for hours on end without human needs for relaxation, fun, and pleasure."[20] Associated variously with an American work ethic, Confucian values, or an inhuman mechanical efficiency, the same model minority traits lauded for exemplifying American self-sufficiency can just as easily signify an un-American lack of playfulness, and even forebode the ascendance of Asia. The "tiger cub" then not only updates the model minority myth but also extends fears of the yellow peril, joining a line that includes "Marco Polo's Mongol soldiers," Fu Manchu, and, more recently, the figure of the Asian gangster.[21]

Chua's detractors indeed seized on the very characteristics that Okihiro identifies as blurring the line between the model minority and the yellow peril. As Wang observes, "Parenting blogs reviled her mothering style as child abuse, pathologized the (narrowly defined) success achieved by Asian American kids as the product of excessive discipline and rote practice, and extolled the virtue of balance, sleepovers, and play."[22] In defending "Western" parenting, critics found fault in Chua's practices *and* the kinds of children her practices presumably shaped. They asked, even if "tiger" mothers produced children better equipped for contemporary economic challenges, would that be the ideal outcome for Americans? Such concerns echo allegations in the late nineteenth century that white workers would have to eat rice, live in deplorable conditions, and otherwise lower their standard of living to compete with Chinese labor. Exemplifying a pattern documented throughout this book, the purported habits of Asian and Asian American children simultaneously embodied the promise and the threat of dissipating difference.

The stereotype of Asian youths as uncreative test-taking machines, used to rebuff Chua, makes a strange appearance in the memoir itself when she recounts that she did not want her daughters to turn into "one of those weird Asian automatons who feel so much pressure from their parents that they kill themselves after coming in second on the national civil service exam" (8). Chua suggests a desire to distinguish her ideal children from this stereotype, but implies that such perceptions of Asian students are accurate and that fears of propagating more automatons are warranted. Her description of the Juilliard waiting room, with "Asian parents everywhere, pacing back and forth, grim-faced and single-minded," then renders these adults, with their robot-like determination, older versions of "those weird Asian automatons." Just as responses to her memoir expressed fears of becoming *and* not becoming like the "Chinese," Chua reveals her own ambivalent relationship to those whom she holds up as models when she encounters her "doubles" in the Juilliard waiting room.

A persistent trope in Asian American cultural productions, the double surfaces in Chua's memoir to express a fraught desire to identify (provisionally) with the model minority's others. In *Better Luck Tomorrow* and *Ching Chong Chinaman*, the performances to which I now turn, the double becomes a means of critiquing as well as expressing this desire. In her seminal work on the "racial shadow" in Asian American literature, Sau-ling C. Wong cites numerous literary examples in which "a highly assimilated American-born Asian is troubled by a version of himself/herself that serves as a reminder of disowned Asian descent."[23] Building on psychoanalytical theories, Wong argues that this racial shadow elicits both "revulsion and sympathy" from the protagonist, who in "disowning" the double realizes their connection as much as their difference.[24] Josephine Lee engages with Wong's study to offer a modified view of the double in works of Asian American drama: she proposes that the double conveys not just a struggle within the psyche of Asian Americans, but "the interactions of Asian Americans caught up in myths of individual success promoted by a capitalist ideology."[25] Lee contends that while the Asian American characters in these plays initially reject ethnic ties in favor of individualism, their relationships with their doubles hint at ethnic affiliations that might offer an alternative to capitalist notions of self and other.[26]

The characters in *Ching Chong Chinaman* and *Better Luck Tomorrow* exhibit an impulse to reject associations with "Asianness" that recalls Wong's study of the "racial shadow" and an acceptance of individualist notions of success that resonates with Lee's analysis. Yet in these recent performances, attraction and wishfulness exert as strong a force in the production of doubles as the mix of repulsion and sympathy at the crux of Wong's theory.[27] Like the parents whom Chua encounters at Juilliard, these doubles are objects of envy and vehicles for furthering personal ambitions. Furthermore, unlike the plays examined by Lee, which suggest the oppositional potential of ethnic affiliations, Lin's film and Yee's drama link the double's appeal to the contradictions of the model minority stereotype, which incentivizes both intimacy with and distance from those who seem to constitute the model minority's others. These performances demonstrate both the longevity of the double in Asian American cultural productions and the new forms and meanings it has developed as a result of increasing divides *within* Asian America, a situation that Wong predicted would be "most conducive to formation of the double."[28]

What I call the mundane, although not the focal point of Wong's study, nevertheless emerges as a crucial facet of her argument when she shows in her reading of Maxine Hong Kingston's *The Woman Warrior* that the double forces the Chinese American narrator to recognize "manner can be changed, but not skin color."[29] The racial shadow reveals, in other words, an apparent disjuncture between the narrator's "race" (or what Robert E. Park might describe as her "racial uniform") and her everyday behaviors. This dynamic is also evident in *Better Luck Tomorrow* and *Ching Chong Chinaman*, but quotidian enactments in these works serve more crucially to facilitate and constrain relationships between characters with model minority aspirations and the others who become their doubles. The former adopt different habits, exchange daily tasks, and generally stretch and manipulate the mundane to accommodate their desire to be another kind of Asian or Asian American. They thus attempt to take advantage of the ostensible paradox of Asian American racial formation, its vacillations between the yellow peril and the model minority, performing its inconsistencies to expand and change their lives. Yet they come to a point of crisis when confronted with those who reflect back the deficiencies of their performance, either by demonstrating its dependence on the affirmation of an unreliable audience or by revealing their material investment in privileges they seek to deny. Furthermore, the mundane, which initially seems to offer a way to double as the other, becomes a force of resistance when the lines between self and other become blurred.

Through various forms of doubling, *Better Luck Tomorrow* and *Ching Chong Chinaman* highlight the sharp economic stratifications that have come to characterize Asian America, stratifications that are alternately uncovered and covered over in debates about the model minority. They capture the fantasies and the anxieties generated by these divides, and the material and imaginative forces that compel as well as circumscribe crossings.

Playing the Part, Burying the Body

Heralded as a breakthrough work in Asian American cinema, the feature-length narrative film *Better Luck Tomorrow* became the center of controversy at the 2002 Sundance Film Festival.[30] The film portrays a group of Asian American high school students who run scams, sell drugs, and hire prostitutes—when not applying to top universities and participating in respectable extracurricular activities like the Academic Decathlon. The film's plot bears many similarities to the 1992 murder of teenager Stuart Tay in a suburb of Southern California. News stories dubbed the crime the "honor roll murder," emphasizing the victim and the perpetrators' reputations as good students and stimulating interest in the apparent inconsistency between this reputation and the grisly murder. While only loosely following the details of Tay's death, *Better Luck Tomorrow* builds on the premise of studious Asian American teenagers who lead double lives.

During a postscreening discussion at Sundance, an audience member criticized the film as an amoral depiction of Asian Americans and asserted that the filmmakers had a responsibility to represent their community more positively. This comment in turn incited an angry response from film critic Roger Ebert, who countered that he would not have similarly reprimanded a white filmmaker. Asian American characters, Ebert insisted, "do not have to 'represent' their people."[31] In an article about the incident, he elaborated, "[Director] Justin Lin said he senses a moral disconnect in some of today's teenagers and wanted to make a movie about it. His cast was all Asian-American because—well, why not?"[32] Quoted in the same piece, Lin explained that the film reflected "a reality among teenagers of any race."[33]

Although both the audience member and the film critic claimed to speak on behalf of Asian Americans and indicated that they recognized a history of racial discrimination, by giving precedence to either appearances or behaviors, they directed their accusations of racial insensitivity at separate targets. In other words, by privileging either how the characters in the film *looked* or how they *acted*, they located responsibility for racial identifications—or for color blindness—at different sites. The audience member suggested that given the visibility of the characters' "race," their behavior reflected badly on an entire community. Meanwhile, Ebert and Lin argued that the characters' behaviors resembled those of teenagers in general, and viewers therefore should not have seen their "race" at all.

These divergent attributions of responsibility reveal opposing assumptions about the point at which racial difference materializes and disappears: on the body of the actor, in the behavior of the characters, or in the vision of the spectator. Missing, however, is a sense of how these points might align or clash, thus prompting the kind of dispute that arose at Sundance. The terms of the argument moreover elide the conceptions of class and national identity couched within claims about the film's relationship to race. Although most accounts of the dispute mention only that the audience member deplored its negative depiction of Asian Americans, Daniel Yi reports that he actually criticized the filmmakers for making a movie "so empty and amoral for Asian Americans and for *Americans*" (emphasis added).[34] If Yi's report is accurate,[35] Ebert's response may have deflected attention away from the film's depiction of Americans (as well as Asian Americans) and the question of how its representations of "Asian Americans" and "Americans" might be related.

Curiously, the film itself explicitly engages with the issues of race and representation debated at the Sundance screening. The prominent place it gives to these issues belies Ebert and Lin's insistence that it is not specifically about Asian Americans, even as it cynically predicts the kind of audience response that first provoked Ebert's defense. In a case of life unwittingly imitating art, both the film and the argument that followed the screening manifest the contradictory demands of racialization, understood as the framing of corporeal traits as markers of innate differences, and assimilation, understood as the adoption of normative behaviors (here, within a particular national context). These dual pressures are crystallized in *Better Luck Tomorrow* by the characters' double lives, which parallel—too neatly for coincidence—the stereotypes of the model minority and the yellow peril. The film asks how one body might simultaneously hold the model minority and the yellow peril as identifications—both burdensome and useful—that must be constantly managed in negotiation with others. By splitting Asian Americans between "good" and "bad," the model minority and the yellow peril create a space of *desire* as well as a restrictive dichotomy. These figures offer different temptations to the teenagers of *Better Luck Tomorrow*. Simultaneously seduced and threatened when they encounter images of themselves and others as stereotypes, they move between roles by expanding their repertoire of the mundane.

In its depiction of high school students who alternately embrace and resent their identification as Asian, *Better Luck Tomorrow* reflects a distinctly contemporary ambivalence about race. This ambivalence is the peculiar offshoot of the major social and institutional changes brought about by the social struggles of the 1960s and 1970s, and the reaction against identity-based politics that followed. Racial identity in the film is not a clear basis for either oppression or resistance, but exerts a more nebulous force. Situated firmly in the middle class and headed for an elite university, Ben, the central character, seems to exemplify the success—or, as some argue, the current obsolescence—of efforts to combat racial inequality. Yet even as Ben initially rejects the idea that race has any bearing on his life, he continuously finds escape either impossible or undesirable. As Ben and his friends shift between reluctant and deliberate enactments of the yellow peril and the model minority, the abject body (figured unambiguously as a corpse in the backyard) warns of the deeper stakes of their performance.

The film begins with a tall gate sliding open, inviting viewers into a clean suburban community lined with identical, pastel-colored homes. An ice cream truck then rolls down the street, chased by a group of excited children. With this belabored first image of American suburbia, *Better Luck Tomorrow* emphatically sets itself in the United States (more precisely, in Southern California) before focusing the camera's gaze on two teenagers, Ben and Virgil, as they lounge in a backyard. Virgil asks Ben, "Are you done yet? Early admissions? Ivy Leagues love it. Gets 'em all wet. All that studying finally pays off and you get to leave this hellhole a year early." As Ben silently tolerates Virgil's rambling, an electronic ringing interrupts their leisurely sunbathing. When the two boys realize that the noise is coming from the ground instead of their pockets, they look at each other with alarm and frantically begin to dig into the yard, eventually coming upon a lifeless hand. As Ben contemplates in a voice-over, "You never forget the sight of a dead body," the film flashes back four months to show the series of events that led to this moment.

The first scenes of *Better Luck Tomorrow* emphasize that it is telling a distinctly American story, one set *after* those once excluded from entry have passed through the gates and made themselves at home. As David Palumbo-Liu argues, "The move to the suburb by assimilated ethnics underscores the perpetuation of a particular narrative of ethnic mobility deeply linked to a closing off of space to any who have not passed through a specific process of becoming American."[36] From this perspective, the presence of two Asian American teenagers in an idyllic American suburb seems to represent the end of a journey from outsider to insider, hardship to success. Furthermore, the complete absence of parents, who are mentioned but never shown, distinguishes *Better Luck Tomorrow* from earlier Asian American films, many of which, as Jun Xing points out, are family dramas.[37] Lisa Lowe contends that familial relations in Asian American novels often symbolize a process of swapping an "original" Asian culture for an American one, an argument also applicable to Asian American films.[38] With parents and older generations kept out of sight, *Better Luck Tomorrow* establishes firm spatial and temporal boundaries around its characters, neatly avoiding any suggestion of migration or transnational affiliations.

Under the sun's glare, however, Ben and Virgil look simultaneously relaxed and uncomfortable. In the spotlight, they are not only the central subjects of the film, but also objects of scrutiny, and the deceptiveness of the innocent ice cream truck that traverses the opening scenes becomes quickly apparent. Virgil's monologue, despite its focus on college applications, describes early admission in explicitly sexual terms and reveals that he sees college as an opportunity to leave "this hell-hole," presumably the pristine suburban setting. The ringing of the cell phone further disrupts the prosaic scene, and the appearance of the hand, which recalls the dismembered ear found at the beginning of David Lynch's *Blue Velvet* (1986), reveals that the pleasant surroundings disguise a grim underside. As the camera fixes on a worm crawling on the corpse, it becomes clear that the seemingly passive American backdrop can suddenly intrude into the narrative and pull the characters from their rest. Although the scene begins as a picture of suburban ease, the unearthing of the dead body, which leads into the flashback that absorbs most of the film, suggests that *Better Luck Tomorrow* will expose what the teenagers' presence in this landscape buries and erases.

When the film moves into the past, presumably to explain the corpse, it presents two possible beginnings to the story. Ben selects one beginning himself. Early in the flashback, Ben successfully tries out for the school basketball team, only to have Daric, the editor of the campus newspaper, ask him, "How do you feel about being the token Asian on the team?" Although the question bewilders and angers Ben, Daric subsequently writes an inflammatory story that incites students to protest Ben's benchwarmer status and eventually leads to his withdrawal from the team. The incident appears to be a humorous interlude and a jab at identity politics without significant consequence, particularly since Ben and Daric become friends. Yet near the end of the film, after Ben and Daric have murdered another student (the one buried in the backyard) and Virgil has attempted suicide, Ben asks Daric why he wrote the story. Daric responds with a confused look, suggesting that he does not understand why the article is relevant in the aftermath of such violent events. Daric's article, however, is significant for drawing attention to Ben's racial difference. Claiming that racialization *begins* with the article would ignore the larger social forces from which ideas of "tokenism" emerge. Daric's story nevertheless seems to *activate* Ben's awareness that his body is racially marked. However firmly he is planted in the film's overstated depiction of American suburbia, Ben must reckon with the susceptibility of his body to signify "otherness."

Ben's unexpected reference to the article after the murder connects it to the dead body, and consequently links the racial awareness that it sparks to the corpse that haunts the film. While *Better Luck Tomorrow* insists on depicting its characters as quintessentially American, it unsettles the teleology of assimilation by inserting racialization as a lurking, interruptive force. Abrupt jumps in chronology and repeated images of gates opening and closing throughout the film capture these disruptions by undermining a sense of temporal linearity and spatial stability. In contrast to the passage from racial difference and conflict to assimilation conceptualized by Robert E. Park's "race relations cycle,"[39] the film's more erratic rhythms suggest continual movement between inclusion and exclusion. Lowe argues that narratives of immigrant inclusion are paradoxically "driven by the repetition and return of episodes in which the Asian American, even as a citizen, continues to be located outside the cultural and racial boundaries of the nation."[40] The variable position of Asian Americans, which makes inclusion always tentative, reveals a symbiotic rather than oppositional relationship between racialization and assimilation: Anne Cheng contends, "Racialization in America may be said to operate through the institutional process of producing a dominant, standard, white national ideal, which is sustained by the exclusion-yet-retention of racialized others."[41] In a circular process, the persistence of racial hierarchies, however implicit, encourages racialized minorities to seek assimilation *and* sets racial limits on its fulfillment, such that the promise of assimilation maintains the very racial hierarchies that it would seem to undermine. This contradictory dynamic exemplifies what Lauren Berlant calls a relation of "cruel optimism," one that exists "when the object that draws your attachment actively impedes the aim that brought you to it initially."[42]

When Ben names Daric's article as the origin of the violent events that subsequently take place, he assumes that racialization and assimilation are separate processes; by racially marking him, the article disrupts his progress toward a good life. Yet the film coyly undermines this assumption by showing that assimilation is itself deeply racialized, and that notions of racial difference persist through, and not despite, the teleology of assimilation. Whereas Ben traces the corpse back to Daric's article, the actual beginning of the flashback is a sequence of images of Ben diligently working, studying, doing community service, and applying to college. Quickly displayed photographs of Ben and each of his friends—Daric, Han, Virgil, and Stephanie—then give a glimpse of their backgrounds and interests. While not all of the characters match Ben's proximity to popular conceptions of the model minority high school student, many of these photographs associate them with typically American experiences: Ben singing in a church choir and wearing a cub scout's uniform; Daric smiling with President George W. Bush; and Stephanie holding a hunting rifle and wearing a cheerleader's outfit. Pictures of hapless Virgil and cool Han fill out *Better Luck Tomorrow*'s breakfast club.

In addition to these photographs and the opening shots of the ice cream truck and suburban homes, the camera lingers early in the film on a fast-food restaurant, a baseball diamond, and high school hallways full of the adolescent types that invariably populate American teen films and television shows. As Cheng points out, "We so often think of stereotypes as about the minority that sometimes we fail to see that the norm is of course itself a stereotype: a stereotype that has been legitimated, a performative expression par excellence."[43] By overloading its introductory scenes with activities and places that collectively accentuate the characters' Americanness, *Better Luck Tomorrow* arguably caricatures these expressions of national identity, offering the kind of "hyperbolic citation" of norms famously theorized by Judith Butler in relation to gender performativity. Butler argues that "acts, gestures, enactments, generally construed, are *performative* in the sense that the essence or identity that they otherwise purport to express are the *fabrications* manufactured and sustained through corporeal signs and their discursive means."[44] Asserting that behaviors that seem to reflect an identity are what produce and maintain it, she theorizes that gender is not something one displays, but something one does. Butler moreover emphasizes that the citation of norms is compulsory to the extent that it is necessary for the formation of legible subjects, as well as exclusionary in its production of a constitutive "outside" of abject bodies and disavowed identifications.[45] The impossibility of perfectly occupying any normative identity and the possibility of repeating conventions inappropriately or excessively, however, allow for a space of potential resignification. Butler posits, "Paradoxically, but also with great promise, the subject who is 'queered' into public discourse through homophobic interpellations of various kinds *takes up* or *cites* that very term as the discursive basis for an opposition. This kind of citation will emerge as *theatrical* to the extent that it *mimes and renders hyperbolic* the discursive convention that it also *reverses*."[46] Without assuming the subversiveness of such exaggerated and improper performances, Butler proposes that they may hold critical potential.

It is tempting to apply Butler's analysis to the initial scenes of *Better Luck Tomorrow* and to argue that its portrayal of prototypical American settings and lifestyles "mimes and renders hyperbolic" conventions of Americanness, the performativity of national identity. The model minority stereotype, however, complicates this argument by insinuating a ready frame through which to see the characters' behaviors. To the extent that the model minority stereotype "renders hyperbolic" the *assimilation* of Asian Americans, and thus racializes assimilation itself, it casts supposedly normative behaviors as performances of racial difference. In other words, the stereotype characterizes as remarkable and peculiar the very movement engrained in the national imaginary as the natural course of becoming American.[47] While praised for being hard-working and self-reliant, the model minority can never *be* American, but can only mimic Americanness, performing it badly, partially, or so well that the performance elicits incredulity.

Better Luck Tomorrow asks viewers to attend to Ben's daily activities by presenting them in a highly exaggerated, repetitive style that lends them an uncanny quality. The flashback begins with Ben at work in a fast-food restaurant, where the employee of the month plaque shows that he has held that honor for several months: shots of these awards in quick succession emphasize the repetitiveness of this achievement. Similarly, when Ben practices free throws at a neighborhood basketball court, abrupt cuts move the film quickly through multiple images of the ball flying toward the basket; these recurrent shots then match the regular series of Xs that he records in a notebook to track his progress.

Yet what is the relationship between the activities depicted in these scenes and the representational modes used to depict them? Is the film attempting to convey the repetitive, excessive quality of Ben's behaviors, or are its formal manipulations instead generating the impression of excessive repetitions? By introducing each character through a series of photo stills—through images that are explicitly cut, framed, and stacked—*Better Luck Tomorrow* highlights the selectiveness of its depiction; yet when it shows Ben's many awards and his diligent basketball practice, it blurs the line between what Ben does and how his activities are represented. Locating strangeness in the execution of these activities renders Ben a figure of robotic dedication, the "weird Asian automaton" eschewed by Chua and implied in characterizations of Asian and Asian American students as adept at rote exercises, but not creative thinking. Locating strangeness in the representational mechanism, by contrast, exposes the dangers (or the redundancy) of defamiliarizing the American mundane through bodies already regarded as imitative, suspicious, and alien. By making it difficult to distinguish between enactment and representational apparatus, the film simultaneously mimics and critiques the naturalization of racialized perception, a process by which the racially marked body comes to seem expressive of—and thus becomes confused with—the mode in which it is seen.

Thus, although Daric's question about tokenism seems to mark the moment when Ben becomes cognizant of his racial identification, the exaggerated, repetitious quality of the preceding scenes that show Ben's daily activities slyly evokes popular depictions of the model minority high school student. A 2005 *Wall Street Journal* article titled "The New White Flight" exemplifies these depictions, even as it concurrently documents their pernicious influence.[48] The article reports that white students in Northern California are leaving schools with large numbers of Asian Americans because of the latter's intense competitiveness and focus on math and science over the liberal arts. According to some of the white and Asian American parents and students interviewed, Asian Americans are not just successful in school, but excessively and inappropriately so. The article concludes with the story of a white student who decides to move to a school with lower test scores where "Friday-night football is a tradition," in a revealing conflation of a smaller population of Asian American students with the retention of hardy American athletic traditions.[49]

This article sheds light on why, despite their stylized portrayals, none of Ben's activities attract much attention *within* the film until he joins the basketball team, after which Daric's story and a student's joke that Ben is the "Chinese Jordan" explicitly frame this activity as peculiar.[50] These distinct modes of "defamiliarizing" Ben's everyday behaviors (loosely, extradiegetic and diegetic) suggest that although the Asian American model minority and the Asian American athlete are both objects of curiosity, the former has been naturalized—body, behavior, and perception aligned in stereotype—while the latter, at least at the time of the film's release, contradicted accepted distributions of bodies and behaviors. Although Ben would like to be "just" another basketball player, the other students continue to remind him of a disjuncture between his racial identification and his choice of extracurricular activity. Together, the curiosity directed at the model minority as a racial type and the keen attention given to the Asian American basketball player as a racial anomaly regulate racial boundaries by flexibly calibrating standards of "typical" behavior for different groups. Although Ben continues to practice free throws by himself after leaving the basketball team, it is only when basketball becomes a purely personal and often solitary activity with no connection to public spectacle or to college applications (he notes earlier that even if he is a "benchwarmer," he can include the team as an extracurricular activity) that the film conveys his time in the basketball court more naturalistically. Only then does basketball become a reprieve from his other pursuits, which pull him toward the opposite extremes of Asian American racial formation.

The film reveals early in the flashback that Ben enjoys occasionally deviating from his routines of work and study to run small cons and pranks with Han and Virgil. "I guess it felt good," Ben explains, "to do things that I couldn't put on my college application." He insinuates that these transgressions provide him with a measure of independence, a space outside the voracious college application, which demands and consumes countless academic achievements and extracurricular activities. Soon after Ben leaves the basketball team, Daric invites him to join a lucrative cheat-sheet scam, and while initially reluctant, Ben develops a tentative business partnership and friendship with Daric. Such activities, however, remain largely contained affairs. The significant break occurs when an athlete at a party ridicules Ben as the "Chinese Jordan." Daric instigates a fight in response and eventually brandishes a gun. As the other student lies helplessly with Daric's gun aimed at his head, Virgil begins gleefully kicking him and encourages Ben to participate. When the group returns to school the next day, rather than face punishment from school officials, the police, or parents as they had expected, they find that the other students now treat them with fear and respect.

The film therefore presents the fight at the party as a transformative moment for the group: with their new reputation, Ben and his friends become the center of illicit activities at their school. Yet the filmmakers insert a curious encounter immediately following the fight that shadows the double life that they subsequently cultivate. As they drive away from the party, Virgil talks excitedly while Ben, Daric, and Han sit in silence. While Virgil remains oblivious, a group of young men (whose ambiguous racial identifications I address below) drive up next to them and begin yelling and making threatening gestures. One even holds up a gun much more intimidating than Daric's. As Virgil recalls the fear on the student's face when Daric wielded his gun ("Did you see the look on that guy's face? You put the fear of God into him, man. The fear of gods"), the camera focuses on Ben's nervous visage as he stares at the car next to them (Figures 4.1 and 4.2). Meanwhile, Daric lowers the volume on the music that had been playing in their car. The film never allows us to hear what those in the other car are actually shouting; Virgil's chattering is the only audible speech during this scene, and he eventually shifts from reveling in the scuffle to panicking at the thought of being punished. As the group waits tensely, the other car finally drives way.

The scene establishes both a parallel and an opposition between the two cars, which seem to mirror each other even as they clearly divide the two sets of occupants. Given that Ben and his friends seem to be middle-class high school students, the appearance of the other car might point to the dangers of conflating the performances of these relatively privileged teenagers with the experiences of those who live in conditions of daily violence and economic hardship, experiences the boys cite but from which they are insulated by the gates of the suburban community that open *Better Luck Tomorrow*. Yet how do we determine that those in the other car are more *real* as gangsters than the main characters of the film? Such a reading depends on the assumption that the performances of those in the other car more accurately reflect their everyday conditions within the world of the film. Their masculine displays, however, are no less hyperbolic than those of Ben's group: they blast music while flashing a gun and looking intensely at the teenagers. The threat they pose seems, within the limited space of the film, less affirmed by evidence of their fearsomeness than by the fear evident in the expressions of Ben, Daric, and Han, whose faces and behaviors reflect back the "authenticity" of the performance. The dynamic between the bodies in the two cars, then, constructs a reality for the other group of young men retroactively, generating a network of relationships between their performance and the experiences and material pressures it might index. Thus, although the scene accentuates the difference between the two cars and casts the film's central characters' performance as inadequate, this difference is ultimately as unverifiable as that perceived by Chua in the Juilliard waiting room. The space between the cars constitutes an *opening*, an invitation to cross, as well as a divide. Similarly, when Virgil's recollection of the other student's terrified look converges with

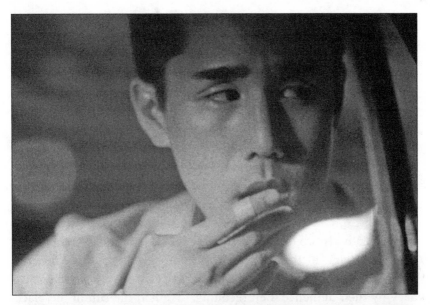

Figures 4.1 and 4.2. Ben stares nervously as young men in a car begin yelling and making threatening gestures. *Better Luck Tomorrow*, directed by Justin Lin. MTV Films, 2003.

Ben's uneasy expression while staring at the other car, this juxtaposition undermines the triumphant tone of Virgil's story (reinforcing a sense of difference between the cars) *and* conjures a moment when they were also able to instill the "fear of gods" in others (suggesting a resemblance between the cars).

This strange moment in *Better Luck Tomorrow* marks a crossroads in the film. The turn in Virgil's long speech from excitement to anxiety and his friends' subdued demeanors as they watch the other car suggest that they accept their performance at the party as a brash and unsustainable act that they already regret. Yet they find at school the next day that their peers now mirror the apprehensive expressions that they transmitted to the other car, realizing them as figures of threat. The lesson that they consequently absorb from the other car is not that they should be wary of trying to emulate the model minority's others, but that the efficacy of their performance depends on its persuasiveness, on what gets reflected back by their audience. Ben recounts, "We had the run of the place. Rumors about us came and went fast and furious. One had us linked to some Chinese mafia. It was fine with us because it just put more fear into everyone." Although Daric's branding of Ben as a token Asian and the teenagers' reputation as part of a "Chinese mafia" derives from a similar stereotyping of their bodies, Ben willingly accepts the latter for the power that it offers him. Daric's article indeed gives Ben his initial education on the measurements made on the racialized body. If, despite Ebert's appeal, Ben is made to represent Asians and Asian Americans, that is, if he cannot elude the racialization of his body, what are his options for performing within its constraints? Newly wise to the ease with which racialized bodies get attached to certain roles and not others, Ben seeks alternate experiences by assuming the role of the model minority's other, in this case, the yellow peril gangster.

In criticizing the film's preoccupation with the teenagers' subsequent spiral into criminal behavior, the audience member at Sundance registers the negative impact it may have on perceptions of Asian Americans, but fails to recognize the *appeal* that such depictions may hold for Asian American men who find themselves frequently portrayed as weak, effeminate, and asexual. When the preface to the influential Asian American anthology *Aiiieeeee!* (1974) made its rallying figure the "wounded, sad, angry" yellow man,[51] it tied Asian American cultural nationalism to the project of recuperating Asian American manhood. The continuing influence of this project is evident in Asian American cinema, about which Celine Parreñas Shimizu observes, "Contemporary Asian American male filmmakers and actors see the Asian American male body as a site of racial wounding, gender grief, and sexual problems in ways haunted by the framework of falling short of the norm."[52] Shimizu suggests, however, that films like *Better Luck Tomorrow* also make it possible to explore alternate forms of manhood through their representation of "the plenitude of Asian American male actualities and desires."[53] The film indeed presents a diverse set of Asian American men, from clownish Virgil to quietly assured Han. Yet while offering several models of manhood, *Better Luck Tomorrow* also highlights the continuing allure of hypermasculine roles for those who are racialized—and gendered—as less than men. The antics of Virgil and Daric in particular express a desire to be other than the emasculated Asian man, other than the model minority—even by adopting an equally stereotypical role. As Josephine Lee points out, "Stereotypes of Asian Americans are no longer simply the seductive images of the Orient rendered for consumption by white audiences. Instead, they have become woven into the complex fantasies Asian Americans have about identity, community, and gender."[54]

Embracing the label of the "Chinese mafia" for the fear it incites and charging the role with hypermasculine displays, the characters' performance of a sexualized yellow peril is symptomatic of the temptation, against which Butler warns, to regard the enactment of social identities as simply a matter of voluntary role-playing. As the friends repeatedly embody the Asian gangster before those who assume the "reality" of their performance, the lines between "self" and "role" prove difficult to sustain. Becoming increasingly invested in his performance, Ben recounts, "I soon learned along with image came maintenance. I needed something to expand my days. It's literally a full-time job just to make people believe who you're supposed to be." While Ben still insists on making a distinction between who he is "supposed to be" and the person he actually is, when he wakes up one morning with a bloody nose from taking too many drugs, we are reminded of his remark while memorizing words for the SAT test: "They say if you repeat something enough times, it becomes a part of you." Following this advice, Ben repeats SAT words and their definitions at regular intervals in the film, and the word that he recites reflects some aspect of his life or behavior at that moment. The first word, "punctilious," and its definition are superimposed on a shot of Ben as he lies in bed while memorizing the word; the word is therefore literally impressed on his body as it is being impressed on his mind (Figure 4.3). As he then moves through "temerity," "quixotic," "catharsis," and "inextricable," the alignment of these words with the action of the film insinuates that the words themselves are shaping him, are indeed becoming a part of him. The designation of "Chinese mafia" has a similar effect on Ben: thus interpellated by the other high school students, Ben finds the words infiltrating his body. Repeatedly enacting the role of the Asian gangster, he is unable to maintain his sense of certainty in a "self" separate from the character he plays. Although Ben would like to believe that his act as a member of a "Chinese mafia" is "not him," his embodiment of the stereotype also makes it "not not him" (the double negativity that Richard Schechner ascribes to performance), and he must grapple with the uncertain boundary between the two. Through their daily repetition, the very performances that Ben initially understands to be artificial infiltrate the mundane, forcing him to "expand [his] days" to accommodate their demands on his body and routines.

Yet even this taxing blurring of "self" and "other" proves insufficient to secure with consistency the audience's belief in his various roles. Enjoying their new wealth and reputation as the "Chinese mafia," the teenagers hire a stripper for one of their parties. At the end of the night, she asks, "So what are you guys?" Although her question initially suggests that she sees them as mysterious Asian gangsters, when Virgil tells her that they are a club, she responds, "Oh, like a math club, or something?" The expression of displeasure on Daric's face indicates that she misinterpreted their performance. If Ben and his friends want to play racial stereotypes, they must also accept the highly contextual and audience-dependent nature of all performances. While they might try to change what their racialized bodies signify, they can never fully dictate the effects of their performance. Whether the characters demonstrate their assimilation by adopting behaviors that promise the American dream or attempt to take advantage of racial fears, their conferrals and struggles with multiple audiences delimit what they ultimately perform, and what their performances ultimately do.

punc·til·i·ous *adj.*
marked by or concerned about precise exact
accordance with the details of codes or conventions

Figure 4.3. Ben memorizes words for his SAT exam. *Better Luck Tomorrow*, directed by Justin Lin. MTV Films, 2003.

Furthermore, whether the characters in *Better Luck Tomorrow* see the embodiment of stereotypes as a burden or an opportunity, their performances take shape and significance not just in their encounters *with* other bodies, but also *against* other bodies in a complexly multiracial and gendered landscape. The backdrop of American suburbia is itself a racialized space, and the emphatic images of a middle-class neighborhood and high school that open the film make the setting particularly salient. Implicitly, it is whiteness against which the teenagers' achievements are assessed, while activities that fall outside its bounds tend to evoke other racial stereotypes. In his comparative study of the works of Frank Chin and Ralph Ellison, Daniel Y. Kim draws attention to a scene in Chin's essay "Confessions of the Chinatown Cowboy," in which Chin bitterly recalls a police officer berating his black and Latino friends for not being more like the (well-behaved) Chinese. Reading this moment, Kim argues, "In the multiracial culture [Chin] describes, in which none of the acknowledged models of racialized masculinity are yellow, the only way for an Asian American male to pass as masculine is to engage in a kind of interracial performative mimesis. Yellow manhood is presented here as a signifying practice—as something one communicates through the repetition of stylized bodily gestures that belong, properly speaking, to men of other races."[55] Kim contends that in Chin's writings, popular conceptions of Asian American masculinity as lacking become connected to a "kind of defective or failed *mimesis* . . . a certain impoverished modality of assimilation."[56] The apparent unavailability or illegibility of "yellow manhood" means that imitating the "stylized bodily gestures" of other men comes to serve as limit *and* possibility. The frustrations expressed by Chin find an echo in *Better Luck Tomorrow* as efforts by characters to assert their manhood often misfire, returned as unconvincing or as derivative. The epithet "Chinese Jordan," used to taunt Ben, and Virgil's cringe-worthy citations of blackness,[57] for example, revive stereotypes of other racialized bodies while casting Ben and Virgil's behaviors as imitations, whether through the voice of another character or through the excesses of the performance itself.

Racial identification is a necessarily comparative exercise, one that involves making simultaneous assessments of the fit between bodies and behaviors across multiple racialized groups. The film dramatizes this process in the moments described above, particularly in skeptical responses to Ben's membership in the basketball team. Yet the process also becomes evident in *responses* to the film, as Manohla Dargis's review for the *Los Angeles Times* demonstrates. Referring to the fateful scene when the two cars drive next to each other, Dargis describes, "Without warning, the beats floating off the car stereo are drowned out by a louder, more insistent rhythm as a car carrying four Latino gangbangers slides next to the Mustang."[58] Reading this review, I was struck by our discrepant perceptions of the so-called gangbangers' "race," for I had presumed that the actors were Asian American. This scene would then establish a contrast between the double lives of Ben and his friends, and the doubles who embody the role of Asian gangsters more persuasively, a meeting that stages the paradox of Asian American racial formation as an unraveling dichotomy, spinning between opposition and equivalence. On the one hand, Dargis's review is a useful reminder that the model minority's "other" comprises not just the yellow peril (as an opposing stereotype) or struggling communities within Asian America (as a counterexample), but also the minority groups against which Asian Americans are set as the "model." On the other hand, the review also raises the uncomfortable question of how she came to see the actors as Latino. The review does not necessarily *affirm* the stereotype of "Latino gangbangers" (in other words, it does not assume the validity of the representation), but it nevertheless *replicates* its alignment of bodies and behaviors, while implicitly casting such performances by Asian American men as a "defective mimesis," the enactment of bodily gestures that "belong . . . to men of other races."[59] Stereotypes are not simply attached to bodies already categorized by race, but impact how such identifications are made.

Discrepancies in racial identification evince the fundamental untenability of such classifications, yet they also illustrate that regardless of "accuracy" (already a dubious criterion for assessing questionable distinctions), such identifications are always meaningful and efficacious. For those who are racially marked, the credibility of a performance, determined in often swift and half-articulated assessments of the relationship between how one looks and how one behaves, has significant consequences that extend beyond casting questions to questions of who gets to live and how. Despite changing conceptions of race that have weakened essentialist claims, racialized measurements of the fit between body and behavior continue to shape how people and institutions distinguish between the normative and the deviant, the credible and the implausible. These measurements influence everyday social relationships and play an important if often implicit part in debates about domestic and foreign policy and the distribution of resources. Both the model minority and the yellow peril stereotypes, for example, imply that certain groups are more or less deserving of economic aid and success. While policymakers have deployed the model minority stereotype to argue against affirmative action and welfare programs, the yellow peril found renewed salience in the 1980s amid fears that Japan posed an economic threat to the United States. The murder of Vincent Chin, a Chinese American man, by two automobile workers in Detroit allegedly resentful of the Japanese car industry, is but one infamous example of how racialized perceptions take on a reality with significant material consequences, in both the corporeal and the economic sense.[60]

The *Better Luck Tomorrow* teenagers, however, embrace the stereotypes of the model minority and the yellow peril for the privileges they afford: monetary gains from their various ventures, the trust of adults who assume their good behavior, and the respect of students who fear them. In their efforts to play the "Chinese mafia" while continuing their academic and extracurricular pursuits, they dwell in the space between their car and the car of their more intimidating counterparts. They seek to manage this ambiguous space—which, as I argued above, is both a divide and an opening, a threat and a temptation—by becoming similar enough to their doubles to benefit from the proximity, but not so similar that they erase the difference between them. Hinting at the impossibility of this task, the film continuously draws attention to the various factors that affect the teenagers' attempts to make these partial crossings: the fear in the eyes of other students facilitates their passage, but the stripper's cheerful query about their math club obstructs it; the demands of maintaining their grades and winning Academic Decathlon competitions keep them close to a certain kind of life, while the expansion of days through drug use pulls Ben too far into another kind of life.

Better Luck Tomorrow's version (or reversal) of the coming-of-age narrative tracks Ben's unraveling sense of self as he struggles to retain control over his numerous performances—those required to meet standards for school and college admissions, as well as those he adopts to play a member of the "Chinese mafia." Although he initially clings to his activities as a responsible high school student as his real life and even attempts at one point to give up the group's illegal schemes, his rival for Stephanie's affection—her boyfriend Steve—undermines his remaining sense of agency. Claiming that Ben is working toward submission rather than achievement, Steve entangles him in a minor plot to reject the system of incentives that encourage "model" behavior. In the violent struggle that then transpires, Ben's most vehement assertion of will materializes the very constraints that Steve had intended to challenge with his help.

A rich private school student, Steve is an enigmatic figure who appears largely untouched by the anxieties and desires of the other teenagers. When Ben and his friends approach Steve's home, they encounter a gate that prevents them from entering. Steve seems to have passed through a second "gate" dividing the model minority middle class from the wealth and privileges of the elite classes. Despite his perfect grades and certain future at an Ivy League university, Steve emphasizes connections, rather than diligence, in achieving success. He offers to get Ben an internship, saying, "I know some people, I'll give them a call." Steve is not the stereotypically hard-working model minority; instead, he seems to have access to the "old boys' network" associated with white privilege.

Steve moreover explicitly dissociates himself from other Asian Americans. Arriving at a party inebriated, he jokes, "So this is where the Asians hang out." When Daric sarcastically affirms, "Yup, the library was closed," Steve responds, "Hey, you're a funny guy. For an Oriental." By insisting on his lack of familiarity with the routines of other Asian Americans, Steve emphasizes his difference. Daric's reply registers the importance Steve places on not engaging in the "typical" behaviors of Asian Americans by, for example, hanging out in the library. Yet the fragility of the distinction that Steve tries to enforce between himself and the other characters nevertheless becomes clear when Virgil sees Steve in his characteristic long, dark coat and jeers, "I'm Chow Yun-Fat," comparing Steve to a well-known Hong Kong action star. By taking on Steve's voice, Virgil implicates himself in the name-calling he directs at Steve, highlighting their mutual interpellation as, and attempted disaffiliation from, "Orientals." Attaching his insult to the exceptional rather than the ordinary, Virgil's remark suggests that even if Steve could distance himself from everyday activities associated with Asian Americans, he would not be able to extricate himself completely from the spectacle of racial difference.

Distinguished from Ben's group by his easy privilege, yet sharing an uneasy racial association, Steve offers a seductive model of what they might attain. When he subsequently rejects the privilege that inspires the other teenagers' envy and resentment, he triggers a violent response that reinforces the boundaries of acceptable behavior. Success, Steve warns Ben, demands compliance with existing social structures while giving the illusion of agency. At a batting cage, Steve asks, "You happy, Ben?" to which Ben replies, "I don't know." Steve responds, "Fuck. That's the most truthful thing I've ever heard. At least you have a choice. I have everything—loving parents, top grades, Ivy League scholarships, of course, Stephanie. . . . I'm so fucking happy I can't stop it." Slamming baseballs throughout his monologue, Steve continues, "It's a never-ending cycle. When you got everything, you want what's left. You can't settle for being happy. That's a fucking trap. You got to take life into your own hands, do whatever it takes to break the cycle." The image of Steve partaking in a traditional American pastime as he gives his monologue evokes the reproduction of national values and customs, with Steve embodying the attainment of the American dream. The scene, however, emphasizes Steve's sense of confinement rather than accomplishment, affirming that his present happiness is one of passive acceptance, a "trap" that brings success without agency. The batting cage, enclosing Steve on three sides, visually re-creates his feelings of imprisonment, while his repetitive acts of hitting the ball suggest the "never-ending cycle" of acculturation and accumulation. Cinematic techniques further stress a sense of endless, inescapable repetition: the scene switches strangely from day to night, and abrupt cuts juxtapose in an unrelenting series multiple meetings of bat and ball and Steve's persistent question of "What?" when Ben begins to laugh.

In order to "break the cycle" and "take life into [his] own hands," Steve proposes giving his parents a "wake-up call" by robbing them. The significance of this puzzling scheme (how exactly would this liberate Steve?) is legible only within the particular symbolic associations established in the film. Steve's idea of breaking the cycle perpetuates the wider disavowal of parental figures in *Better Luck Tomorrow*, but it also reflects his resistance to a broader societal parenting. If, as Steve insists in his rant to Ben, the comforts of abiding by established conceptions of achievement deplete real agency, asserting control requires a complete rejection of the privileges they afford. While this scheme exposes Steve's avaricious impulse to possess even *lack* if that is what remains after having everything else, its aborted execution reveals the other characters' collective investment in safeguarding the possibility of being as "happy" as Steve. Steve's plot to see what might happen by breaking the cycle not only fails, but it also ends with his death when those whom he solicits as accomplices—Ben, Daric, Virgil, and Han—turn against him and decide to give him, rather than his parents, a "wake-up call."

The scenes that depict their assault on Steve repeatedly disrupt the viewer's expectations by switching between styles. Thus disorienting the audience, the film replicates the confusion between real and fake, self and role, experienced by Ben and his friends in their double life, and insinuates that this confusion reaches a crisis point with Steve's murder. As Steve enters a dimly lit garage, Daric, Virgil, and Han surround him with menacing looks. Daric even coolly smokes a cigarette. The spotlight of a garage lamp adds an exaggerated quality to the encounter, imbuing their behaviors with an affected air and suggesting that the teenagers created an overtly theatrical scene. Once they begin beating Steve, however, close-ups and erratic lighting replace this distanced view with a sense of immediate, palpable chaos, which escalates in the subsequent struggle for a gun. The gun goes off, but the film then cuts to an image of Ben, Virgil, Han, and Daric in a car heading to a New Year's Eve party. The sudden break leaves the viewer in a state of suspense but insinuates that Steve has been shot.

The film eventually returns to the scene in the garage to show what transpired: Ben, who had been acting as a lookout, rushes in upon hearing the gun fire and finds that no one has been hit by the bullet. The filmmakers thus manipulate the theatrical convention of the gun that appears in an early act and goes off before the play's end, encouraging then undermining the viewer's assumption that someone will be shot. Instead, Ben suddenly begins to beat Steve with a baseball bat, spraying blood across Han's face. The close-ups of the expressions of terror and disbelief on Han, Virgil, and Daric capture their visceral reactions to the beating, and invite the audience to share their repulsion. The film then shifts from graphic violence to discordant comedy when the owner of the garage, Jesus, enters and exclaims, "What the fuck? We didn't agree to this. This is going to cost you extra." The wider shot of the dramatic solo lighting that accompanies Jesus's response further lends the moment a farcical quality. When Steve's body begins to shake, however, Daric completes the murder by stuffing his mouth with a gasoline-soaked cloth while Virgil holds his head. Close-ups again directly involve the audience in the unpleasant physicality of Steve's murder. Moving between a visceral, graphic style and a more distanced view with comedic shades, the film encourages continual adjustments in audience expectation and perspective without destroying our faith in its narrative realism: the characters must clean up the blood, get rid of the body, and contend with questions once people begin to notice the victim's absence. Collectively, these scenes induce viewers to experience the destabilizing interface between styles in shifts that are registered by the body as it laughs or turns away. If the real effects of illusory roles are what drew Ben to his double life, the discomfiting realness of these scenes and the momentary relief offered by the comical interludes simulate an impossible desire to turn back the doubling, to assume, as before, a neat alignment of identity and identification, and a clear boundary between voluntary and involuntary enactments.

A shadow of the Vincent Chin murder crosses the film during this climatic scene: Ben beats Steve with a baseball bat, the very object used to kill Chin, as well as one of the weapons used to beat Stuart Tay. Despite the very different circumstances surrounding the murders of Chin and Tay, they were national scandals in part because they unsettled the notion that Asian Americans were on the right track, that they constituted a chosen minority immune to racism and untouched by the violence that troubled other racialized communities. That a baseball bat was used in these attacks connects these incidents, with lamentable poignancy, to a symbol of national belonging. The baseball bat moreover directly links Steve's death to his speech at the batting cage. Repeatedly pummeling Steve as Steve had pummeled baseballs, Ben offers him the absolute abjection of "what's left": in becoming the buried, the invisible, and the shattered, Steve embodies not a break in the cycles he deplores, but their constitutive remains. Ben indeed enacts the unspoken demands of total assimilation directly onto Steve's body, fulfilling the process that he had wished to disrupt. Josephine Lee muses, "If the Asianness of the body is read as a nonpermeable boundary, passage of the Asian body through the boundaries of racial categorization requires radical violence."[61] It is exactly through "radical violence" that Ben offers Steve a final transcendence of his racialized body. By then burying Steve, he incorporates him directly into the land itself.

The execution of the imperative to assimilate oneself *invisibly* into the American landscape by those similarly racialized points to the difficulty of "breaking the cycle" when it continues to promise "better luck tomorrow." This promise still calls to Ben's group, as the friends disarm whatever threat Steve may have posed, then avoid, each in his own way, the consequences of the murder. Yet as the ringing of Steve's cell phone at the beginning of the film reminds them, they will have to continue to reckon with the bodies that refuse a neat suburban burial. Returning near its conclusion to the scene of Virgil and Ben sunbathing, the film seems to accept, through its circular structure, the persistence of the cycles so frustrating to Steve. Importantly, however, it reimagines a tale of progress and triumph as one of burials and hauntings. Although the film initially presents Ben as a paragon of the model minority stereotype, it resists the embrace of what Palumbo-Liu terms "model minority discourse":

> Model minority discourse provides a particularly potent site of subject construction and ideological containment because it achieves its force from the fact that it *appears*, by dint of mobilizing "ethnic dilemmas," to be contestatory. Yet the sublation of ideological contradiction within the recuperative operations of individual "healing" vindicates the dominant ideology while rewarding the subject with a particular form of individual well-being freed from both the constraints of collectivity (that is, "I am no longer 'labeled as Asian American,' I am an *individual*") and its obligations ("I am *myself* first, and my 'Asian Americanness' only partially coincides with that Self, and I can access it at will").[62]

According to Palumbo-Liu, the "model minority discourse" prevalent in Asian American literature replicates the ideology it seems to critique by privileging individual achievement over collective responsibilities. This discourse charts a movement from "ethnic dilemma" to "individual 'healing,'" a trajectory that *Better Luck Tomorrow* overturns. The image of Virgil, lying with bandages around his head in a hospital bed after attempting suicide, makes clear that rather than moving toward progressive "healing," the film receives its momentum from the resurfacing of violence. Insisting on the constant intrusion of the abject body into axiomatic tales of assimilation, the film gestures toward the ghosts hidden beneath their well-groomed settings.

As *Better Luck Tomorrow* draws to a close, we see Ben back at school, sitting alone at a lunch table while students move about him. He later goes to a basketball court, but just as he is about to shoot the ball, he puts it under his arm; he then stands still as the camera captures him from various angles. The film's emphasis on Ben's immobility in the midst of movement (whether that of the other students or the camera) suggests his inability to choose between two evident options: to turn himself in for murder and face the legal repercussions of his actions, or to continue his life as before. Ben's "choices," however, merely ensure that the same cycles of racialization and assimilation will continue by casting him in the familiar molds of the yellow peril or the model minority. His stillness, then, seems to come from standing outside these pressures, which not only propel the film's plot, but also constitute Ben as a legible subject.

Ben's passivity is nevertheless not offered as a solution; instead, it calls attention to the unfeasibility of acting in a vacuum without an audience or a script. It thus sets Ben in what Berlant calls an impasse, "a space of time lived without narrative genre."[63] Finding Ben as he walks home from the basketball court, Stephanie invites him into her car and expresses some concern that she has not heard from Steve. She further implies, however, that she has chosen Ben over Steve, and kisses him. The camera focuses on Stephanie's tentative smile and Ben's more ambiguous expression. As the film closes with an image of the two riding off together, through a sunny street lined on each side with identical suburban homes, Ben reflects in a voice-over, "For the first time in my life, I don't know what my future will hold. I don't even know what the other guys are going to do. All I know is that there's no turning back." Deferring any solution or resolution until "tomorrow," the film poses the question of how to move forward after confronting the limits of potential action, when the scripts that guided one's decisions no longer seem viable. It offers a conventional denouement (the protagonist finally winning his love interest), but only as an impossible ending. When the film suddenly cuts to a black screen in the middle of Ben's last sentence (following "All I know"), it insists on concluding not with an image of an illusory happy ending, but with a brief void (before the credits) that reflects a state of unknowing.

Trading Places: Servants, Orphans, and Gaming Champions

The doubles that the *Better Luck Tomorrow* teenagers encounter while driving reflect back the inadequacy of their performance and showcase the fierceness they wish to emulate. Although the fearful response of Ben and his friends suggests that they "don't have what it takes," the teenagers, like Chua, dedicate themselves to becoming more like their doubles while retaining their privileges.

A desire to be like the model minority's others also preoccupies Desdemona Wong, an ambitious American high school student in Lauren Yee's satirical drama *Ching Chong Chinaman*. Since its first readings in 2007, *Ching Chong Chinaman* has received productions by the Pan Asian Repertory Theatre in New York, Mu Performing Arts in Minneapolis, and Impact Theatre in Berkeley. The play depicts the foibles of the Wong family, particularly the two children, Desdemona and Upton. While sharing some resemblance to Ben, Desdemona is not interested in living as both the model minority and the yellow peril, but seeks to secure her status as the model minority by associating herself with those who lack her privilege. In an echo of Chua, Desdemona believes that in order to get into Princeton, her dream school, she has to borrow from the experiences of those who have struggled. Yet what she hopes to borrow is not a particular way of living (for example, the focus and discipline that Chua tries to re-create through classical music), but rather a story that bridges suffering and success, poverty and comfort. In contrast to Desdemona, her brother Upton is concerned only with winning an online gaming competition in South Korea. While Desdemona focuses on excelling in every task demanded of an American high school student, Upton finds that fulfilling his daily obligations to school and family prevents him from devoting all of his time to gaming. He consequently feels that he must, like Ben, expand his days. Rather than turning to drugs to fuel a double life, however, Upton hires someone to carry out his everyday duties.

Desdemona and Upton therefore seek to supplement their lives with, respectively, the narratives and the labor of others. While Desdemona solicits tales of hardship for her college applications from an orphan in Korea whom she decides to sponsor financially, Upton also looks to Asia to meet his goals and employs a man from China to act as his "indentured servant." Through Desdemona and Upton's relationships with these surrogates, Yee dramatizes the desires and the anxieties generated by the class divides that cut across Asian America and, more broadly, the Asian diaspora.

Ching Chong Chinaman portrays Desdemona, Upton, and their parents Ed and Grace as emphatically assimilated, much like the characters in *Better Luck Tomorrow*. While the drama is unable to show the accoutrements of middle-class American life with cinematic verisimilitude, it exaggerates the family's investment in this identity, which expresses itself most clearly in how they continually differentiate themselves from those who are working class, immigrants, or foreigners. Such tendencies show themselves most strongly in Ed and Grace. Grace insists that she cannot understand her Chinese American doctor's fluent English, while Ed assumes that peripheral Asian characters are all undocumented immigrants or maids.

Although Upton specifically hires Jin Qiang, or "J," to do his schoolwork and chores while he trains for his gaming championship, J is soon engaged in or at least proposed for a variety of activities for the entire family. Between completing homework assignments for Upton and Desdemona, J becomes Grace's lover and Ed's confidant. Both of these roles make him a vehicle for highlighting the couple's befuddlement when confronted with seemingly basic tasks. However confident they are as American suburbanites, Grace and Ed are unable to satisfy the expectations of family and home attached to this identity. Ed tells Jin Qiang, "Sometimes I think my wife's silly. Sometimes I think her demands are stupid. 'Take out the trash.' 'Mow the lawn.' 'Make me a baby.' What does she want me to make it out of? Money?"[64] Ed, whom the play implies is impotent, sets procreation at the end of a list of chores, suggesting that Grace's unfulfilled desire to get pregnant has taken on the character of an everyday burden. Meanwhile, Grace is simply inept at all quotidian functions. Ed explains to the audience, "My wife, she's just not very good at anything. She can't work, she can't turn on a computer, she can't cook—we're always ordering takeout—but there it is" (287). Grace's clumsy attempts to manage the household bear out Ed's characterization. As soon as Grace remembers to wake her children for school, alarm clocks go off and make her cries superfluous. Desdemona then enters the scene already getting ready for school, and Grace offers vain assistance (281). Desdemona's independent execution of her morning routines only emphasizes the redundancy of her mother's attempts to help.

The difficulty that Grace has inserting herself into the routines of her family paradoxically seems to intensify her desire for a baby, for someone, she explains, who needs her. In an attempt to distract her, Ed tries to occupy her with the very activities that disorient her:

ED: You have to drive Desi to her thing today. That's probably very
important. What you need . . . you need a hobby. Garden. Bake. Knit.
No, wait, don't knit.

GRACE: Music. I love music. And dancing.

ED: Or crosswords. There's one of those every day.

GRACE: It takes two to tango.

ED: What about tap dancing? Takes two feet to tap. (*Beat.*) Wait. Wait a
minute. You know what came this morning? (*Sings, as he retrieves a
box.*) "I'm dreaming of a white Christmas." (*Ed hands Grace a large
box of cards and a list. He pulls out a Christmas card.*) Someone's got
a nice family, hmm? (280)

Dismissing the shared activities that Grace proposes, Ed directs her to
solitary hobbies that, instead of fulfilling her wish for a baby, will simply
fill up her days. His one momentary concession to her desire for something more exciting than driving her daughter to school and writing
Christmas cards is tap dancing. When Grace subsequently takes up tap
dancing with J, who is secretly an aspiring dancer, and finally tap dances
away from Ed with a girl who represents her "love child" with J, she not
only contradicts Ed's notion that tap dancing is only a two-feet activity,
but also rejects his attempts to keep her in the family by absorbing her
in chores and hobbies that require her regular attention.

Desdemona and Upton share their parents' assurance that they are
not like any of the other Asian or Asian American characters and pres-
ences in the play, but they are savvier about developing relationships
with the latter that might help them achieve certain goals. While Ed and
Grace struggle to perpetuate the everyday practices of their middle-class
life, Desdemona and Upton actively work to manage its limitations without giving up their place within it. As Upton explains in a recording he
makes for a school essay, his basic academic and familial duties conflict
with his larger ambitions:

Podcast for Yankee Ingenuity, an essay by Upton Sinclair Lewis Wong.
Take one. (*Beat.*) Now say I am a fifteen-year-old male whose greatest
ambition is to qualify for a coveted spot in the World of Warcraft international arena tournament. An objective that requires several months

of diligent playing. Now I'm on this computer game, World of Warcraft, eight to ten hours a day. The rest of the time I am at school or I am asleep or I am doing homework/chores. In order to win my spot at the international arena tournament, I must play during nearly all of my waking hours. Yet there are also tasks in my life that must be fulfilled—education, family obligations, food, sleep, personal hygiene. But is there a way I can get both done? (273)

Despite having a name that combines references to two authors known for their critiques of American society, Upton expresses his unabashed faith in "Yankee Ingenuity." He understands that the reiteration of everyday practices, whether it involves doing homework or training for a gaming championship, is necessary to cultivate and maintain a certain social position. Yet the repetition and persistence required of the mundane makes it difficult to be two people at once. Upton's solution to this quandary takes advantage of the perceived flexibility of the mundane, its uncertain relationship to the body that carries out its exercises. By delegating some of his everyday practices to J, Upton believes that he can sustain two lives. Yet as J takes on more and more of Upton's duties and even begins developing close relationships with his parents, Upton finds that the rest of the family easily accommodates his absence. By the time Upton learns that he has qualified for the championship in Korea, they largely ignore him. Betting that he can control the mundane's distribution of tasks and roles, Upton realizes that by not participating in the routines of his family, he has lost his position within it.

Upton mistakenly believes that he is too different from J to be replaced by him. His identity, in other words, seems safe from threat, even if he gives away its associated practices, since J is his indentured servant, a "displaced person," as Desdemona calls him, who comes from poverty and does not speak English. Yet from J's first appearance, the play casts doubt on the distinction that Upton makes between them, and, more generally, on the family's sense of difference from anyone and anything that is legible as "Asian." When *Ching Chong Chinaman* opens, the Wongs breezily chat about Manifest Destiny, racism, and anti-Semitism while posing for a family portrait; meanwhile, "In the middle is a Chinese man in his twenties doing math homework. He would blend right in if he weren't wearing traditional Chinese clothing and a coolie hat"

(267). By introducing J as a silent, busy presence at the center of the picture before showing the family's quick embrace of his labor, the play proposes to explore what quietly sustains middle-class American life. In an introduction to Yee's script, Josephine Lee argues, "As the play progresses, elements of their American home, Ivy League schools, leisure activities, white-collar jobs are increasingly exposed as fantasies of invisible labor."[65] The play thereby conveys how thoroughly the mundane of American middle-class life is dependent on the unrecognized work of others. If J's main task—doing Upton and Desdemona's homework—bends credibility for comic effect, his continuing presence in the family as Upton's indentured servant emphasizes the conditions of inequity that become quickly normalized as intrinsic to maintaining a certain standard of living.

J's invisibility—first suggested when he is ignored by the family as they take their picture—is reinforced in the following scene when Ed and Grace come into the kitchen where he is working but do not seem to notice him. The reason they disregard him at this moment, however, is that they mistake him for their son. However much the family might disavow any resemblance to J, he is unseen not only because of his unrecognized labor, but also because of his *similarity* to the Wongs. The stage directions, which stipulate that J resemble the Wong family except for a stereotypically "Chinese" costume, reinforce this idea and give J's invisibility an added valence. The difference between J and the Wongs must be both spectacular and precarious. J is like the family and yet not like the family, and what holds the border is his overtly outrageous costume. If J were to take off his costume, he might very well "blend right in" with the family and attain a different kind of invisibility. The reverse is also presumably true: if the entire Wong family were to put on J's hat and clothes, they would be indistinguishable from him.

Yee's drama thus sets as a primary point of interest the line between the Wong family and those, including J, who are similarly racialized but occupy different social positions. Although Yee initially intended to write a play about a white family hiring a Chinese indentured servant, she decided instead to make the play about a Chinese American family that is "ultra-assimilated" (267). The play humorously presents their detachment from anything that might seem Chinese through their inept use of chopsticks, their limited understanding of Chinese food, and an extended dialogue in which Grace and Ed's inability to pronounce Jin Qiang's name (they only hear it as "Ching Chong") compels Upton to shorten it to "J." Yet while *Ching Chong Chinaman* extracts much humor from the family's uncomfortable relationship to ethnicity, it also lends the play a critical edge as an exploration of the stakes of identification.

The weakness in Upton's plan to hold onto two lives through a surrogate lies in his inability to see the two-sidedness of J's invisibility: J is invisible both because of his difference from the Wongs (he embodies the unseen labor that sustains the family's way of living) and because of his similarity to them (without his costume, he could be mistaken for one of them). Missing this duality, Upton depends on J's difference to prevent a slippage between J's execution of familial duties and his inclusion within the family. The performance moreover situates Upton's oversight in a broader "post-identity" context in which established modes of identification no longer exert the same influence. The audience learns that Upton's idea to hire an indentured servant comes from his knowledge of the Chinese laborers who worked on the American transcontinental railroad. In a lengthy monologue framed as another recorded essay, Upton explains,

In 1865, in the midst of construction on the Transcontinental Railroad, building superintendent Charles Crocker was faced with a conundrum. Due to the harsh conditions and back-breaking labor, his workforce was hemorrhaging at an alarming rate. He needed able-bodied men, and fast. It was not until he finally started hiring Chinese workers—workers who could not have gained entry into America otherwise—that Crocker began to make progress. Four years later, thanks to Chinese sweat and Crocker's ingenuity, the railroad was completed, leading the country one step closer toward Manifest Destiny. This example from yesteryear can provide us with ways to improve our own lives today. So say I want to progress in World of Warcraft AND lead a healthy, normal life. How can I achieve both? The answer can be found in Crocker's brilliant scheme from nearly 150 years ago: indentured servants. Workers from Third World countries whose time is worth far less than my own. I, hypothetically speaking, of course, buy them a one-way plane ticket to America and forge a student visa. They complete my homework, my chores, and my familial obligations. Like Crocker, I am able to achieve my goals painlessly, and they receive opportunities far beyond what they could get in their home countries. (278–79)

The crucial role that Chinese laborers played in the construction of the railroad and the subsequent erasure of their contribution have been important subjects for Asian American history and cultural productions. This topic has received major dramatic treatment in off-Broadway stagings of Frank Chin's *The Chickencoop Chinaman* (1972) and David Henry Hwang's *The Dance and the Railroad* (1981), which was revived in New York in 2013. While not without humor, these plays took seriously the project of recuperating an erased history. In *Ching Chong Chinaman*, a narrative that has deepened the historical reach and the political stakes of an Asian American identity serves an entirely different kind of lesson. In his retelling, Upton echoes the mistaken belief that these early Chinese laborers were indentured servants or "coolies." He moreover identifies not with the workers, but with Charles Crocker, the construction supervisor and a key railroad investor, whom he regards as a model of "Yankee Ingenuity." What Upton derives from this history, in other words, is not a sense of solidarity with the workers, but a justification for benefiting from cheap labor. The call of Manifest Destiny, the betterment of lives that are "worth less" than his, and the preservation of his way of life become the grounds for bringing J from China.

Yet even as Upton's monologue undermines the expectation that because he is Chinese American he will automatically identify with the Chinese railroad workers, the story he provides to explain why he hired J as a so-called indentured servant also transmits a lesson from Asian American history and—if read ironically—a critique of global labor practices. The play thus asks what happens when narratives used to advance a political sensibility and a historical basis for identifying with the struggles of immigrants and workers no longer hold power. In a context where personal goals are accommodated through flexible identifications, what might compel someone to align herself or himself with those who are less advantaged?

Ching Chong Chinaman provides one cynical answer to this question through Desdemona. The relationships that appeal to Desdemona are those that link her to the hardships absent from her middle-class life.

Determined to get into Princeton, Desdemona feels disadvantaged by her advantages as well as her racial identification. She complains to her mother, "If I had cancer, if you disowned me, then I could be myself. Then I'd have a chance. Then I could say something interesting in my personal statement" (282). She explains, "I'm an Asian American female with a 2340 [a very high SAT score] and a 4.42 GPA at an elite public high school. That's like the worst thing in the world. Nobody's gonna want me" (282). Desdemona's crude complaint about her too-easy life reveals her blindness to how the very advantages of class and education that she wishes to deny have brought her to the threshold of an elite university, if not yet into its halls. When she explains, however, that she is a less desirable candidate because admissions officers see her as indistinguishable from other Asian American women, she echoes the real frustrations of Asian American students who have suspected universities of imposing racial quotas to suppress their numbers. Such frustrations have spurred government investigations from the 1980s to the present, and various institutions have acknowledged that implicit biases in admissions criteria as well as explicit preferences for legacies and athletes have worked against Asian American applicants.[66]

In addition to its salience for Asian American college aspirants, the issue of Asian American acceptance rates—namely, their possible subjection to racial quotas—has also been raised to support arguments for barring all considerations of race in college admissions. Most Asian American organizations have consistently voiced their support for affirmative action, but the recent Supreme Court case *Fisher v. University of Texas at Austin* highlighted the issue's polarizing effects. Abigail Fisher, a white applicant who was denied admission, claimed that the university violated the Equal Protection Clause of the Fourteenth Amendment and the Civil Rights Act of 1964 by discriminating on the basis of race. A handful of Asian American organizations filed briefs in favor of Fisher (thus complementing the primary brief in which Asian Americans were repeatedly invoked to buttress Fisher's case), while close to a hundred Asian American groups responded with competing briefs on behalf of the University of Texas.[67] Despite the former's much smaller numbers, efforts by the 80–20 Educational Foundation to bring organizations together to support Fisher represent a major break from what has been the more common position taken by Asian American organizations vis-à-vis affirmative action.

Desdemona's obsession with being admitted into Princeton thus sets a particularly fraught issue for Asian Americans at the center of the play, but empties it of any significance beyond its implications for fulfilling personal goals. Desdemona is unconcerned with why one might either defend or reject affirmative action, or with changing the overall system. She is interested only in how existing preferences might be manipulated to support her own application. In a perversion of efforts by Asian American organizations to defend affirmative action by emphasizing the crucial opportunities it provides to certain Asian American communities and other racial minorities, efforts that prioritize broader social commitments over the fate of individual applications, Desdemona associates herself with those less advantaged only to make a case for her own admission. Yet as Desdemona assumes the stories of others, these figures begin to exert unexpected pressure on the facile analogies and links that she attempts to construct.

Recalling the early montage of Ben in *Better Luck Tomorrow*, Desdemona moves swiftly among self-care, schoolwork, college applications, and extracurricular activities. These tasks bring her closer to her goals, but she regards them as ultimately insufficient because her life lacks crucial experiences of hardship. Whereas Steve conspires to reject the system of incentives that traps him in a "never-ending cycle," Desdemona understands that effectively narrating one's relationship to deprivation (namely, how it was overcome) is an integral part of perpetuating those cycles: such tales ensure continued participation in the system while casting failures as expressions of individual shortcomings. Desdemona accordingly sponsors a parentless seventeen-year-old girl in Korea, Kim Lee Park, who becomes the subject of her college application essay on "a person who has influenced you in a significant way." The inspiration that Desdemona draws from Kim for the essay is staged in the play as a dialogue between the two characters. With Desdemona's prompt, "Kim was born in Seoul, South Korea," lights rise on Kim, who continues, ". . . at the mouth of a river, under the full moon of August" (277). Kim then recounts that she was an abandoned "love child without love," who was saved only by Desdemona's donation. The money, she explains, allowed her to buy a yak that provided her with food, heat, and transportation. Kim concludes dramatically, "Without Desdemona, I do not know where I would be. Her passion for academics and dedication to instigating community change have been the factors that prevented me from throwing myself into the river" (277).

The moon, the love child, and the water together recall "No-Name Woman," the memorable opening chapter of Maxine Hong Kingston's *The Woman Warrior*, in which the narrator tells of her aunt's suicide after giving birth out of wedlock. Yet the story that in Kingston's seminal work propels the narrator's efforts to recuperate a condemned aunt becomes, in Yee's satire, a letter of recommendation—disguised as personal statement—attesting to one teenager's fitness for Princeton. Furthermore, in contrast to Kingston's narrator, who ponders, "What is Chinese tradition and what is the movies?"[68] Desdemona is not particularly concerned with parsing truth from fiction. Instead, as her attempts to revise her essay demonstrate, she exploits the difficulty of verifying her claims about Kim's life:

KIM LEE PARK: I'm not very well at English. I don't feel anymore like doing this. (*Kim Lee Park sighs. Desdemona grabs her roughly.*)

DESDEMONA: Now listen, you stupid little girl: I need an essay and I can't wait 'til you FEEL like it! (*Desdemona slaps Kim Lee Park. Pause.*)

KIM LEE PARK: I apologize. Do you want to start again?

DESDEMONA: "Seventeen years ago, Kim was born in Seoul, South Korea, at the mouth of a river, under the full moon of August. Abandoned by my mother—"

KIM LEE PARK: "Beaten by my mother?"

DESDEMONA: Oh, good. "—beaten by my mother, I was headed for a life of emptiness and sadness—" (*Stops.*) That just seems a little vague. What kind of emptiness?

KIM LEE PARK: Malnourishment?

DESDEMONA: ". . . malnourishment and . . . abuse . . ."

KIM LEE PARK: That sounds sad.

DESDEMONA: Yeah, that's better. (*Pause.*) You're my best friend, Kim. I'm glad I didn't let you die.

KIM LEE PARK: Me, too, Desdemona. (278)

As benevolence turns to rage, Desdemona's exertion of physical force makes tangible the power that she holds over Kim as her sponsor. In return for providing the financial means to turn a particularly bleak life into a slightly more viable one, Desdemona seeks to adopt the story of that transformation: the more maudlin her description of Kim's life, the more compelling the change that Desdemona ostensibly helped effect. To give her personal statement interest and thus differentiate herself from other applicants, Desdemona looks to Asia to extract an appropriately purple narrative. As Desdemona herself comments, however, the essay "seems a little vague." Changing "emptiness" to "malnourishment" and "sadness" to "abuse," she attempts to fill out the essay with details that might lend credibility to her account. Kim's hesitant additions, punctuated with question marks, suggest her understanding that it is not veracity that matters, but the cultivation of its likeness through more concrete language. In her nonchalant willingness to deceive, Yee's Desdemona embodies the version of her Shakespearean namesake that torments Othello's imagination.[69]

During the process of writing the essay, however, the pronouns shift to conflate Desdemona and Kim, and the lines between them begin to blur. By slapping Kim, Desdemona also breaks the conceit that the two are corresponding from a distance, and thus lends their interaction a more physical *and* a more fantastical quality. In other words, by hitting Kim and thus giving her a more real presence on the stage, Desdemona raises the possibility that Kim (or at least this version of Kim) is a figment of her imagination—available for such attacks because she is not in Korea, but in her mind. The play gives other indications that Kim might be more imaginary than real. If the preposterous descriptions of the all-purpose yak are not enough to render Kim suspicious, her name raises a flag for those familiar with Korean appellations, as Kim Lee Park is simply an amalgam of three common last names.

Whether Kim is real or fictive in the world of the play, Desdemona soon abandons her as a source of struggles to enhance her essay. Coming across another one of Desdemona's essays about Kim, Upton points out that the prompt asks, "Tell us about a major struggle in your life" (286), and thus solicits an account of the hardships that Desdemona herself has faced. Desdemona subsequently turns her attention to the film version of Amy Tan's *The Joy Luck Club* and a genealogy website,

InstantHeritage.com, in search of a more personal link to suffering. Desdemona is particularly delighted to find out through InstantHeritage.com that because her great-great-grandfather was denied entry to the United States, he immigrated to Mexico instead. This, she happily announces to her less pleased father, would have made their family Chinese Mexican:

> ED: But Mexicans are so poor. And noisy.
> DESDEMONA: Dad, those are totally not the right adjectives for your ancestors.
> ED: Mexicans don't even speak English. (*Contemplates this news.*) Sorry it turned out like that, Desi. Hope you're not disappointed.
> DESDEMONA: About being Latino? Are you kidding? This is so much better. I've researched it: Hispanic girls like me face huge obstacles in their lives. Discrimination, lack of access to education and contraception, machismo—(301)

Stereotypes and generalizations are the norm in this exchange between Desdemona and Ed, as Desdemona protests Ed's choice of adjectives but makes similarly sweeping claims. While Ed lists stereotypes about class and behavior to differentiate himself from his "ancestors" and hints at a fear of transfer, Desdemona seizes on everyday challenges that she hopes to adopt as part of her identity, but not her life. It is the broad reach of such characterizations that Desdemona anticipates will connect her to the obstacles faced by those "like" her. The analogous relationship that she asserts here performs a distinct function. The link opened up through a weakly shared Mexican heritage allows Desdemona to claim the experiences associated with certain communities as her own without "facing huge obstacles" herself. Her imagined relationship to "Hispanic girls" sounds remarkably like her relationship to Kim, but she embraces the direct familial connection as a justification for telling this narrative as her own.

Although Desdemona's ploy could be read as either a critique of affirmative action or a mockery of certain understandings of affirmative action, her turn to Mexico as a new direction for her college essay and her great-great-grandfather's detour to Mexico are both responses to the inconsistent gatekeeping of opportunities and access. The stories of Chinese immigrants that inspire Desdemona and Upton underscore the arbitrary regulation of borders, which facilitated the passage of laborers to help build the transcontinental railroad, but closed entry after its completion and compelled later immigrants to enter via Mexico. Similarly, while the *bracero* programs brought Mexican workers to the United States, Mexican immigrants were later subject to nativist ire and calls for new immigration restrictions. Desdemona thus misses the larger connection between the histories of Chinese American and Mexican American immigration suggested by her great-great-grandfather's path. While the play gives Desdemona's frantic efforts to get into Princeton a satirical treatment that elicits little sympathy, it sets her misguided endeavor in a historical frame that illuminates what she might actually share with those whose experiences she casually borrows.

Yet while Desdemona like Chua looks to prior generations of immigrants to aid her ambitions, and like the teenagers of *Better Luck Tomorrow*, seeks to supplement her middle-class life by identifying with other minorities and Asian and Asian American types, she forgoes one crucial component of their performances: their sustained enactments of the mundane. Whereas Ben becomes so enmeshed in carrying out the tasks of the "Chinese gangster" alongside his usual routines that his body begins to degrade and Chua translates the discipline she identifies with first-generation immigrants into a regular schedule of practice and study, Desdemona's attempt to embody the narratives she solicits from others remains purely rhetorical or decorative.

Desdemona's understanding of her "Mexican" identity becomes clear during a family trip with Ed and Grace, presumably to celebrate her (already passed) fifteenth birthday. Yee asks that performances spare no detail in caricaturing Desdemona and Ed's superficial embrace of their "Mexican" heritage. The trip is interrupted, however, when Kim suddenly reappears:

> *Mexican hotel room. Desdemona in a hideous quinceañera dress. She hums "Feliz Navidad" as she applies sunscreen. Kim Lee Park, looking emaciated and desperate, enters.*
> KIM LEE PARK: Desdemona . . . Desdemona . . . I am so hungry.
> DESDEMONA: Go eat your yak. (*Ed enters with a Corona, a piñata, and piñata bat, which he leaves on the bed. Desdemona appeals to him and points to Kim Lee Park.*) Dad! (*Ed shoos Kim Lee Park out.*)

ED: All right, nothing to see here. You can make the room up in half an
hour. (307)

From Desdemona's quinceañera dress to Ed's Corona beer and piñata,
the scene emphasizes their specious conception of ethnic identity.
This critique becomes more serious when Kim enters the scene to
remind Desdemona of her previous dabbling in the suffering of others.
Although her appearance here arguably manifests Desdemona's feelings of guilt after abandoning Kim, Ed's interactions with Kim make
her presence real. By pointing to Kim when Ed returns, Desdemona
indicates a character visible to her father as well as herself. Thus, while
slapping Kim in the earlier scene turned the figure from an embodiment
of someone corresponding with Desdemona from a distance to a more
ambiguous and potentially imaginary presence, pointing at Kim in this
scene makes her real to both characters. Yet the gesture that makes Kim
visible to Ed also initiates her banishment. To point to something is to
draw attention to it, but also to signal one's distance from the object.
By pointing, Desdemona indicates her separation from Kim, and just
as Kim establishes a more concrete presence in the play, she is quickly
sent away. While Desdemona embraces the possibility of conjuring Kim
whenever necessary, she enlists Ed to control her when she appears at
an inconvenient moment. When Ed tells Kim, "nothing to see here," he
suggests that Kim should not be seeing Desdemona; yet by ushering
Kim out at the same time, he also insinuates that Kim herself should
not be seen. Interpellating Kim as a maid by telling her to make up the
room later, Ed enforces a strict divide between his family and the invisible labor that Josephine Lee identifies as a central aspect of the play.

When Kim next appears, however, she does so specifically as the double
that forces Desdemona to see resemblance where she only saw difference.
After sending Kim away, Ed gives Desdemona a bracelet as part of her
quinceañera celebration and reveals that it came from her birth mother in
Korea. Desdemona is distraught to realize that she is an abandoned child,
and Kim materializes at exactly this moment to articulate her fears:

KIM LEE PARK: Dear Desdemona: Mother Superior told me the won-
derful news. I cannot wait until you come to visit me at the orphan-
age, where we will become best friends.

DESDEMONA: Shut up, you are not me!

KIM LEE PARK: I am also working on my application to Princeton for next year. Thanks to you, I am inspired to write about deep and tragic things. (*Reads from essay.*) "Eighteen years ago, Desdemona Wong was born in Seoul, South Korea—at the mouth of a river, under the full moon of December. Abandoned by her mother—" (*Desdemona tackles Kim Lee Park and beats her up.*) (309)

In giving Desdemona the bracelet, Ed gives her exactly what she had purportedly sought: a story of "deep and tragic things" that she can claim as her own. Unlike her discovery of a "Mexican" heritage, however, this news does not delight Desdemona, but horrifies her, belying her wish for difficult experiences to include in her personal statement. The difference between discovering she is adopted and finding out about her "Mexican" heritage is subtle as both disclosures involve her lineage and are accompanied by prescribed stereotypes and narratives. Yet when Desdemona learns that she is adopted, the "like" that separated her from "Hispanic girls like me" collapses, leaving her not like Kim, but as Kim. When Kim then claims that they will be best friends, Desdemona notably responds, "Shut up, you are not me!" While "I am not you" would emphasize Desdemona's fear of becoming Kim, "You are not me" more strongly suggests a fear of Kim becoming Desdemona: "you," she insists, cannot be "me." While the stories and lives of others must seem permeable for Desdemona to borrow from them (thus, for her to become like them in her college essays), she anxiously protects her own deliberately concocted identity from appropriation. Kim affirms Desdemona's fear of reciprocal infiltrations when she begins reading her application essay to Princeton, which exactly mimics Desdemona's essay about Kim. When Desdemona begins to beat Kim, it is specifically Kim's use of Desdemona's story, which was once a story about Kim, that provokes her. The recursivity of this relationship threatens to collapse the border between them, a border that Desdemona had carefully regulated to allow certain passages, and not others.

In *Better Luck Tomorrow*, the two cars that drive next to each other create a mirror that illuminates their incongruity, a divide that tempts crossings. In *Ching Chong Chinaman*, Kim's "letter" to Desdemona upon learning that she is also adopted similarly holds up a mirror, but one that threatens to negate their difference. In both of these scenes, characters confront doubles that force a crisis of identification. While the *Better Luck Tomorrow* teenagers and Wong siblings all want to stretch their identifications as much as possible—to play multiple parts, to maintain and change their identities simultaneously, and to be the model minority and its antithesis—the limits of their efforts become clear when the others they invoke come close enough to reflect back the inconsistencies in their performance, or threaten to become them.

Better Luck Tomorrow and *Ching Chong Chinaman* moreover share critical scenes in which beatings lead to incomplete erasures. As discussed above, Steve's corpse in *Better Luck Tomorrow* rests uneasily beneath the film's suburban landscape as a reminder of the contradictory demands placed on the racialized body. In *Ching Chong Chinaman*, Kim's body holds parallel significance as the threat of Desdemona and Kim converging is augmented by their common racialization. Comparable to the stylistic shifts that accompany the scene of Steve's murder, Desdemona's last interaction with Kim switches between the imaginary and the actual to capture the confusion that Desdemona experiences once she realizes that her "real" relationships (with her family) are invented, and her "invented" relationships (with Kim) are real. In beating Kim, Desdemona seeks to make her disappear, yet paradoxically makes her more present by interacting with her physically and requiring Ed to stop the attack: "Ed rips Desdemona off Kim Lee Park, who remains bashed on the floor for a moment. They wait awkwardly" (309). Ed suggests to Desdemona, "We'll just wait until she, uh, goes away," and after a moment, Kim finally "dematerializes" (309). The pause before Kim dematerializes recalls the first sight of the unearthed hand in *Better Luck Tomorrow* as the characters are compelled to be with a body that reminds them of a shared racialization, a body that is the repository of desires as well as apprehension. In both the film and the play, these damaged bodies refuse to disappear on request, forcing Desdemona and Ed to "wait awkwardly," and Ben and his friends to wait fearfully.

When Desdemona beats Kim, she rejects the idea that the difference between them is mere illusion and that they might therefore be exchangeable. Her enraged response is ironic given her earlier appropriation of Kim's stories, but it is also especially fitting because of the multiple roles that the actor playing Kim takes on throughout the play.

Aside from the Wong family, the play's character list includes two additional roles, Chinese Man and Chinese Woman. Chinese Man is J, and remains a consistent character throughout the performance. By contrast, Chinese Woman moves between several roles, including Mrs. J (J's mother), Kim Lee Park, a reporter, an Asian schoolgirl, and the Little Chinese Girl, who represents the child conceived during Grace's affair with J. Furthermore, Mrs. J is a character that takes on multiple voices, a Midwestern accent when working as an Intel customer service agent and an "imitation Eastern European accent" (304) when working for a phone sex hotline. Thus, the roles assigned to Chinese Woman seem to proliferate, as role-doubling breeds even more role-playing. All minor roles, these characters materialize and dematerialize around the family. Some of them, like Grace's doctor and J's mother, are presumably characters that exist alongside the Wong family in the world of the play. A few of the characters embody objects such as a fortune cookie message, Desdemona's essay on her ancestors, and a Spanish-speaking pregnancy test that Grace buys in Mexico. Other characters, like the Asian schoolgirl whom Upton envisions will worship him when he wins the World of Warcraft championship, the not-yet-born Little Chinese Girl, and Kim Lee Park, are situated more ambiguously within the play's distribution of "real" and "imagined" characters. As mentioned above, when the actor plays Kim, she could be embodying someone corresponding with Desdemona from a distance, a figment of Desdemona's imagination, or a hotel maid. Kim's name, stitched together from three different last names, matches the conglomeration of roles that the actor must play.

Despite their differences, all of the characters that fall under the category "Chinese Woman" are similarly racialized and gendered. Even the character of Pregnancy Test, which initially seems to differ from the others by not having any connection to Asia, is revealed to be "Hecho en China" (313). It seems that either race and gender *limit* the range of roles that the actor takes on during the performance, or they are what enable her shifts in character. The other alternative, of course, is that they do both: the perception of similarity—articulated in Desdemona's complaints about female Asian American applicants' lack of distinctiveness in the eyes of admissions officers—makes the characters seem interchangeable, but only within the bounds of race and gender. If J's mother can, by contrast, pretend to be a Midwestern Intel employee or a Bulgarian seductress, she can do so only as a voice that projects a different body.

When Desdemona beats Kim, she is also attacking the body of the actor who has been performing the very shifts among Chinese, Korean, and American; doctor and phone sex worker; and real and imagined that Desdemona intensely fears. Until this moment, Desdemona staves off the threat of becoming too intimate with those not middle-class and American (except as useful to her) by turning to the mundane as an impermeable border, or at least one that should not be crossed. When presented with the possibility that the figures represented by Chinese Man and Chinese Woman might infiltrate her life, Desdemona insists that a lack of knowledge about their habits imposes a limit on their interactions. The need for each person to stay in her or his "natural environment" becomes Desdemona's refrain. When J first joins the Wongs, for example, Desdemona protests, "We need to return him to his natural environment. We don't know anything about his diet, his lifestyle, his basic wants. We don't even have the right sensitivity training to even begin to cater to his needs as a displaced person" (270). Similarly, when Ed suggests adopting Kim to alleviate Grace's unhappiness, Desdemona declares, "Kim is staying in Korea, her *natural* environment. And she is not mine; she is an independently sponsored child" (270). In statements replete with contradictions, Desdemona characterizes a relationship between financial unequals in terms of independence and turns to the idea of a "natural environment" to stress that passages must be regulated, even as she herself violates these strictures as a tourist and the progeny of immigrants.

Lecturing Ed on how to interact with J, or someone outside their "natural environment," Desdemona advises, "If you don't speak his language, don't talk to him. It's insulting" (273), and later instructs him, "Just sit there. Don't look at him [J]; don't acknowledge him" (274). In suggesting that one should neither leave one's natural environment nor engage someone who is displaced, Desdemona uses the mundane as an alibi: differences in "diet, lifestyle, basic wants" as well as language become the grounds for not bringing someone into her space and for not seeing those who nevertheless enter. For Desdemona, the cultivation of bodies by different "natural environments" establishes firm borders.

Yet like the shifting state borders that confronted earlier generations of Chinese immigrants, distinct patterns of daily life form a boundary that is fiercely but inconsistently patrolled. Indentured servants, railroad workers, and maids make it possible for those who employ them to, as Ben puts it, "expand [their] days." Despite her protests that J and Kim should stay in their natural environments, Desdemona nevertheless uses J to do her calculus homework and cultivates a financial relationship with Kim to strengthen her college application. In order to sustain and improve their lives, both Upton and Desdemona depend on unequal relationships with those whose everyday possibilities must be distinct from their own.

The play's mysterious conclusion, however, suggests a profound breach in the border that Desdemona erects between the Wongs and Chinese Man and Woman. After Ed leaves to drop J off at the U.S.-Mexico border and Grace tap-dances away with Little Chinese Girl, Upton and Desdemona find themselves alone with only food to keep them company. Reaching his sister on the phone, Upton tells her that he received a Christmas card from their family. At that moment, a family portrait in which Ed and Grace sit with J and Little Chinese Girl briefly appears:

> *Lights up on Ed and Grace posing for the picture. J and Little Chinese Girl stand where Desdemona and Upton should be. Upton and Desdemona look at the family portrait warmly.*
>
> UPTON: It's nice.
>
> DESDEMONA: Yeah. We do look happy. (*Flashbulb. The family portrait dematerializes.*)
>
> UPTON: What time is it there?
>
> DESDEMONA: Right about midnight. (*The clock strikes twelve. A snowflake. Another. It's unclear whether we are in Korea or Mexico. Upton and Desdemona watch the snow fall.*)
>
> UPTON: The snow sure is pretty, huh?
>
> DESDEMONA: Yeah.
>
> UPTON: Merry Christmas, Des.
>
> DESDEMONA: Merry Christmas.
>
> UPTON: See you at home.

DESDEMONA: OK. (*Desdemona and Upton don't hang up but stay on the line as they watch the snow. We perhaps hear "Feliz Navidad" in the background.*) (317)

In placing J and Little Chinese Girl where Upton and Desdemona should be, the play suggests that Upton may have been replaced by J, to whom he had outsourced his everyday tasks, while Desdemona may have been replaced by another love child, her mother's "real" daughter, or, more abstractly, a figure that represents the instability of identity. Finding her claim to the family "illegitimate" given the criteria of blood and natural environment that she had propounded, Desdemona, like Upton, finds herself discharged from the Wongs.

The substitution suggested in the family portrait makes sense as a reversal of Upton and Desdemona's fortunes and a critique of their conceptions of the mundane, but it nonetheless presents some mysteries. As a portrait of Ed, Grace, Grace's lover, and their love child, it might show a modern family. Read symbolically, however, it also materializes a different kind of Asian American family. The portrait of a highly assimilated, model minority family becomes one that includes "indentured servants" and, through the actor playing Little Chinese Girl, a range of figures from the Asian diaspora. Yet if we consider Upton and Desdemona's relationship to the portrait, other readings offer themselves. From Mexico and Korea, respectively, Desdemona and Upton might well be staring at a portrait of their imagined family, one which they have not yet joined. The wistfulness with which Desdemona and Upton admire the portrait might then move the play from a satire of the model minority stereotype to an expression of its continued power: in other words, it becomes a fantasy of the life that Desdemona and Upton seek to have.

The distinct forms of communication staged in the performance lend support to the idea that Upton and Desdemona have become, or perhaps always were, its "displaced persons." The surrogacy offered by J and Kim, then, does not simply allow Upton and Desdemona to delegate certain responsibilities and functions; it enables them to displace their position as the model minority's others onto imagined figures. The play frames Upton and Desdemona's respective accounts of the history of the Chinese railroad workers and the personal struggles of Kim Lee Park as essays required for school assignments and college applications.

Such essays are critical to assessing their fitness as model minorities, and the examples read in the play emphasize American enterprise and triumph over adversity. They thus parody the kinds of narratives into which Upton and Desdemona must insert themselves in order to fulfill their roles in an ideological project that carefully manages the terms of acceptable difference. Because Desdemona and Upton overhear or read each other's writings, the essays also serve as an indirect form of communication between the two siblings throughout the performance. At the end of the play, however, Desdemona and Upton converse over the phone, which until that moment is primarily a medium of communication between J and his mother. The loneliness and displacement expressed in these earlier phone calls are shared in the play's last moments by Upton and Desdemona, even as all their wishes—for Upton, to become a gaming champion and to be free of familial duties, and for Desdemona, to have a story of triumph over hardship and to get into Princeton—have come true. Communicating directly through the phone, rather than indirectly through essays that justify their use of surrogates, Desdemona and Upton end the play in a quiet moment of being both together and apart.

Ultimately, however, the play gives few definite clues about how to understand Desdemona and Upton's place within the revised family portrait. Ending with Desdemona and Upton admiring a picture they claim represents their family, yet from which they are conspicuously absent, the drama concludes with an image of surrogacy not as the solution to their adolescent dilemmas, but as an unresolved mystery. A comprehensive reading of *Ching Chong Chinaman* requires establishing a relationship between Desdemona and Upton and their doubles in the final family portrait, yet the similarities and the differences that give meaning to earlier exchanges fail here because the reversal makes all four characters suddenly unknowable. After playing for scenes with the potential for one character to become another, *Ching Chong Chinaman* ends with a substitution that suggests only an unarticulated connection.

*   *   *

In 2012, the Pew Center echoed a familiar narrative in its report "The Rise of Asian Americans": it claimed that while a century ago, "most Asian Americans were low-skilled, low-wage laborers crowded into

ethnic enclaves and targets of official discrimination," they now constitute "the highest-income, best-educated and fastest-growing racial
group in the United States."[70] In response, the Association for Asian
American Studies issued a statement that countered, "The reality is,
there is a significant body of our community who are not happy, educated, or high-income earners. In fact, these invisible Asian Americans
are among our poor and with limited opportunities for education."[71] In
emphasizing the socioeconomic diversity of the Asian American community and warning that the Pew report affirms seemingly positive but
ultimately harmful conceptions of Asians and Asian Americans, the
AAAS press release reiterated arguments put forward to counter the
model minority stereotype. These arguments generally stress the inaccu-
racy of the stereotype and its damaging effects. They also, however, have
an important—if less recognized—performative function. Namely, they
continually pledge responsibility to the very populations whose needs
may be pushed aside by the model minority stereotype and encourage
reassessments of the borders of Asian America. Rebuttals of the model
minority stereotype therefore insist on building affiliations based on difference, not sameness, and assume the accountability of the majority to
the minority, of those who are successful to those who are struggling.
They are performances of collective interests, even as they emphasize the diversity that makes difficult the *uniformity* of those interests.
Rejections of the model minority stereotype by Asian Americans, Asian
American organizations, and Asian Americanists are not attempts to
claim a perpetually oppressed status, but efforts to perform solidarity
in difference. In other words, they lay bare and resuture the seams that,
always precariously, hold Asian America together.

In their insistence on disrupting the narratives of ambitious, successful characters with the presence of the model minority's others (from the
yellow peril gangster to the effectively indentured worker), *Better Luck
Tomorrow* and *Ching Chong Chinaman* share something of the spirit
that propels these rejections of the model minority stereotype. While
neither the film nor the drama is interested in engaging with questions
about the accuracy of the stereotype or in seriously presenting its consequences, they use the model minority stereotype as an occasion for
dramatizing gaps, both seductive and threatening, within Asian America. These fissures are provisionally crossed with the mundane as ac-

complice, but never completely bridged. Ending with Ben and Stephanie driving away without resolving Steve's disappearance, and Desdemona and Upton staying on the phone but not speaking, *Better Luck Tomorrow* and *Ching Chong Chinaman* offer images of the tentative companionship that follows their efforts to turn others into their doubles, and then their doubles into others. With these ambiguous and open endings, the film and the play suggest that given the stratifications that put pressure on articulations of an Asian American identity, differences must be confronted not to dismantle affiliations, but to redefine them.

The Everyday Asian American Online

The short Internet videos that constitute "Rick's Man Tutorials" promise their viewers advice on how to attract women, only to reveal the ineptitude of their teacher. In the video "Good Hygiene Gets Girls" (2010), Rick counsels his viewers to wash their face, take showers, and apply lotion, which he pronounces "lo-tee-on" and proclaims an exciting discovery.[1] Peppering his advice with homophobic and sexist remarks, Rick exhibits a befuddled machismo that recalls *Better Luck Tomorrow*'s Virgil. Yet whereas Virgil's hypermasculine displays become increasingly spectacular in Lin's film, "Rick's Man Tutorials" sit firmly in the everyday: in addition to advising good hygiene, Rick gives suggestions on cooking and exercise.[2] Ridiculing Rick's notion of attractive masculine behavior through his ineffectual performances of the mundane, these videos also spoof the Internet tutorial, one of many popular online genres that, through both their form and content, insinuate themselves into the everyday practices of viewers.

"Rick's Man Tutorials" are the invention of Wong Fu Productions, a company that creates online media featuring Asian American performers and artists. Their short film "Yellow Fever," which the founders made while students at the University of California, San Diego, became one of the first videos starring Asian Americans to attract a substantial viewership on the Internet when it was posted in 2006. Since then, and in contrast to their small presence in traditionally distributed American films and television shows, Asian Americans have become major producers of online media.[3] For performers who have struggled to acquire financial backing and industry access, videos offered through websites such as YouTube provide a valuable new means of circulating their work. The *New York Times* reported in 2011 that three of the top twenty most subscribed channels on YouTube star Asian Americans: Michelle Phan

provides makeup tutorials, while Ryan Higa (also known by his user-
name Nigahiga) and Kevin Wu (KevJumba) produce short spoofs and
humorous video logs (or "vlogs") in which they share their thoughts on
a variety of subjects.[4] The interest of these videos in the routine concerns of makeup application, dating, and snacking aligns them with the
cultural productions explored in previous chapters. They draw even
closer to the everyday, however, by presenting the mundane in a form
distinctly suited for casual consumption. Given the importance of this
new medium for young Asian American performers and artists and its
extraordinary dissemination of quotidian performances (even the most
banal moments of daily life find themselves captured and broadcast on
the Internet), a study of the racial mundane would be incomplete without a consideration of the short online video.

These videos are closer to the newspaper, the radio, and the television
show than the theater or the cinema in their chumminess with everyday
practices, but they also defy the spatial and temporal confines of earlier
media. With the increasingly common use of mobile devices, content on
the Internet is often (literally) at hand for multiple viewings at any time.
Videos can be consumed in a casual, perfunctory manner, while waiting
in line, taking a break, or chatting with friends. YouTube has been especially influential not only in facilitating the widespread consumption of
online videos, but also in encouraging their production by anyone with
access to digital recording equipment and the Internet. Jean Burgess and
Joshua Green have noted that the integration of YouTube into the everyday lives of its users blurs the boundaries set by traditional media,
expanding and diversifying participation in the creation of online content.[5] Amateur videos on YouTube can easily attract as many viewers as
those posted by established artists, and with access to computers and
cameras growing, producing as well as consuming content on the Internet is becoming more common practice.

Videos by Higa, Phan, Wu, and Wong Fu Productions share several
features that enhance the impression that they are part of the quotidian
practices of both producers and viewers. They are short (usually about
two to eight minutes in length); the performers often establish a sense of
familiarity with their viewers by addressing them directly and adopting
an informal tone; and new pieces appear continually on their respective
YouTube channels and websites, but not according to a fixed schedule.

While capturing the rhythms and tenor of daily life, these videos also evince a savvy understanding of the possibilities of defamiliarizing the mundane—for comic effect, to demonstrate expertise, or to establish the ordinariness of Asian Americans. The transformation of everyday activities into spectacles in these videos confers on the Asian American performer the role of the "straight man" (or woman), sometimes to an alter ego or an altered image of themselves. Setting markedly stylized, spoofed, and embellished characters against the more natural personae crafted and maintained by the videos' stars, these performances emphasize the latter's familiarity. The mundane thus does double duty: it establishes the videos' concerns as commonplace, and makes possible a turn to caricature and theatrics that sets the Asian American performer, by contrast, as ordinary.

My choice of the comedy routine term "straight man," however, also purposefully evokes colloquial associations of "straight" with heterosexuality. A steadfast investment in heteronormative relations across the videos facilitates their efforts to deflate perceptions of racial difference. Yet this investment also limits their reconception of the ordinary. Here, the term "ordinary" describes a quality of seeming common and familiar that sits between the everyday, which has more diffuse and neutral connotations, and the normative, which suggests a more coercive force. Accordingly, in their engagements with everyday behaviors, these videos take advantage of normative conceptions of gender and sexuality to claim the ordinariness of Asian Americans.

Wong Fu Productions' "Yellow Fever" stands as an early example of this dynamic.[6] The fifteen-minute film was initially available for download through the creators' website and later posted on YouTube by fans. The popularity of "Yellow Fever" helped to launch Wong Fu Productions,[7] which continues to make a steady stream of short Internet films and music videos, including collaborations with Ryan Higa and Kevin Wu. Like Better Luck Tomorrow, "Yellow Fever" defamiliarizes the mundane to engage with stereotypes of race and gender specific to Asian American men. Yet in contrast to Better Luck Tomorrow's stylized depictions of hypermasculine behaviors, "Yellow Fever" emphasizes the ordinariness of Asian American masculinity by satirizing the racialization of desire.

Accompanied by portentous music and shots of a college campus, a voice-over begins "Yellow Fever" with a provocative statement: "There is an enormous injustice plaguing our country right now, a social issue that has been kept under the rug for far too long." The injustice, we soon learn, is that a disproportionately large number of white men are dating Asian American women. The opening of "Yellow Fever" thus echoes the 1974 preface to *Aiiieeeee!* which reported that "more than 50 percent of Japanese American women were marrying outside their race" and that Chinese American women were also following this trend.[8] For the anthology's editors, these numbers reflected more than a simple dating preference; they also exposed a deeper crisis in Asian America: "These figures say something about our sensibility, our concept of Chinese America and Japanese America, our self-esteem, as does our partly real and partly mythical silence in American culture."[9] "Yellow Fever" and the preface to *Aiiieeeee!* decry the tendency of Asian American women to partner with non-Asian men, and frame this statistic as part of a broad social problem, "an enormous injustice plaguing our country," or a crisis of self-esteem in Asian America. Each work moreover positions itself as an effort to counter silences—either the silence surrounding imbalances in dating habits, or the general silence of Asian Americans in mainstream American culture.

The popularity of "Yellow Fever," which was produced several decades after *Aiiieeeee!*, suggests that its interest in interracial dating resonated with contemporary viewers, or that it at least lent the subject a renewed currency. The film, however, quickly undermines the grave tone of its opening by presenting a series of humorous exchanges between college students, and its focus on dating rather than marriage also gives it a less serious edge. In the course of the film, Phil, an Asian American college student, attempts to account for dating patterns that indicate racial preferences. For *Aiiieeeee!* editors Jeffrey Paul Chan and Frank Chin, the stereotype of Asian and Asian American men as submissive and unmanly manifested white "racist love" and patterns of exogamy revealed the internalization of racism;[10] by contrast, Phil regards discrepancies in dating habits more as a personal inconvenience than as a manifestation of larger social dynamics. When he announces that he will investigate the matter in order to improve his own chances of securing a date, the film reveals—and mocks—the self-interest that drives his critique of interracial dating.

An ambivalence about the contemporary significance of race percolates through "Yellow Fever" as it maneuvers around the question of whether or not race continues to influence social possibilities. The film repeatedly implies that the situation troubling Phil is a matter of individual choice and resolve, only to cast doubt on this idea by shifting to stylized presentations of the mundane. Phil's conversation with Richard, a South Asian American student who speaks with an accent and performs a stereotypical "guru" persona, exemplifies this equivocation. Reprimanding Phil for being self-centered, Richard advises him "to always look at the big picture" and launches into a passionate speech: "The blame is not on the white boys or the Asian girls, the blame is on the individual. It is because Asian guys just don't have the confidence and the assertiveness needed to start up a conversation with a girl. It's not because white boys have this or that or have this magical power. It is because the majority of Asian guys are too pansy, and they have very very small . . . [long pause] confidence." After Richard's lengthy monologue, Phil concurs, "You're totally right. Thank you so much for opening my eyes." Richard then drops his "guru" accent and tells Phil, "Good. Well, I'm glad I could help, but I gotta go. Catch you later, all right?"

This exchange, which the film presents as resolving Phil's concerns, is playfully contradictory despite Richard's blunt message. Richard vacillates throughout his speech between making generalizations about racial groups (including reiterating stereotypes of Asian men), and insisting that only individuals are to blame for social patterns they find unfair. Thus, while asserting that Asian American men simply need to be more confident, Richard also echoes the very stereotypes that have associated them with a deficient masculinity, that is, one presumably diminished by its proximity to femininity and queerness. When Phil then claims that Richard has offered sound and illuminating advice, their conversation seems to affirm prevalent stereotypes of race, gender, and sexuality, while conferring the responsibility of making them untrue on those who are stereotyped.

Not all viewers of "Yellow Fever" will read against or beyond Richard's words to Phil, but the film nevertheless presents a more ambiguous perspective than the one explicitly articulated by their dialogue. The choice to have Richard adopt an exaggerated accent and a stereotypical persona at the beginning of their conversation and then abandon them by the end of the scene suggests that the film is interested at some level in critiquing racial representations. This project is at odds with Richard's advice, which perpetuates rather than rejects stereotypes of Asian men. Furthermore, the sudden transformation in Richard's character implicates the audience in a moment of comic self-reflexivity that makes viewers complicit in enjoying both a caricature of South Asians commonly found in American popular culture *and* a reversal that mocks the caricature. The film thus draws attention to its management of audience expectation and engagement, and casts doubt on how seriously we are to take Richard's insistence that Asian American men simply need to behave differently—particularly when he makes this argument in a "guru" voice that he later discards. The sudden shift in Richard's speech simultaneously enacts the fantasy of willfully casting aside stereotypes *and* exposes the thickly mediated lens through which viewers might read his performance. Embodying similar contradictions, the laughter that the reversal incites registers the heavily accented speech as caricature; yet it also contributes to the caricature of accents (including those not purposefully exaggerated) by affirming one kind of speech as "normal" and the other as comical, and thus establishing the casual talk of American college students as the Asian American ordinary.

Two parallel scenes that bookend Phil's investigation further undercut Richard's confident assertions by again switching between representational modes. Phil explains to a friend that an incident involving his white roommate Andrew sparked his curiosity about interracial dating. He had invited two Asian American students, both women, to his apartment, and as they were walking past the kitchen, his guests suddenly became mesmerized by Andrew, who stood at the counter making a sandwich. The film first offers a naturalistic shot of Andrew spreading peanut butter on bread. Then, presenting Andrew as the women might see him, or as Phil *imagines* they see him, it shifts into a more stylized shot of Andrew with wind blowing through his hair and extradiegetic rock music accompanying his suddenly seductive poses. Recounting this moment, Phil explains to his friend, "I don't get it. It's like they saw something I didn't see." This scene then repeats at the end of the film—after Phil's decisive conversation with Richard—but with one key difference. Phil, ostensibly comforted by Richard's advice, is playing poker with an African American friend, who asks if he can make himself a sandwich. When Andrew and his date, an Asian American woman, walk into the apartment, the woman stops at the kitchen and stands captivated by Phil's friend. Like Andrew, the friend is shown first in a naturalistic shot, and then in a more stylized fashion reminiscent of a glamorous photo shoot, complete with jazzy music and provocative poses. While Andrew looks on with a horrified expression, Phil gloats and the film ends.

The repetition of the sandwich-making scene, first with Andrew and then with Phil's African American friend, suggests that what Asian American men lack is not confidence, but a flattering screen through which others might see their everyday behaviors as irresistibly alluring. While Richard argues that white men do not have a "magical power" that allows them to attract women more effectively than Phil, these scenes imply that racialized conceptions of manhood (or gendered conceptions of race) frame bodies differently, lending some a magical aura (manifested in the film by the extradiegetic music, stylized shots, and contrived performances of seductiveness), while leaving others without this advantage. Thus, instead of countering stereotypes of Asian American men as sexually "unnormal" through opposing images of hypermasculine behavior,[11] "Yellow Fever" sets Phil's persistent *ordinariness* against exaggerated depictions of his roommate and his friend. The choice to have the other two men mesmerize women while performing overtly banal activities in the kitchen—a space associated, moreover, with women's domestic work—emphasizes that what makes them attractive is less an inherent quality than the mediation of desire by race. The exaggerated shots expose the historically and socially developed lens through which bodies exert their force, or settle innocuously into the background. In this context, Richard's advice to Phil—and not just Phil's grievances—misses the "big picture": given the power of established, pervasive patterns of seeing, individual action is inseparable from this mediating lens.

"Yellow Fever" converges here with *Better Luck Tomorrow* in presenting these negotiations with existing perceptual habits as a particularly vexing problem of representation. The two films moreover highlight this problem by shifting to a more stylized mode when presenting the desire incited by other racialized masculinities ("Yellow Fever"), or displaying the machismo of young Asian American men (*Better Luck To-morrow*). Yet they persist in naturalizing certain types of desire even as they critique others. As I mentioned above, it is unclear whether the exaggerated sandwich-making shots in "Yellow Fever" represent how the men appear to women or how Phil *envisions* they must appear to women. Nevertheless, the *direction* of desire (from men to women, and women to men) is unambiguous. Furthermore, women's desires are seen through and understood only in relation to the desires of straight men. (Phil strangely does not solicit advice from Asian American women while on his mission to uncover why they ostensibly choose not to date Asian men.) In *Better Luck Tomorrow*, Stephanie also serves primarily as the love interest of three boys, although the film strives at moments to portray her as a complex character.

While these recent productions are more explicitly self-reflexive and ironic than early cultural nationalist writings when they include homophobic and sexist remarks, David Eng's observation about Asian American cultural nationalism applies to them as well: "racial problems consistently manifest themselves in questions of sexual relations be-tween Asian American men and women, with the figure of the Asian American homosexual entirely banished from this heterosexual land-scape."[12] By tracing the shape of ordinary Asian American masculin-ity over dominant patterns of sexual relations and gendered behaviors, "Yellow Fever" ultimately stakes narrow parameters. Many of the videos made by Wong Fu Productions after "Yellow Fever," including "Rick's Man Tutorials," echo its focus on heterosexual relationships, although not all share its explicit concern with how racialized perceptions inform dating habits. The robust collection of videos, performers, collaborators, and viewers brought together by Wong Fu Productions suggests the cul-mination of the project of Asian American cultural nationalism without its polemic anger and working-class affinities: namely, the creation of a community of Asian American artists and audiences defined as much by normative gender and sexual identities as by ethnic affiliation.[13]

Although the increasing participation of young Asian Americans as creators of online content is shifting the center of Asian American cul-tural expression away from traditional forms and reshaping contempo-rary popular culture more generally, the intimate relationship between these productions and the mundane has ambiguous implications. On the one hand, their success demonstrates the potential for those who are underrepresented in mainstream media to produce widely circulated works that target everyday practices. These videos facilitate the redistribution of the familiar and the unfamiliar through their incisive depictions of quotidian behaviors and advise habits of interaction and perception. On the other hand, by making such strong claims on the everyday, these videos also encourage viewers to see the specific lifestyles and concerns they portray as typical.

Along with Wong Fu Productions, other Asian American performers and entrepreneurs have taken advantage of the new opportunities afforded by Internet media, with Higa, Phan, and Wu among the most successful. In addition to making short narrative films like "Yellow Fever" available to a wide audience, YouTube has helped to propagate a number of video genres that focus on quotidian matters. For example, Phan is famous for her makeup tutorials, while Higa and Wu first established themselves with their video logs or "vlogs." In these videos, form and content align as the qualities of online media that allow for casual consumption and production complement their everyday subject matters. All three began uploading videos to YouTube around the same time (Higa in 2006, Phan and Wu in 2007), and since then, they have each garnered millions of subscribers on their channels. Although each performer has diversified her or his offerings over the years, their videos collectively reveal an aspiration (more or less serious) to influence viewers' quotidian behaviors, whether through advice on personal care and interpersonal relationships, or through caricatures of daily habits. Phan's videos most clearly exemplify this objective with their step-by-step instructions on makeup application, or item-by-item review of products, all given in the manner of a helpful friend. Higa and Wu likewise cultivate the sense that they are addressing familiar audiences. Whereas Phan's videos largely employ voice-overs (presumably so that she does not have to talk as she applies makeup on herself), the "vlog" form that Higa and Wu favor calls for them to speak directly into the camera and thus creates the impression that they are sitting in the room with the viewer or engaged in a personal video chat. Anecdotes, rants, and reflections on everything from ice cream to pimples occupy the "vlogs" and inspire the spoofs and web series also on their YouTube channels.[14]

The appeal of these videos depends on their stars' proficiency in dissecting experiences and concerns that seem common—that is, shared, pervasive, and recurrent. Higa, Phan, and Wu collect audiences by demonstrating that they are adept at articulating the nuances of quotidian activities and interactions. While Phan carefully explains the layers of products required to achieve even a "natural," everyday look, Wu and Higa identify what is funny about apparently unremarkable situations such as living in a college dormitory or shaking someone's hand. These videos' domains of expert and satirical insight, however, extend beyond the quotidian to the spectacular offerings of popular culture, which are then set against their engagement with daily concerns. For example, in "Expectations vs. Reality: Romance," Higa juxtaposes scenes that illustrate the unreasonable expectations generated by romantic films (chance meetings, emotional conversations, and symbolic gifts) with those that show the realities of contemporary dating (contacting someone through Facebook, reconciliations via text, and criticisms of the other person's appearance).[15] Higa skillfully spoofs both the contrived plots and grave language of Hollywood love stories, and the more cavalier attitudes expressed in the "reality" segments, but begins and ends the video by directly addressing his audience and offering frank thoughts on being single. He accordingly establishes an additional layer of contrast, namely between the humorous side-by-side comparison of "expectation" and "reality," and the "actual" reality suggested by the framing monologues. He thus presents himself as a cutting eye on popular culture and quotidian interactions, but ultimately assumes a pose of familiarity that establishes him as the viewers' everyman.

Exemplified by the "Expectations vs. Reality: Romance" video, interactions between men and women are a common concern in Higa and Wu's works and, as in "Yellow Fever," simultaneously affirm the ordinariness of Asian American masculinity and the ordinariness of normative sexual relations. But whereas "Yellow Fever" explicitly connects this project to racial stereotypes, race occupies a more nebulous place in Higa and Wu's videos. As a short narrative film, "Yellow Fever" has more clearly defined boundaries than a "vlog," which, diary-like, implies regular entries and extended relationships. Higa and Wu's respective YouTube channels add to the impression that they are establishing a casual, ongoing relationship with their viewers. Other than the date of upload, the number of views and comments, and, on rare occasion, a number in the title that places the selection in a series, the channels do not offer any logic of hierarchy or order among videos. Videos are gathered together but loosely organized, uploaded frequently but not systematically. While a short, relatively coherent series may appear within the channels, the performances collectively lack an overarching message or trajectory. These YouTube channels therefore complement the mode of the "side-by-side" that Yoon Sun Lee discerns in many works of Asian American literature, a form of the everyday that she argues manifests "a reluctance to single out a dominant, continuous chain of causality initiated by a human act."[16]

Cultivating a sense of informal continuity, the common genres and distribution systems of online media allow race to appear in the videos of Asian American performers as a significant but not totalizing influence. In a study focusing on the works of Asian American singer-songwriters, Grace Wang argues that race is both visible and incidental in the "Asian movement" (so named by one of the artists) that is purportedly taking place via the Internet. While these performers disavow the centrality of race, they also invoke an Asian American community of artists and fans.[17] By contrast, some of Higa and Wu's signature videos address issues of racialization and racism directly. One of Wu's earliest successes, for example, offers a sustained diatribe about racial stereotypes.[18] Yet with over a hundred videos on each of their channels, race is, as Wang argues, both visible and incidental in their body of work. With one performance poking fun at racial stereotypes and another ruminating on handshakes, the videos suggest that race informs some of their everyday experiences, but not the entirety, and that these experiences are both ordinary and exceptional. The YouTube format allows these topics to move flexibly between primary and secondary importance, to prompt a lengthy rant in one work and a bemused pause in another.

Even within videos, race can suddenly move from background to foreground, and vice versa. Phan and Higa offer strikingly similar representations of their early encounters with racism in their respective "Draw My Life" videos.[19] These videos, which became popular in 2013, consist of short illustrated autobiographies: users draw stick figures on a whiteboard to depict scenes from their lives, which they explain through voice-over narration. Thousands of "Draw My Life" videos have appeared on YouTube, and Internet personalities receive fan requests to add their own. In both of their videos, Phan and Higa recount their experiences of being taunted and bullied at school. Whereas their narrations offer more general accounts of the difficulties they faced in their youth, the specific racial epithets and stereotypes that other students threw at them are only written into the illustrations. Unlike Phan, who at one point talks about feeling different because of her "race" in the voice-over for her "Draw My Life" video, Higa never mentions in his narration that the bullying he experienced was racially inflected. This silence, however, only makes the sudden appearance of racialized goading in his drawings (a bully telling him to "Go back to China") all the more startling, and all the more revealing. The incongruity between the explicit drawing and the vague narration suggests that not only is racism uncomfortable to recount, but it has also become something unacceptable to discuss in a pointed, serious way. Even as the videos seem to pass over these incidents, to speak around them in order to move ahead to the happy ending, they nevertheless pause long enough for the derogatory words to be written out. The parallel manners in which Phan and Higa present these moments suggest that although race exerts a palpable force in their everyday lives, they must accommodate a simultaneous pressure to treat it parenthetically. In the uneven alignment of spoken and written words, the videos manifest a tension between recognizing and obscuring the influence of race on how they draw their lives.

In contrast to the sober deflections of these videos, Wu's series on his father, "My Dad Is Asian," offers an extended engagement with racial caricature not as the object of critique—humorous or otherwise—but as a vehicle for comedic expression.[20] In the series, Wu plays the straight man to his father's exaggerated performance of the "Asian parent," now an established type in popular culture as a result of Internet memes and books such as Amy Chua's memoir. Wu's father explodes in rage and threatens to whip his son when he does not excel at school, sings karaoke songs, practices tai chi, and goes to extreme measures to save money. Yet while these videos perpetuate certain stereotypes, it would be unfair not to mention their deviations from blatant racial caricature. The father's blissful swaying to hip-hop music and energetic role-playing as James Bond, for example, reveal a loving portrayal of a quirky parent. Furthermore, the father's inability to keep a completely straight face in the videos lets slip that he is ultimately a parent indulging his child's requests to play for the camera. The absurd *character* of Kevin's dad thus serves as a foil to both Kevin, the Asian American teenager whose embarrassment proclaims his relative ordinariness, and the off-camera father who occasionally peeks through.

Although the father is the star of these videos, the comedic vision that they manifest is clearly that of the son. This difference reflects the distinct opportunities that online media provide to younger, tech-savvy Asian Americans attuned to American popular culture and older immigrants who remain objects of caricature, if ironically and even lovingly rendered. Born in 1990, Higa and Wu were teenagers when they became recognized Internet celebrities; born in 1987, Phan is only slightly older. While websites like YouTube provide a more democratic platform for distributing media, they are nevertheless not available to everyone, or at least not available to everyone in the same way. As Burgess and Green note, "Access [on YouTube] to all the layers of possible participation is limited to a particular segment of the population—those with the motivations, technological competencies, and site-specific cultural capital sufficient to participate at all levels of engagement the network affords."[21] Lisa Nakamura similarly points out, "The Internet is a paradox: notable for the ways in which scholars have predicted its 'ubiquity,' it is nonetheless far from universally accessible inside or outside the context of the living room."[22] This "digital divide" is starkly evident within Asian America. Although a Pew report in 2001 (and then again in 2011) identified Asian Americans as the demographic group with the heaviest Internet use,[23] Nakamura notes, "As the Pew report did not sample non-English-speaking respondents, it is unlikely that it was able to survey immigrants or recently arrived and undereducated Asian Americans, exactly those people most likely to work as the 'interacted' in the circuit of informatic labor."[24] Missing from the Pew survey, Nakamura suggests, are those who provide the material labor for technological products and systems, but are unable to participate fully in the production and consumption of online media. This group constitutes part of the global underclass of workers who make possible the Internet Age through their labor, yet are largely absent from the cultural productions that circulate through digital networks.

Despite these significant limitations on the accessibility of online media, the emergence of overnight YouTube sensations perpetuates the appearance of boundless opportunity. The success stories exemplified by Internet personalities like Higa, Phan, and Wu entwine the narrative of the model minority with seductive tales of ordinary people who become web celebrities. When Phan or Higa emphasize the isolation, failures, and disappointments of their pasts in their "Draw My Life" videos, they provide encouragement to adolescent viewers who might face similar struggles, but also turn their vehicle of representation into a vehicle for salvation. The medium of the online video is simultaneously the mode of communication and the path to success.

Phan's "Draw My Life" video offers a particularly compelling account of her background, stressing her family's financial struggles and even hinting at an abusive home environment. Coming after Phan had already become an Internet celebrity and successful entrepreneur, the video provides a narrative in which to situate the tutorials that have made her famous. Over the years, Phan's tutorials have taken on an increasingly polished look, accruing numerous global sponsors, including cosmetics companies whose products appear in the videos, and leading to Phan's own makeup line. Phan epitomizes the cosmopolitan professionalism that Nhi T. Lieu finds in the many "makeup guru" videos by women of Asian descent that have appeared in recent years.[25] The rags-to-riches story narrated in her "Draw My Life" video affirms a particular model of uplift in which economic disparities and racial bigotry are challenges for an individual to overcome and Asian American women can become paragons of a new kind of global entrepreneur.

Phan's "Draw My Life" video nevertheless leaves traces of what remains unspoken and unseen: her generally upbeat narrative suddenly becomes eerie when she recounts her gambling-addicted father's sudden departure from the family in a quiet voice or mysteriously scratches out the face of her stepfather, only later explaining in vague terms that he made her miserable. While these tiny fissures do not significantly unsettle Phan's glossy image, they nevertheless introduce an unexpected element of disquiet into the video and set the routines of beauty and fashion over which she asserts expert control in tension with her day-to-day coping with precarious father figures.

Although makeup tutorials might seem less amenable to the intimate anecdotes and commentary that are common in "vlogs," a popular video or channel can allow (sometimes oblige) performers to cultivate a distinct personality. The genre of the "Draw My Life" video enables YouTube personalities to participate in a playful, collective project of sharing biographical details without disrupting the style and form of their trademark productions. Phan's usual makeup tutorials offer occasional glimpses into her private life, but they primarily convey intimacy through the tone of her voice-over and the friendliness of her facial expressions. The popularity of Phan's videos indeed depends on a balance between establishing a cozy relationship with her viewers and retaining a professional distance that affirms her expertise. Furthermore, while the performance of a specific personality helps to distinguish her videos from dozens of similar tutorials, Phan must ultimately offer advice that appears widely applicable; in other words, her skills in this context are valuable insofar as they are *transferable*. The differences that matter in the tutorials are those between the "makeup guru" and the novice viewer, and those between the face as it appears in the beginning and the face as it appears in the end. The videos must promise simultaneous passage between these points: as Phan changes her face with makeup, her viewers must concurrently acquire the skill to change their faces in the same way. Whatever distinctness Phan claims as a personality, her success depends on the possibility of passing on her abilities and her finished "looks."

For this process to be maximally effective, however, differences in physical appearance, including specific attributes that have been utilized to classify people by race, must also seem malleable, ready to be copied, enhanced, obscured, or altered by makeup. Phan offers the possibility of drastically changing one's features in tutorials that show the viewer how to use makeup to look like a specific actor, type, or character, such as celebrity Angelina Jolie, a Korean pop singer (as a group, not a particular performer), and Disney "princesses." While some of these videos simply display a look inspired by these figures, others strive toward meticulous imitation. The specificity of Phan's references allows her to defer to accuracy when instructing the viewer to contour the face with darker makeup to create the illusion of a narrower nose (Angelina

Jolie), draw dramatic "cat eyes" that slant upward (Korean pop stars), and use bronzer to darken the skin (Jasmine, from Disney's animated film *Aladdin*).

Yet in reproducing the appearance of others, whether living actors or cartoon characters, Phan enters the controversial territory of racial masquerade. Although Phan's detailed tutorials show that the features of any one figure resist neat categorization into racial types, they nevertheless recall practices of making actors look like characters of a different "race," most commonly, attempts to make white actors resemble other racialized groups, which extend from minstrel shows and plays like *The Yellow Jacket* to the contentious yellowface performances in the musical *Miss Saigon* (1990).

A video in which Phan re-creates the Chinese folk heroine Mulan as she is drawn in Disney's animated film (1998) reveals a careful avoidance of the problematic history of yellowface and other cross-racial performances that her tutorials might evoke.[26] Yet Phan's attempt to emulate this character, with whom she would be racially categorized, also generates suggestive tensions. Sianne Ngai has shown the persistent associations made between animatedness, both as a condition of liveliness and its simulation, and those who are racially marked; she argues that these associations establish the latter as "excessively emotional, bodily subjects."[27] Ngai further proposes, however, that animation might nevertheless afford a "nexus of contradictions with the capacity to generate unanticipated social meanings and effects."[28] Phan's video is replete with such contradictions as the racialized subject is both the object of animation and the one who animates.

Wearing a pink silk robe, Phan begins the five-minute tutorial by applying heavy white face paint and explaining that in China at the time (presumably Mulan's time), pale faces were favored as a sign of the privileged classes. She then builds dramatic "cat eyes" with thick coats of black eyeliner before moving on to the rest of her face (Figure A.1). The painstaking process by which Phan transforms herself into Mulan and the highly exaggerated look that she creates highlight the work required to become the character, despite a shared racial identification. The video thus shows that Mulan is not simply a representation of an Asian woman, but a highly contrived image, a conglomeration of unlikely features that only give the impression of semblance. When

Figure A.1. Makeup tutorial on how to look like Disney's Mulan. "Mulan Bride," YouTube video posted by Michelle Phan, 2011. http://youtu.be/ebcc1WXJS6A.

Phan declares, "I don't think I've ever been this pale," while brushing on white face paint to mimic Mulan's makeup, she visually and verbally sets herself at a distance from the character. Paradoxically, it is by drawing Mulan on her face that Phan is able to insist that she is *not* Mulan. Yet while the tutorial dramatizes the labored process by which the ordinary Asian American becomes the animated Asian of American creation, it also includes moments in which Phan implies a particular intimacy with Mulan. For example, Phan's remark that white skin was desirable "back then" in China is revealingly vague (when exactly is this time?), but assumes an authority to speak on this matter. Phan also uses this video to respond to speculation that she had plastic surgery to create folds on her eyelids. Rejecting this idea, she explains that not all Asian people have "monolids," and adds that Asian eyes come in "all shapes and sizes." She makes these assertions just as the video shows her trying to imitate Mulan's face by creating sharp black angles at the corners of her eyes. Visually, this moment further stresses the difference between Phan and Mulan; the voice-over, however, conveys Phan's recognition that she is viewed through a racial lens, one that sees identity rather than difference between her and Mulan. Even as she must apply exorbitant layers of makeup to look like Mulan, the Disney character's eyes already inform how her eyes are seen (i.e., as unusual for an Asian woman). By taking on the task of animating Mulan herself—and *on* herself—Phan is able to stage the misalignment of their faces as well as the tendency to superimpose narrowly racialized features over less neatly defined ones.

Although Phan explains early in the video that Mulan is one of her favorite Disney characters because she is a warrior, she chooses to emulate instead an image of Mulan as a bride. When disguised as a man to take her father's place in the army, Mulan wears no makeup (thus, no white face paint needed), ties her hair back, and dresses in much simpler outfits. Replicating this more ambiguously gendered figure would have entailed a much less intensive transformation. It is the exaggerated femininity of Mulan the bride, with her painted face, coiffed hair, and pink robe, that allows Phan to showcase the dramatic contrast between her own features and those of the cartoon. This choice intensifies a sense of spectacle that is concomitantly racialized and gendered, but also exposes its careful engineering.

The process of re-creating some form of idealized feminine beauty is, of course, depicted in all of Phan's makeup tutorials, as she begins with a clean face and slowly adds layers of cosmetics until she achieves a desired look. The success of her videos, however, depends on not a critique of this meticulously constructed face, but a naturalization of it, with excursions into cartoons, celebrities, and fantastical creatures affirming the unaffectedness of the other looks. The Mulan tutorial offers a rare deviation when it sets images of Phan's profuse application of eyeliner as the backdrop to her rejection of narrow conceptions of "Asian eyes." This incongruent intersection of performance and commentary hints that naturalized conceptions of physical appearance, gendered and racial, are not far from the exaggerated representations circulated in cartoons. Yet whatever critique might be smuggled into this strange juncture in the video, it remains a tutorial intended to show viewers how to fashion a feminized yellowface look, complete with exaggerated "Asian" features and bridal costuming and accessories. Phan's brief disquisition on eyes is quickly followed by instructions for creating the two-dimensional look of a cartoon. When Phan, as a final touch, draws a black curl on her forehead to represent a lock of hair, the same black lines that changed the shape of her eyes insist that Mulan is, after all, just an animated character, not to be taken too seriously. At the same time, it completes the process of transforming the racialized subject into an animated object, reducing her to a collection of exaggerated features by drawing *over* her actual body.

In offering to show her viewers how to look like someone else by cultivating their skills in makeup application, Phan affirms the notion, traced throughout *The Racial Mundane*, that the execution of seemingly minor tasks opens up the possibility of traversing racial demarcations. What Phan proposes more dramatically, however, is an opportunity to change physical features themselves, not through permanent bodily alterations, but through the development of certain quotidian skills. Her videos claim that with the right tutorials and practice, anyone can layer other faces over her or his own. Phan mediates as the one whose hands must be imitated in order to effect such transformations, but she must ultimately disappear in order for her tutorials to achieve their ostensible goal: the simultaneous transmission of everyday proficiencies and new looks. The viewer, after all, is hoping to look like Mulan, not Phan-as-Mulan, and in the process, to assimilate Phan's abilities so that the tutorials become unnecessary. Yet for those like Phan who maintain YouTube channels, continued success requires that viewers keep returning for more, as the number of views serves as the key barometer of a video and a channel's relevance. The necessity of securing habitual, long-term viewing thus conflicts in some ways with the actual adoption of Phan's specialized skills as daily practice. As a "guru" of the everyday, Phan must hover between the ordinary and the exceptional, continuously performing a partial disappearance while remaining a part of her audience's routine viewing practices. The mundane returns as a contradictory force, promising passage, and thwarting it.

As this book has argued, the mundane equivocates thus when rendered available for dissection, transformation, and transmission—in gloomy reports on Chinatown living conditions, through the ritualization of routines to counter pressures to disappear, through an actor's efforts to replicate another's voice and posture, and in debates about the proper balance of study and play for American students. And yet, as the Mulan tutorial hints, the mundane also has untold currents that continually escape capture, scrutiny, and staging. In Phan's final trans-formation into Mulan, these currents press against the thick lines of simulated animatedness to hint at the untenability of the performance. In the very closing moments of the tutorial, as she displays her finished look, Phan explains through the voice-over that she is going to end the video because "all this posing is getting kind of awkward." In jokingly pointing out the endurance required to sustain her performance, Phan recalls the skills attributed to the actor who played the Property Man in *The Yellow Jacket*: "For two hours and a half this property man moves among the actors as though invisible to them and to the spectators. The slightest bit of overplaying, the least stooping to buffoonery, the merest suggestion of theatricals on his part would ruin his impersonation and mar the whole play."[29] *The Yellow Jacket* asks that the actor who plays the Property Man maintain the impression that his performance is natural, which will paradoxically make his behaviors seem even more peculiar to the audience. Emphasizing the difficulty of this performance is nec-essary in order to affirm the boundary between the white actor and the Chinese role, particularly since the play itself repeatedly stages the per-meability of racial and cultural lines. In other words, the actor's attempt to inhabit the everyday body of the other must remain a challenge in order to preserve their difference.

By contrast, when Phan remarks on the difficulty of posing at the end of her Mulan video, she is trying to maintain not a role that must seem unaffected, but one that embraces its own artificiality, its explicit fusion of cartoon and racial caricature. If this yellowface performance is hard to sustain, it is not because racial difference is indelible, but because it is a perpetually collapsing project. In pointing to the moment after the per-formance's end, when the recursive production of yellowface unravels, the video exposes the impossibility of sustaining what might be called the racial foreshortening of the live body—that is, not the lively ani-mated body, but the one that is present and continues on in the everyday.

NOTES

INTRODUCTION

1. Maxine Hong Kingston, *Tripmaster Monkey: His Fake Book* (New York: Vintage, 1990), 34. Subsequent citations in text.

2. At the risk of seeming inconsistent, I place the word "race" in quotation marks only when the context of a sentence might suggest that I am thinking of the term uncritically (for example, when I refer to someone's "race," as opposed to when I mention debates about race). This choice reflects the book's understanding of racial identifications as social constructs (thus, the quotation marks when I use the term to describe particular individuals or peoples) that nonetheless have real effects (thus, the lack of quotation marks when I use the term to discuss how it circulates and functions in society).

3. Performance is a key term in this book because of its dual meanings—"doing" and "presenting"—but its multiple uses can also lead to confusion, particularly when J. L. Austin or Judith Butler's work on "performativity" is also part of the analysis. I therefore use the term "performativity" only when referring to the notion of the performative as elaborated in speech act theory and in Butler's theory of gender. In addition, I use the term "theatrical performance" even when it might sound redundant to indicate performances, including those outside the theater proper, that have a theatrical quality; as I explain in the introduction, my understanding of theatricality derives from semiotic and phenomenological analyses provided by Umberto Eco and Bert O. States.

4. I refer here to Judith Butler's work on gender performativity and Richard Schechner's definition of performance as twice-behaved or restored behavior. Judith Butler, "Performative Acts and Gender Constitution: An Essay in Phenomenology and Feminist Theory," in *Performing Feminisms: Feminist Critical Theory and Theater*, ed. Sue-Ellen Case (Baltimore: Johns Hopkins University Press, 1990), 270–82; Richard Schechner, *Between Theater and Anthropology* (Philadelphia: University of Pennsylvania Press, 1985), 36.

5. The mundane is linked to but does not completely coincide with the affective present and the everyday conceived specifically as a condition of capitalist modernity. The bodily repetitions that it describes are transhistorical, although their shape, significance, and effects vary historically. On the affective present, see Lauren Berlant, *Cruel Optimism* (Durham, NC: Duke University Press, 2011). On the modern everyday, see Henri Lefebvre, *Critique of Everyday Life*, vols. 1–3, trans. John Moore (London: Verso, 1991); and see Yoon Sun Lee's *Modern*

Minority: Asian American Literature and Everyday Life (New York: Oxford University Press, 2013) for an analysis of its representation in Asian American literature.

6. Richard Dyer, *White* (London: Routledge, 1997), 14.

7. Ibid., 14–15.

8. Homi Bhabha, *The Location of Culture* (London: Routledge, 1994), 89.

9. Robert E. Park, "Behind Our Masks," in *Race and Culture*, ed. Everett C. Hughes et al. (Glencoe, IL: Free Press, 1950), 244–55. For an extended discussion of Park's work, see Chapter 1.

10. Pierre Bourdieu, *The Logic of Practice* (Stanford: Stanford University Press, 1990), 56.

11. Y. S. Lee, *Modern Minority*, 13.

12. Butler, "Performative Acts," 278, and *Bodies That Matter* (New York: Routledge, 1993), 232; Bourdieu, *Logic of Practice*, 67 and 73.

13. Bourdieu, *Logic of Practice*, 73.

14. Erving Goffman, *The Presentation of Self in Everyday Life* (New York: Anchor Books, 1959), 17–20.

15. Ibid., 15.

16. Butler, "Performative Acts," 279.

17. W. E. B. Du Bois, *The Souls of Black Folk* (New York: Signet Classic, 1995), 45.

18. Hartman explains, "The interchangeable use of performance and performativity is intended to be inclusive of displays of power, the punitive and theatrical embodiment of racial norms, and the discursive reelaboration of blackness, and the affirmative deployment and negation of blackness in the focus on redress." Saidiya Hartman, *Scenes of Subjection: Terror, Slavery, and Self-Making in Nineteenth-Century America* (New York: Oxford University Press, 1997), 57.

19. Bert O. States, *Great Reckonings in Little Rooms: On the Phenomenology of Theater* (Berkeley: University of California Press, 1985), 35.

20. Ibid., 20.

21. Umberto Eco, "Semiotics of Theatrical Performance," *TDR: The Drama Review* 21 (1977): 110.

22. Schechner, *Between Theater*, 113.

23. Karen Shimakawa, *National Abjection: The Asian American Body Onstage* (Durham, NC: Duke University Press, 2002), 57.

24. Role-doubling appears in film and television but less frequently than in theater, and it usually serves a comedic purpose or advances a story about twins or doppelgangers. In terms of cross-racial performance, other than in satires, films and television shows either ask audiences to disregard a possible misalignment of racial identifications or, more controversially, perpetuate practices of making white actors look like another ethnicity or "race." See extended discussions of cross-racial performances in Chapter 3.

25. Shimakawa, *National Abjection*.

26. Mary Yu Danico, "Association for Asian American Studies Responds to the Pew Center Report: 'Rise of Asian Americans'" (Association for Asian American Studies, July 16, 2012).

27. Lefebvre, *Critique*, 1:12.

28. Butler cautiously differentiates between normative embodiments that "do" gender, and performances *in* the theater where it is possible to separate acting from the real, but also contemplates the critical possibilities of hyperbolic citations of norms (*Bodies*, 232). In her reading of Luce Irigaray, Elin Diamond makes a complementary argument about mimesis-mimicry, "in which the production of objects, shadows, and voices is excessive to the truth/illusion structure of [patriarchal] mimesis, spilling into mimicry, multiple 'fake offspring.'" Elin Diamond, *Unmaking Mimesis: Essays on Feminism and Theater* (New York: Routledge, 1997), 65.

29. Lefebvre, *Critique*, 2:226.

30. Ibid., 1:12.

31. Michel de Certeau, *The Practice of Everyday Life*, trans. Steven Rendall (Berkeley: University of California Press, 1984), 30.

32. De Certeau, *Practice*, 58.

33. Colleen Lye, "Racial Form," *Representations* 104.1 (Fall 2008): 96.

34. Susan Koshy offers an important critique in "The Fiction of Asian American Literature," *Yale Journal of Criticism* 9.2 (Fall 1992): 315–46.

35. "CNN/YouTube Democratic Presidential Debate," CNN, July 23, 2007.

36. Patricia J. Williams, *Seeing a Colour-Blind Future: The Paradox of Race* (London: Virago Press, 1997), 3.

37. Diana Taylor, *The Archive and the Repertoire: Performing Cultural Memory in the Americas* (Durham, NC: Duke University Press, 2003).

38. Alain Badiou, *Rhapsody for the Theatre*, trans. Bruno Bosteels (London: Verso, 2013), 2.

39. Elin Diamond, "Introduction," in *Performance and Cultural Politics*, ed. Elin Diamond (London: Routledge, 1996), 1.

CHAPTER 1. TRYING ON *THE YELLOW JACKET* AT THE LIMITS OF *OUR TOWN*

1. Thornton Wilder, *Our Town* (New York: HarperCollins, 2003), 4. Subsequent citations in text.

2. Thornton Wilder, "Preface to *Three Plays*," in *American Characteristics and Other Essays*, ed. Donald Gallup (New York: Harper & Row, 1979), 109.

3. San Francisco Board of Supervisors, "Report of the Special Committee of the Board of Supervisors of San Francisco on the Condition of the Chinese Quarter and the Chinese in San Francisco, July 1885" (San Francisco Municipal Reports for the Fiscal Year 1884–1885, San Francisco Board of Supervisors, 1885), Appendix 166.

4. Andrew Gyory, *Closing the Gate: Race, Politics and the Chinese Exclusion Act* (Chapel Hill: University of North Carolina Press, 1998), 1.

5. California State Senate, "An Address to the People of the United States upon the Evils of Chinese Immigration," in *Chinese Immigration; Its Social, Moral, and Political Effect. Report to the California State Senate of Its Special Committee on Chinese Immigration* (Sacramento: State Office, 1973), 8–9.

6. San Francisco Board of Supervisors, "Report of the Special Committee," Appendix 209.

7. The 1885 municipal report claimed, "The facility with which [the Chinese] put on habits of decency when they become cooks and servants simply adds other testimony to their ability to adapt themselves to circumstances when it is their interest to do so" (San Francisco Board of Supervisors, "Report of the Special Committee," Appendix 180). Even Mark Twain, who was generally critical of hostility directed at Chinese immigrants, asserted, "[The Chinese] do not need to be taught a thing twice, as a general thing. They are imitative." Mark Twain, *Roughing It*, vol. 2 (Hartford: American Publishing, 1901), 130.

8. Nayan Shah, *Contagious Divides: Epidemics and Race in San Francisco's Chinatown* (Berkeley: University of California Press, 2001), 27.

9. San Francisco Board of Supervisors, "Report of the Special Committee," Appendix 174.

10. Shah, *Contagious Divides*, 17–18.

11. San Francisco Board of Supervisors, "Report of the Special Committee," Appendix 172.

12. Shah, *Contagious Divides*, 166.

13. San Francisco Board of Supervisors, "Report of the Special Committee," Appendix 184.

14. Erika Lee, *At America's Gates: Chinese Immigration during the Exclusion Era, 1882–1943* (Chapel Hill: University of North Carolina Press, 2003), 26.

15. California State Senate, "Address to the People," 47.

16. Adam McKeown, "Ritualization of Regulation: The Enforcement of Chinese Exclusion in the United States and China," *American Historical Review* 108.2 (April 2003): 377.

17. Kitty Calavita, "The Paradoxes of Race, Class, Identity, and 'Passing': Enforcing the Chinese Exclusion Acts, 1882–1910," *Law and Social Inquiry* 25.1 (Winter 2000): 17.

18. McKeown, "Ritualization of Regulation," 391.

19. E. Lee, *At America's Gates*, 89.

20. For literacy tests, see E. Lee, *At America's Gates*, 89; for the texture of hands and feet, see Calavita, "Paradoxes of Race," 25; McKeown, "Ritualization of Regulation," 391.

21. Calavita, "Paradoxes of Race," 25.

22. Ibid., 25–26.

23. E. Lee, *At America's Gates*, 107.

24. Ibid., 209.

25. Erika Lee emphasizes that the coaching books demonstrate their writers' extensive and precise knowledge of the kinds of questions asked by inspectors; one book gave more than four hundred sample questions (*At America's Gates*, 196).

26. Calavita, "Paradoxes of Race," 2.

27. Shah, *Contagious Divides*, 225.

28. Ibid., 15.

29. San Francisco Board of Supervisors, "Report of the Special Committee," 204.

30. Ibid.

31. Ibid., 205.

32. Henry Yu, "The 'Oriental Problem' in America, 1920–1960: Linking the Identities of Chinese American and Japanese American Intellectuals," in *Claiming America: Constructing Chinese American Identities during the Exclusion Era*, ed. K. Scott Wong and Sucheng Chan (Philadelphia: Temple University Press, 1993), 191.

33. Ibid., 194.

34. Park, "Behind Our Masks," 249.

35. Park, "The Problem of Cultural Differences," in *Race and Culture*, 3.

36. Park, "Culture and Cultural Trends," in *Race and Culture*, 26–27.

37. Park, "Behind Our Masks," 251.

38. Park, "A Race Relations Survey," in *Race and Culture*, 159.

39. Park, "Racial Assimilation in Secondary Groups," in *Race and Culture*, 206.

40. David Palumbo-Liu, *Asian/American: Historical Crossings of a Racial Frontier* (Stanford: Stanford University, 1999), 86.

41. *The Yellow Jacket*, advertisement, *New York Times*, October 30, 1912, 22, *New York Times* Historical, http://proquest.umi.com, accessed June 16, 2005.

42. "J. Harry Benrimo, Actor, Playwright," *New York Times*, March 27, 1942, 23, *New York Times* Historical, http://proquest.umi.com, accessed June 16, 2005.

43. The play refers to the yellow jackets worn as a sign of imperial favor during the Qing dynasty. While the authors make use of the idea that the jacket is a sign of high social status, the drama does not suggest a familiarity with the actual practices surrounding its distribution and use.

44. Today, *Aladdin* is more commonly associated with the Middle East; these nineteenth-century theatrical productions, however, were set in China. For an extended discussion of *Aladdin* and *Kim-ka!*, see Krystyn Moon, *Yellowface: Creating the Chinese in American Popular Music and Performance, 1850s–1920s* (New Brunswick, NJ: Rutgers University Press, 2005), 23–26.

45. George C. Hazelton, Jr. and J. Harry Benrimo, *The Yellow Jacket*, in *The Chinese Other, 1850–1925: An Anthology of Plays*, ed. Dave Williams (Lanham, MD: University Press of America, 1997), 235. Subsequent citations in text.

46. James Harbeck, "The Quaintness—and Usefulness—of the Old Chinese Traditions: *The Yellow Jacket* and *Lady Precious Stream*," *Asian Theatre Journal* 13.2 (1996): 241.

47. Moon, *Yellowface*, 99. *Huaju*, or Chinese spoken drama, emerged in the early twentieth century. A 1907 adaptation of *Uncle Tom's Cabin* by Chinese students in Japan is generally regarded as the first work of *huaju*.

48. Colin Mackerras, "The Drama of the Qing Dynasty," in *Chinese Theater: From Its Origins to the Present Day*, ed. Colin Mackerras (Honolulu: University of Hawaii Press, 1983), 92.

49. I am thinking here of Peggy Phelan's argument regarding the ontology of performance: "Performance's only life is in the present. Performance cannot be saved, recorded, documented, or otherwise participate in the circulation of representations of representations: once it does so, it becomes something other than performance." Peggy Phelan, *Unmarked: The Politics of Performance* (London: Routledge, 1992), 146.

50. Moon, *Yellowface*, 112–13.

51. Mackerras, "Drama of the Qing Dynasty," 112.

52. Nancy Rao, "Songs of the Exclusion Era: New York Chinatown's Opera Theaters in the 1920s," *American Music* 20.4 (2002): 426.

53. Ronald Riddle, *Flying Dragons, Flowing Streams: Music in the Life of San Francisco's Chinese* (Westport, CT: Greenwood, 1983), 61.

54. Su Zheng, *Claiming Diaspora: Music, Transnationalism, and Cultural Politics in Asian/Chinese America* (New York: Oxford University Press, 2010), 94.

55. Dave Williams, *Misreading the Chinese Character: Images of the Chinese in Euroamerican Drama to 1825* (New York: Peter Lang, 2000), 113.

56. Moon, *Yellowface*, 112.

57. Robert G. Lee, *Orientals: Asian Americans in Popular Culture* (Philadelphia: Temple University Press, 1999), 28.

58. E. M. Green, "The Chinese Theater," *Overland Monthly and Out West Magazine*, February 1903, 7–9, APS Online, http://proquest.umi.org, accessed June 24, 2005.

59. *The Yellow Jacket* may not have always been performed in yellowface when it was produced on smaller community stages. The Collection of Chinese Theater Images in California at the San Francisco Museum of Performance and Design includes a photograph titled *Performance of the Yellow jacket* [sic] *by the Hawaii Chinese Civic Club dramatic chapter in 1950s*, which seems to show a Chinese Hawaiian cast. A study of this performance is outside the scope of this chapter, but such a production attests to the unpredictable lives of dramatic scripts, which are open to multiple, variable enactments.

60. R. G. Lee, *Orientals*, 43; Sean Metzger, "Charles Parsloe's Chinese Fetish: An Example of Yellowface Performance in Nineteenth-Century American Melodrama," *Theatre Journal* 56.4 (2004): 651.

61. Moon, *Yellowface*, 118.

62. Eric Lott, *Love and Theft: Blackface Minstrelsy and the American Working Class* (New York: Oxford University Press, 1995), 234.

63. Bret Harte and Mark Twain, *Ah Sin*, in *The Chinese Other, 1850–1925*, 82.

64. Erika Fischer-Lichte, *The Show and the Gaze: A European Perspective* (Iowa City: University of Iowa Press, 1997), 79.

65. Williams, *Misreading*, 172.

66. "Acting, Acting, All the Time, but Not a Word to Speak," *New York Times*, December 1, 1912, X8, *New York Times* Historical, http://proquest.umi.com, accessed June 16, 2005.

67. Ibid., X8.

68. "Something New and Strange in Drama," *New York Times*, November 3, 1912, X6, *New York Times* Historical, http://proquest.umi.com, accessed June 16, 2005.

69. Clayton Hamilton, "Yellow Jacket," *Bookman*, December 1912, 382, APS Online, http://proquest.umi.com, accessed September 14, 2005.

70. Alexander Woollcott, "Second Thoughts on First Nights," *New York Times*, November 12, 1916, X6, *New York Times* Historical, http://proquest.umi.com, accessed June 16, 2005.

71. J. Harry Benrimo, "Legend and Truth: The Facts about 'The Yellow Jacket,' Again in Revival Here," *New York Times*, November 4, 1928, 118, *New York Times* Historical, http://proquest.umi.com, accessed June 16, 2005.

72. "J. Harry Benrimo, Actor, Playwright," *New York Times*, March 27, 1942, 23, *New York Times* Historical, http://proquest.umi.com, accessed June 16, 2005.

73. Arthur Feinsod, *The Simple Stage: Its Origins in the Modern American Theater* (New York: Greenwood, 1992), 28.

74. Clayton Hamilton, "What Is Wrong with the American Drama?," *Bookman*, May 1914, 314, APS Online, http://proquest.umi.com, accessed June 24, 2005.

75. *The Yellow Jacket*, advertisement, *New York Times*, November 15, 1912, 10, *New York Times* Historical, http://proquest.umi.com, accessed June 16, 2005.

76. *The Yellow Jacket*, advertisement, *New York Times*, December 1, 1912, X8, *New York Times* Historical, http://proquest.umi.com, accessed June 16, 2005.

77. "Something New," X6.

78. "'The Yellow Jacket' Is a Real Novelty," *New York Times*, November 5, 1912, 13, *New York Times* Historical, http://proquest.umi.com, accessed June 16, 2005.

79. Hamilton, "Yellow Jacket," 382.

80. "Something New," X6.

81. Fischer-Lichte, *Show and the Gaze*, 81.

82. Hamilton, "What Is Wrong?," 314.

83. "Something New," X6.

84. "Reading the Heart of the East through the Drama," *Current Opinion*, January 1913, 35, APS Online, http://proquest.umi.com, accessed June 24, 2005.

85. "Play That Went Round the World," *New York Times*, November 26, 1916, X7, *New York Times* Historical, http://proquest.umi.com, accessed June 16, 2005.

86. Woollcott, "Second Thoughts," X6.

87. Harbeck, "Quaintness," 241.

88. Feinsod, *Simple Stage*, 55.

89. Ibid., 28.

90. Helen Caldwell, *Michio Ito: The Dancer and his His Dances* (Berkeley: University of California Press, 1977), 54.

91. "Play That Went Round the World," X7.

92. Jack Tchen, *New York before Chinatown: Orientalism and the Shaping of American Cultures* (Baltimore: Johns Hopkins University Press, 1999), 292.

93. "Play That Went Round the World," X7.

94. Tchen, *New York*, xx.

95. "When Grandees Give 'The Yellow Jacket,'" *New York Times*, March 11, 1917, X5, *New York Times* Historical, http://proquest.umi.com, accessed June 16, 2005.

96. Woollcott, "Second Thoughts," X6.

97. Benrimo, "Legend and Truth," 118.

98. Ibid., 118.

99. Ibid., 118.

100. Ibid., 118.

101. Hamilton, "Yellow Jacket," 382.

102. "Acting, Acting," X8.

103. Feinsod, *Simple Stage*, 67.

104. Sang-Kyong Lee, *East Asia and America: Encounters in Drama and Theatre* (Sydney, Australia: Wild Peony, 2000), 89.

105. Hazel Durnell, *Japanese Cultural Influences on American Poetry and Drama* (Tokyo: Hokuseido Press, 1983), 171.

106. Ibid., 166.

107. Edwin Schallert, "'Our Town' at Biltmore Wins Acclaim as Inspirational Stage Production," *Los Angeles Times*, April 11, 1939, 13. See also Brooks Atkinson, "How They Used to Live," *New York Times*, February 13, 1938, 155.

108. See Atkinson, "How They Used to Live," 155; Brooks Atkinson, "Frank Craven in Thornton Wilder's 'Our Town,' Which Is the Anatomy of a Community," *New York Times*, February 5, 1938, 18; Schallert, "'Our Town,'" 13; E. F. M., "Boston Takes No Wilder Chance," *New York Times*, December 18, 1938, 153.

109. "Wilder Tells Why 'Our Town' Is Sentimental," *Chicago Daily Tribune*, June 5, 1938, E2.

110. Wilder, "Preface to *Three Plays*," 109.

111. In addition to the articles about *Our Town* mentioned above, see Nelson B. Bell, "Strong Family Inheritance Prompted Writing of 'Our Town,'" *Washington Post*, December 11, 1938, TS3.

112. Nancy Bunge, "The Social Realism of *Our Town*: A Study in Misunderstanding," in *Thornton Wilder: New Essays*, ed. Martin Blank et al. (West Cornwall, CT: Locust Hill Press, 1999), 358.

113. Wheatley is specifically criticizing the anthology *American Drama Colonial to Contemporary*, ed. Stephen Watt and Gary Richardson (Fort Worth, TX: Harcourt Brace, 1995). Christopher J. Wheatley, "'Acts of Faith: Thornton Wilder and His Critics': Public Popularity—Academic Neglect," in Blank et al., *Thornton Wilder: New Essays*, 23.

114. "Wilder Tells Why," E2.

115. Wilder, "Preface to *Three Plays*," 109.

116. Thornton Wilder, "A Preface for *Our Town*," in Gallup, *American Characteristics*, 100–101. It was also published in the *New York Times*, February 13, 1938, 155.

117. Paul Lifton, "Theatrical Ragout from a Master Chef," in Blank et al., *Thornton Wilder: New Essays*, 285.

118. Wilder, "Preface for *Our Town*," 101.

119. Wilder, "Preface to *Three Plays*," 109.

120. Bunge, "Social Realism," 351.

121. M. C. Kuner, *Thornton Wilder: The Bright and the Dark* (New York: Thomas Y. Crowell, 1972), 67.

122. Bert Cardullo, "Whose Town Is It, and Whither Goes It? An Historico-Aesthetic, Comparative-Influential Inquiry into *Our Town*," *Studies in the Humanities* 25.1–2 (1998): 14.

123. Bunge, "Social Realism," 358.

124. Mary F. Brewer, *Staging Whiteness* (Middletown, CT: Wesleyan University Press, 2005), 33.

125. David Palumbo-Liu, "Universalisms and Minority Culture," *differences: A Journal of Feminist Cultural Studies* 7.1 (1995): 188.

126. Brewer, *Staging Whiteness*, 33.

127. Bunge, "Social Realism," 358; and David Castronovo, *Thornton Wilder* (New York: Ungar, 1986), 83.

128. Bunge, "Social Realism," 357.

129. "City Children Find 'Our Town' Alien," *New York Times*, August 14, 1969, 26, *New York Times* Historical, http://proquest.umi.com, accessed October 4, 2007.

CHAPTER 2. EVERYDAY RITUALS AND THE PERFORMANCE OF COMMUNITY

1. William L. Worden, "Where Are Those Japanese War Brides?," *Saturday Evening Post* 227.21 (November 20, 1954): 133, Academic Search Premier, http://ebscohost. com/, accessed April 2, 2008.

2. Ibid., 39.

3. Ibid., 134.

4. Ibid., 133.

5. Ibid., 134.

6. In this chapter, I use "Japanese American" to designate those of Japanese descent residing in the United States and "Japanese Canadian" to designate those of Japanese descent residing in Canada, although I recognize the problematic use of "American" to refer only to the United States.

7. Greg Robinson documents Franklin D. Roosevelt's support for dispersing Japanese Americans after the internment camps, and connects it to his endorsement of similar international projects for resettling Jewish refugees after the war.

See Greg Robinson, *After Camp: Portraits in Midcentury Japanese American Life and Politics* (Berkeley: University of California Press, 2012), particularly chap. 1.

8. Roy Miki and Cassandra Kobayashi, *Justice in Our Time: The Japanese Canadian Redress Settlement* (Vancouver: Talonbooks, 1991), 46.

9. Ibid., 50.

10. Lye, "Racial Form," 96.

11. I am mindful of critiques by Canadian literary scholars of a tendency in Asian American studies to appropriate Asian Canadian texts—particularly Kogawa's *Obasan*—as examples of Asian American literature, and to insert them into U.S.-based frameworks. In my reading of *Itsuka*, I strive to attend to the specificities of the Canadian internment and dispersal policies. Furthermore, by juxtaposing *Itsuka* and *Tea*, a play about "war brides," I hope to avoid conflating the two internments while acknowledging both parallels and differences in the representation and treatment of Japanese North Americans during this era. See Guy Beauregard, "What Is at Stake in Comparative Analyses of Asian Canadian and Asian American Literary Studies?," *Essays on Canadian Writing* 75 (Winter 2001): 217–39; and Marie Lo, "Passing Recognition: *Obasan* and the Borders of Asian American and Canadian Literary Criticism," *Comparative American Studies* 5.3 (2007): 307–32.

12. Donald C. Goellnicht, "Joy Kogawa's *Obasan*: An Essential Asian American Text?," *American Book Review* 31.1 (November/December 2009): 5.

13. My discussion of *Obasan* rather than *Itsuka* in relation to these controversies reflects the relatively little critical attention received by the latter.

14. Angela Pao, *No Safe Spaces: Re-casting Race, Ethnicity, and Nationality in American Theater* (Ann Arbor: University of Michigan Press, 2010), 59–60.

15. In his preface to the revised edition of *Beginnings in Ritual Studies*, Ronald L. Grimes acknowledges accusations of conceptual fuzziness, but also suggests that defining ritual too narrowly might limit interdisciplinary collaboration. Ronald L. Grimes, *Beginnings in Ritual Studies*, rev. ed. (Columbia: University of South Carolina Press, 1995), xiii.

16. Paul Connerton, *How Societies Remember* (Cambridge: Cambridge University Press, 2007), 58.

17. Ibid., 59.

18. Bernhard Leistle, "Ritual as Sensory Communication: A Theoretical and Analytical Perspective," in *Ritual and Identity: Performative Practices as Effective Transformations of Social Reality*, ed. Klaus-Peter Kopping et al. (Berlin: Lit Verlag, 2006), 49.

19. Victor Turner, *From Ritual to Theater: The Human Seriousness of Play* (New York: PAJ, 1982), 82–83.

20. Gerd Baumann, "Ritual Implicates 'Others': Rereading Durkheim in a Plural Society," in *Understanding Rituals*, ed. Daniel de Coppet (New York: Routledge, 1992), 99.

21. Catherine Bell, *Ritual Theory, Ritual Practice* (New York: Oxford University Press, 1992), 130.

22. Ibid., 74.

23. Connerton, *How Societies Remember*, 45.

24. Joseph C. Hermanowicz and Harriet P. Morgan, "Ritualizing the Routine: Collective Identity Affirmation," *Sociological Forum* 14.2 (June 1999): 200.

25. Jean Comaroff and John Comaroff, "Introduction," in *Modernity and Its Malcontents: Ritual and Power in Postcolonial Africa*, ed. Jean Comaroff and John Comaroff (Chicago: University of Chicago Press, 1993), xv–xvi.

26. Ibid., xxi.

27. Benedict Anderson, *Imagined Communities: Reflections on the Origin and Spread of Nationalism* (New York: Verso, 1983), 7.

28. Ibid., 26.

29. Grimes, *Beginnings*, 69.

30. Pamela Sugiman, "Memories of Internment: Narrating Japanese Canadian Women's Life Stories," *Canadian Journal of Sociology* 29.3 (Summer 2004): 378.

31. Joy Kogawa, *Itsuka* (New York: Anchor, 1992), 9. Subsequent citations in text.

32. Grimes, *Beginnings*, 72. Grimes's distinction between space and place both resonates with and diverges from that of de Certeau. The latter describes *space* as "practiced place" (de Certeau, *Practice*, 117).

33. Rita Felski, *Doing Time: Feminist Theory and Postmodern Culture* (New York: New York University Press, 2000), 91.

34. Leistle, "Ritual as Sensory Communication," 49.

35. Bell, *Ritual Theory*, 109.

36. De Certeau is interested in how "users make (*bricolent*) innumerable and infinitesimal transformations of and within the dominant cultural economy in order to adapt it to their own interests and their own rules" (*Practice*, xiii–xiv).

37. Kogawa herself was active in the National Association for Japanese Canadians and served as a consultant for its pamphlet, *Justice in Our Time*, which chronicles much of the history fictionalized in her novels.

38. This shift in the novel also seems to mark a move away from Obasan to Emily, both as a role model for Naomi and as a model of a distinct literary style. Scholars have read *Obasan* as setting Obasan and Emily as contrasting models for Naomi. See Shirley Geok-lin Lim, "Japanese American Women's Life Stories: Maternality in Monica Sone's *Nisei Daughter* and Joy Kogawa's *Obasan*," *Feminist Studies* 16.2 (Summer 1990): 288–312; Minh Nguyen, "'It Matters to Get the Facts Straight': Joy Kogawa, Realism, and Objectivity of Values," in *Reclaiming Identity: Realist Theory and the Predicament of Postmodernism*, ed. Paula Moya and Michael Hames-García (Berkeley: University of California Press, 2000), 171–204; and Meredith Shoenut, "'I Am Canadian': Truth of Citizenship in Joy Kogawa's *Obasan*," *American Review of Canadian Studies* 36.3 (Fall 2006): 478–97.

39. Connerton, *How Societies Remember*, 58–59.

40. As *Itsuka* comes to a close, the referent of Naomi's "we" gradually narrows from members of the redress movement to Cedric and herself; the repetitions of "we" then lessen in the final passages as Naomi reflects on what Settlement Day means for her personally.

41. The redress movement's insistence on both individual and community compensation could similarly be seen as affirming the importance of considering personal *and* communal losses in tandem.

42. Ralph Ellison, "Richard Wright's Blues," *Antioch Review* 50.1/2 (Winter–Spring 1992): 62.

43. Sugiman, "Memories of Internment," 383.

44. Roger Daniels, "The Decisions to Relocate the North American Japanese: Another Look," *Pacific Historical Review* 51.1 (February 1982): 71–77.

45. From this perspective, the U.S. government's agreement to acknowledge the injustice of the internment and to provide redress was not inconsistent with the conservatism of the Reagan administration. According to Palumbo-Liu, "The success of the Japanese Americans was used to dispute a structural critique of the U.S. political economy. Yet the very racism away from which conservatives tried to draw attention reappears strongly in the logic of the model minority myth" (*Asian/American*, 172).

46. Tetsuden Kashima, "Japanese American Internees Return, 1945 to 1955: Readjustment and Social Amnesia," *Phylon* 41.2 (1980): 115.

47. Dorothy Swaine Thomas, *The Salvage* (Berkeley: University of California Press, 1952).

48. Caroline C. Simpson, "'Out of an Obscure Place': Japanese War Brides and Cultural Pluralism in the 1950s," *differences: A Journal of Feminist Cultural Studies* 10.3 (Fall 1998): 65.

49. A series of legal enactments after World War II enabled the immigration of Japanese women married to U.S. servicemen during a period when immigration from Japan was still restricted. The Soldier Brides Act (1947) and Public Law 717 (1950) gave couples a small window of time to wed and apply for a visa to enter the United States.

50. Simpson, "'Out of an Obscure Place,'" 49–50.

51. Worden, "Where Are Those Japanese War Brides?," 133.

52. Ibid., 134.

53. Ibid., 133.

54. Ibid., 134.

55. Although anti-miscegenation laws were still in effect in the United States, Worden interestingly casts disapproval of such relationships as a problem in Japan, but not in the United States (ibid., 39).

56. Ibid., 38.

57. Janet Wentworth Smith and William L. Worden, "They're Bringing Home Japanese Wives," *Saturday Evening Post*, January 19, 1952, 27, Academic Search Premier, http://ebscohost.com/, accessed August 14, 2008.

58. Among the many subjects taught at these schools were child rearing, cooking, housekeeping, Christianity, and American history and customs. For an extended description and analysis of these schools, see Regina Lark, "They Challenged Two Nations: Marriages between Japanese Women and American GIs, 1945 to the Present" (PhD diss., University of Southern California, 1999), particularly chap. 4, "From Chopsticks to Forks: Turning Japanese Brides into American Housewives."

59. Smith and Worden, "They're Bringing Home Japanese Wives," 79.

60. Elena Tajima Creef, "Discovering My Mother as the Other in the *Saturday Evening Post*," *Qualitative Inquiry* 6.4 (December 2000): 451, SAGE Journals Online, http://qix.sagepub.com/, accessed April 2, 2008.

61. Creef observes that whereas the army extensively examined the backgrounds of the women, the men only had to show "proof of citizenship, single status, and proof of ability to support a wife" (ibid., 452).

62. Velina Hasu Houston, *Asa Ga Kimashita (Morning Has Broken)*, electronic ed. (Alexandria, VA: Alexander Street Press, 2004), 38.

63. Velina Hasu Houston, *American Dreams*, 1st electronic ed. (Alexandria, VA: Alexander Street Press, 2004), 83.

64. Houston, *American Dreams*, 112.

65. Roberta Uno, "Introduction to *Tea*," *Unbroken Thread: An Anthology of Plays by Asian American Women*, ed. Roberta Uno (Amherst: University of Massachusetts Press, 1993), 157.

66. Velina Hasu Houston, *Tea*, in Uno, *Unbroken Thread*, 171. Subsequent citations in text.

67. Uno, "Introduction to *Tea*," 157.

68. J. L. Austin distinguishes perlocutionary acts as "what we bring about or achieve *by* saying something, such as convincing, persuading, deterring, and even, say, surprising or misleading." J. L. Austin, *How to Do Things with Words* (Cambridge, MA: Harvard University Press, 1975), 109.

69. Production choices can, of course, radically change the implications of these remarks. For example, in the Horizons Theatre production, actors wore transparent kimonos over "Western" clothes, inverting the notion of a Japanese "inside" covered by an Americanized exterior. This costuming choice would thus complicate or contradict Chiz's comment that Himiko's death "made me remember that underneath my comfortable American clothes, I am, after all, Japanese" (170). Susan Haedicke, "'Suspended between Two Worlds': Interculturalism and the Rehearsal Process for Horizons Theatre's Production of Velina Hasu Houston's *Tea*," *Theatre Topics* 4.1 (March 1994): 89–103.

70. Victor Turner, *The Ritual Process: Structure and Anti-Structure* (Chicago: Aldine, 1969), 95.

71. Turner, *From Ritual to Theater*, 80.

72. Jon McKenzie, *Perform or Else: From Discipline to Performance* (New York: Routledge, 2001), 50.

73. Kimberly Jew, "Dismantling the Realist Character in Velina Hasu Houston's *Tea* and David Henry Hwang's *FOB*," in *Literary Gestures: The Aesthetic in Asian American Writing*, ed. Rocío G. Davis and Sue-Im Lee (Philadelphia: Temple University Press, 2006), 195.

74. Marvin Carlson, *The Haunted Stage: The Theatre as Memory Machine* (Ann Arbor: University of Michigan Press, 2001), 53.

75. In her reading of the play, Josephine Lee offers an analysis of this distribution of roles that both converges with and diverges from my own. While Lee argues that the role-doubling sets the other characters as extensions of the "war brides" and thus encourages a conception of Asian American women as vessels that contain and endure hardship, I focus on the indeterminacy of the relationship between the central "war bride" character and the minor roles. Josephine Lee, *Performing Asian America: Race and Ethnicity on the Contemporary Stage* (Philadelphia: Temple University Press, 1997), 204.

76. Shimakawa proposes that this juxtaposition of characters reframes and complicates their seemingly stereotypical traits by encouraging comparisons between and among the women rather than against conceptions of normative American behavior (*National Abjection*, 105–7).

77. See Walter Goodman, "'Tea,' End Of Trilogy," *New York Times*, October 21, 1987, late ed., C23, LexisNexis, http://www.lexisnexis.com; Alvin Klein, "Japanese Wives in U.S. Are Portrayed in 'Tea,'" *New York Times*, November 5, 1989, New Jersey Weekly Desk, late ed., sec. 12, 20, LexisNexis, http://www.lexisnexis.com, accessed November 1, 2008; Lloyd Rose, "'Tea': Steeped in the Familiar," *Washington Post*, March 24, 1993, final ed., B2, LexisNexis, http://www.lexisnexis.com, accessed November 1, 2008; Ed Siegel, "Souls Struggle in Limbo in the Berkshires," *Boston Globe*, August 18, 1999, D1, LexisNexis, http://www.lexisnexis.com, accessed November 1, 2008.

78. Anne Midgette, "Steeped in Female Bonding, Shared with a Troubled Ghost," *New York Times*, May 31, 2007, E7, LexisNexis, http://www.lexisnexis.com, accessed November 1, 2008.

79. Grimes, *Beginnings*, 63.

80. Schechner, *Performance Theory* (London: Routledge, 1988), 157.

81. Schechner aligns efficacy with ritual and entertainment with theater, although he emphasizes that no one performance is solely efficacious or entertaining (*Performance Theory*, 130).

82. Kogawa claims that the bad review led her to publish a substantially revised version of *Itsuka* in 2005 under the new title of *Emily Kato*. As she relates, however, this book received little publicity and fared worse than *Itsuka* in sales. Michael Posner, "Restoring a Book to Life," *Globe and Mail*, March 9, 2006, R3, LexisNexis, http://www.lexisnexis.com, accessed November 26, 2008.

83. Stan Persky, "*Itsuka* pales in *Obasan*'s shadow," *Globe and Mail*, March 28, 1992, LexisNexis, http://www.lexisnexis.com, accessed November 26, 2008.

84. Even favorable reviews of *Itsuka* often echo Persky's criticisms of the novel as too documentary and sociological, and assume an incongruity between politics and aesthetics. See Claire Rothman, "Political Clamor Drowns out Kogawa's Voice," *Montreal Gazette*, March 14, 1992, final ed., H2, LexisNexis, http://www.lexisnexis. com, accessed November 26, 2008; and Brendan Bernhard, "In Short: Fiction," *New York Times*, March 13, 1994, late ed., sec. 7, 18, LexisNexis, http://www. lexisnexis.com, accessed November 26, 2008.

85. Mary di Michele, "Wearing the 'Hairshirt of Ethnicity,'" *Toronto Star*, March 28, 1992, Saturday ed., G17, LexisNexis, http://www.lexisnexis.com, accessed November 26, 2008.

86. Schechner, *Between Theater*, 99.

87. Ibid., 101.

88. Haedicke, "'Suspended between Two Worlds,'" 89.

89. Ibid., 98.

90. Lark, "They Challenged Two Nations," 384.

91. Ibid., 384–85.

92. Michael Omi and Howard Winant, *Racial Formation in the United States: From the 1960s to the 1990s*, 2nd ed. (New York: Routledge, 1994), 99.

93. Ibid., 98.

CHAPTER 3. MAKING CHANGE

1. The image of "the fortuitous encounter upon a dissecting-table of a sewing machine and an umbrella" comes from Comte de Lautréamont's *Les Chants de Maldoror*, first published in 1868. Comte de Lautréamont, *Maldoror* (New York: New Directions, 1965), 263.

2. Anna Deavere Smith, *Twilight: Los Angeles, 1992* (New York: Anchor Books, 1994), 101. Subsequent citations in text. In the published script, the line breaks are meant to capture the rhythm of each character's speech.

3. Ben Highmore, *Everyday Life and Cultural Theory: An Introduction* (New York: Routledge, 2002), 47.

4. Elizabeth Wong, "Kimchee and Chitlins," in *But Still Like Air, I'll Rise*, ed. Velina Hasu Houston (Philadelphia: Temple University Press, 1997), 441. Subsequent citations in text.

5. Ivan Light and Edna Bonacich, *Immigrant Entrepreneurs: Koreans in Los Angeles 1965–1982* (Berkeley: University of California Press, 1988), 22–23, 122–23.

6. Peter Morrison and Ira Lowry, "A Riot of Color: The Demographic Setting," in *The Los Angeles Riots*, ed. Mark Baldassare (Boulder, CO: Westview, 1994), 24–27.

7. Philip Kasinitz, *Caribbean New York: Black Immigrants and the Politics of Race* (Ithaca, NY: Cornell University Press, 1992), 198, 201.

8. Regina Freer, "Black-Korean Conflict," in Baldassare, *Los Angeles Riots*, 190.

9. Heon Cheol Lee, "Conflict between Korean Merchants and Black Customers: A Structural Analysis," in *Koreans in the Hood: Conflict with African Americans*, ed. Kwang Chung Kim (Baltimore: Johns Hopkins University Press, 1999), 119.

10. Rhonda Richards, "Two Sides of American Dream," *USA Today*, May 12, 1992, Money: 1B, LexisNexis, http://www.lexisnexis.com, accessed October 25, 2007.

11. Kathryn Tolbert, "Out of the Mainstream," *Boston Globe*, October 25, 1992, Magazine: 20, LexisNexis, http://www.lexisnexis.com, accessed October 25, 2007.

12. Kyeyoung Park, "Use and Abuse of Race and Culture: Black-Korean Tension in America," in Kim, *Koreans in the Hood*, 69.

13. Nancy Abelmann and John Lie, *Blue Dreams: Korean Americans and the Los Angeles Riots* (Cambridge, MA: Harvard University Press, 1995), x.

14. H. C. Lee, "Conflict," 125.

15. Ibid., 119.

16. Garry Pierre-Pierre, "Something in Common; To Bridge a Gap Korean Grocers Try a Little Creole," *New York Times*, October 18, 1997: B1, LexisNexis http://www.lexisnexis.com, accessed October 25, 2007; Joyce Shelby, "Teaching That Smiles Can Take a Biz Miles," *New York Daily News*, August 7, 1996, 3, LexisNexis, http://www.lexisnexis.com, accessed October 25, 2007.

17. Abelmann and Lie, *Blue Dreams*, 163.

18. See Light and Bonacich, *Immigrant Entrepreneurs*.

19. Freer, "Black-Korean Conflict," 185.

20. Freer observes that during the 1991 boycott of John's Liquor Store in Los Angeles, members of the Brotherhood Crusade and the Korean American Grocers Association insisted that "a solution to the conflict had to come from the two communities alone" (ibid., 193). Thus, they perpetuated the notion that only the parties most visibly involved in the boycott should be responsible for alleviating tensions.

21. Ella Stewart, "Communication between African Americans and Korean Americans before and after the Los Angeles Riots," in *Los Angeles—Struggles toward Multiethnic Community: Asian American, African American, and Latino Perspectives*, ed. Edward T. Chang and Russell C. Leong (Seattle: University of Washington Press, 1994), 41.

22. News stories that addressed both cultural and economic factors tended to conceive of them as separate if cumulative ingredients. In addition to the articles above, see William Schmidt, "For Immigrants, Tough Customers," *New York Times*, November 25, 1990, sec. 4, 5, LexisNexis, http://www.lexisnexis.com, accessed October 25, 2007; Seth Mydans, "Shooting Puts Focus on Korean-Black Frictions in Los Angeles," *New York Times*, October 6, 1991, sec. 1, pt. 1, 20, LexisNexis, http://www.lexisnexis.com, accessed October 25, 2007; Douglas Martin, "Seeking Ties and Clout, Korean Grocers Join Voices," *New York Times*, March 22, 1993, sec. A, 1, LexisNexis, http://www.lexisnexis.com, accessed October 25, 2007.

23. Bourdieu, *Logic of Practice*, 54.

24. Ibid., 60–61.

25. Containing these tensions in economically depressed urban areas could, however, help maintain the constancy of the *habitus* in wealthier areas.

26. Bourdieu notes, "Sociology treats as identical all biological individuals who, being the products of the same objective conditions, have the same *habitus*" (ibid., 59).
27. H. C. Lee, "Conflict," 127.
28. Diamond, "Introduction," 5.
29. Bourdieu, *Logic of Practice*, 67.
30. Bertolt Brecht, *Brecht on Theatre: The Development of an Aesthetic*, ed. John Willett (New York: Hill & Wang, 2001), 192.
31. The play in this respect echoes complaints directed against the media by those involved in and affected by the boycott and the uprising. Abelmann and Lie, *Blue Dreams*, observe that Korean-language newspapers spent much time analyzing mainstream reports of the "Black-Korean conflict," and that Korean Americans organized protests against their local media for their coverage. The interviews recorded in Anna Deavere Smith's *Twilight*, such as the statements by Allen Cooper quoted at the beginning of this chapter, capture similar objections to media coverage of the uprising.
32. Pao, *No Safe Spaces*, 27.
33. Ibid., 5.
34. Ibid., 26–30.
35. Bourdieu, *Logic of Practice*, 68.
36. Freer, "Black-Korean Conflict," 176.
37. Phelan, *Unmarked*, 22.
38. De Certeau, *Practice*, 127.
39. Wong scripts Matilda's dialect for both Soomi's reenactment and Suzie's interview, but it is slightly more exaggerated in the former. The variations in how Wong writes such simulated speech suggest the degree to which characters feel sympathetic toward one another, with more marked distinctions when they perform members of the opposing Chorus.
40. Tania Modleski, "Doing Justice to the Subjects: Mimetic Art in a Multicultural Society: The Work of Anna Deavere Smith," in *Female Subjects in Black and White: Race, Psychoanalysis, Feminism*, ed. Elizabeth Abel et al. (Berkeley: University of California Press, 1997), 65.
41. Modleski recalls, "After seeing the way white women were portrayed in this version my first reaction was one of anger. . . . If Smith was not prepared to acknowledge my oppression as a woman, I felt, I would not recognize hers as an African American" (ibid., 70).
42. Anna Deavere Smith, *Fires in the Mirror* (New York: Anchor, 1993), xl.
43. Smith, *Fires*, xxxix.
44. My use of the term "articulation" is inspired by Stuart Hall's reading of Gramsci: "[Gramsci] draws attention to . . . the complexity of the processes of de-construction and re-construction by which old alignments are dismantled and new alignments can be effected between elements in different discourses and between social forces and ideas. It conceives ideological change, not in terms of substitution or imposition but rather in terms of the articulation and the

disarticulation of ideas" (23). Stuart Hall, "Gramsci's Relevance for the Study of Race and Ethnicity," *Journal of Communication Inquiry* 10.2 (1986): 5–27.

45. See Charles Lyons and James Lyons, "Anna Deavere Smith: Perspectives on Her Performance within the Context of Critical Theory," *Journal of Dramatic Theory and Criticism* 9.1 (Fall 1994): 45; Dorinne Kondo, "Shades of Twilight: Anna Deavere Smith and *Twilight: Los Angeles, 1992*," in *Connected: Engagements with Media*, ed. George Marcus (Chicago: University of Chicago Press, 1996), 316; and Modleski, "Doing Justice to the Subjects," 60–62.

46. Smith, *Fires*, xxiv.

47. Ibid., xxvii.

48. Debby Thompson, "'Is Race a Trope?': Anna Deavere Smith and the Question of Racial Performativity," *African American Review* 31.1 (Spring 2003): 127–28.

49. Ibid., 133.

50. Lyons and Lyons, "Anna Deavere Smith," 47.

51. Ibid., 50.

52. Ibid., 50.

53. Brecht, *Brecht on Theatre*, 198.

54. Ibid., 105.

55. Lyons and Lyons, "Anna Deavere Smith," 60; Thompson, "'Is Race a Trope?,'" 129.

56. Smith's attention to the speaker's body is evident in the published performance script, which notes those moments when a subject's effort to verbalize his or her understanding of an issue intersects with a specific corporeal expression.

57. My analysis here is based on the published script and the performances included in the film version of *Twilight* (dir. Marc Levin, PBS, 2001); it is also informed by my attendance at Smith's performance *Let Me Down Easy* at the Berkeley Repertory Theatre.

58. Bourdieu, *Logic of Practice*, 58.

59. Lyons and Lyons, "Anna Deavere Smith," 45.

60. Modleski calls attention to the problematic assumptions behind such understandings of Smith's work, which reinforce conceptions of black women's bodies as empty vessels ("Doing Justice to the Subjects," 60–62).

61. Kondo, "Shades of Twilight," 316.

62. Smith, *Fires*, xxviii.

63. Phelan, *Unmarked*, 13.

64. Anna Deavere Smith, "Not so Special Vehicles," *Performing Arts Journal* 17.2/3 (May–September 1995): 87.

65. Sandra Kumamoto, "Teaching Identity Politics in a Post-identity Age: Anna Deavere Smith's *Twilight*," *MELUS* 30.2 (2005 Summer): 202.

66. Modleski, "Doing Justice to the Subjects," 65.

67. For an extended study of nontraditional casting practices, see Pao, *No Safe Spaces*.

68. Ann Geracimos, "In her Element, Anna D. Smith Serves up Life's Drama Stage," *Washington Times*, January 30, 1997, pt. C, 8, LexisNexis, http://www.lexisnexis.com, accessed October 25, 2007.

69. Smith, *Fires*, xxxix.

70. Bourdieu, *Logic of Practice*, 68.

71. Cherise Smith, *Enacting Others: Politics of Identity in Eleanor Antin, Nikki S. Lee, Adrian Piper, and Anna Deavere Smith* (Durham, NC: Duke University Press, 2011), 163.

72. Bourdieu, *Logic of Practice*, 73.

CHAPTER 4. HOMEWORK BECOMES YOU

1. Amy Chua, *Battle Hymn of the Tiger Mother*, paperback ed. (New York: Penguin, 2011), 3–4. Subsequent citations in text.

2. Amy Chua, "Why Chinese Mothers Are Superior," *Wall Street Journal*, January 8, 2011, online.wsj.com, accessed June 14, 2013.

3. Richard Bernstein, "Asian Students Harmed by Precursors' Success," *New York Times*, July 10, 1988, late ed., sec. 1, 16.

4. Martin Kasindorf, et al., "Asian-Americans: A 'Model Minority,'" *Newsweek*, December 6, 1982, U.S. ed., 39.

5. Koshy notes that the figure of the model minority sets critics who see it as "assimilationist, homogenizing, and heterosexist" against those "who see it as an economic confirmation of the veracity of their cultural values and have invested it with their class aspirations, plural national attachments, gender norms, and heterosexual arrangements" (Susan Koshy, "Neoliberal Family Matters," *American Literary History* 25.2 [Summer 2013]: 348). For Ninh, a serious consideration of the latter is exactly what has been lacking in investigations of the model minority stereotype: "The heart of the issue is not whether an Asian immigrant family currently meets the socioeconomic or professional measures of the model minority. Rather, the issue is whether it aspires to do so, whether it *applies* those metrics: not resentful of the racializing discourse of Asian success as a violence imposed from without, but implementing that discourse, with ingenuity, alacrity, and pride, from within." erin Khuê Ninh, *Ingratitude: The Debt-Bound Daughter in Asian American Literature* (New York: NYU Press, 2011), 9.

6. Grace Wang, "On Tiger Mothers and Music Moms," *Amerasia Journal* 37.2 (2011): 134.

7. Ibid., 132.

8. Fox Butterfield, "Why Asians Are Going to the Head of the Class," *New York Times*, August 3, 1986, late ed., sec. 12, 18.

9. Ibid., 18.

10. Lori Gottleib, "Amy Chua," *Atlantic Monthly*, November 2011, 50.

11. In a new book, *The Triple Package: How Three Unlikely Traits Explain the Rise and Fall of Cultural Groups in America* (New York: Penguin, 2014), Chua and her coauthor (and husband) Jed Rubenfeld claim to identify the characteristics that explain the success of certain groups in the United States. Rather than the everyday practices of parents and children, this book focuses on three broad "cultural" traits. Critics of *Triple Package* argue that it perpetuates notions of racial

hierarchies and ignores the impact of sociohistorical circumstances on the various groups that it discusses.

12. Annie Murphy Paul, "Tiger Moms: Is Tough Parenting Really the Answer?," *Time*, January 20, 2011, time.com, accessed June 14, 2013.

13. "Tiger Cubs v. Precious Lambs," *Economist*, January 20, 2011, economist.com, accessed June 14, 2013.

14. Butterfield, "Why Asians Are Going," 18.

15. Less blatant than the *New York Times* article by Butterfield, stories about Asian Americans that appeared during this time in *Christian Science Monitor* and the *Washington Post* similarly insinuated a potentially threatening rise in numbers. See John Dillin, "Asian-Americans: Soaring Minority," *Christian Science Monitor*, October 10, 1985, National sec., 3; and Spencer Rich, "Asian Americans Outperform Others in School and Work; Census Data Outlines 'Model Minority,'" *Washington Post*, October 10, 1985, final ed., sec. 1, A1.

16. See Gary Okihiro, "Perils of the Body and Mind," in *Margins and Mainstream: Asians in American History and Culture* (Seattle: University of Washington Press, 1994), 118–47.

17. Koshy, "Neoliberal Family Matters," 345.

18. Ibid., 345–46.

19. Okihiro, "Perils of the Body and Mind," 141.

20. Ibid., 141.

21. Doobo Shim and Joann Lee observe an increasing number of depictions in the late twentieth century of Asians as gangsters in films and news stories, respectively. Doobo Shim, "From Yellow Peril through Model Minority to Renewed Yellow Peril," *Journal of Communication Inquiry* 22.4 (October 1998): 385–409; Joann Lee, "A Look at Asians as Portrayed in the News," *Editor & Publisher*, April 30, 1994, 56–57.

22. Wang, "On Tiger Mothers," 130.

23. Sau-ling C. Wong, *Reading Asian American Literature: From Necessity to Extravagance* (Princeton: Princeton University Press, 1993), 92.

24. Ibid., 92.

25. Josephine Lee, *Performing Asian America*, 168.

26. Ibid.

27. This chapter focuses on what Sau-ling C. Wong describes as a variation of the racial shadow but leaves for future studies to investigate: doubles that manifest what the protagonist idealizes and desires, rather than (or in addition to) what she disowns (*Reading Asian American Literature*, 117).

28. Ibid., 111.

29. Ibid., 90.

30. *Better Luck Tomorrow* (dir. Justin Lin, MTV Films, 2003).

31. Roger Ebert, "No Place for Political Correctness in Film," *Chicago Sun-Times*, January 18, 2002, http://www.betterlucktomorrow.com, accessed November 29, 2003.

32. Ebert, "No Place."
33. Ibid.
34. Daniel Yi, "They're the Bad Seeds?," *Los Angeles Times Calendar Live*, April 6, 2003, http://www.betterlucktomorrow.com, accessed November 29, 2003.
35. Subtitles in video footage of the debate affirm Yi's account, although the audience member's remark is cut off by the voice-over. Video at www.youtube.com/watch?v=LSzP9YV3jbc.
36. Palumbo-Liu, *Asian/American*, 281.
37. Jun Xing, *Asian America through the Lens: History, Representations, and Identity* (Walnut Creek, CA: AltaMira Press, 1998), 125.
38. Lisa Lowe, *Immigrant Acts: On Asian American Cultural Politics* (Durham, NC: Duke University Press, 1996), 62.
39. Park, "Our Racial Frontier on the Pacific," in *Race and Culture*, 150.
40. Lowe, *Immigrant Acts*, 6.
41. Anne A. Cheng, *The Melancholy of Race: Psychoanalysis, Assimilation, and Hidden Grief* (New York: Oxford University Press, 2001), 10.
42. Lauren Berlant, *Cruel Optimism* (Durham, NC: Duke University Press, 2011), 1.
43. Cheng, *Melancholy of Race*, 59.
44. Butler, *Gender Trouble*, 2nd ed. (New York: Routledge, 1999), 173.
45. Butler, *Bodies*, 12.
46. Ibid., 232.
47. Although theories of American assimilation vary in their assessment of the transformation effected by the contact between different groups (Milton Gordon lists "Anglo-conformity," "the melting pot," and "cultural pluralism" as different models), I focus primarily on the dynamic implied by the model minority myth and depicted in the film: the incorporation of a minority group into the majority through socioeconomic advancement and the appropriation of normative behaviors and values. Milton Gordon, *Assimilation in American Life: The Role of Race, Religion, and National Origins* (New York: Oxford University Press, 1964).
48. Suein Hwang, "The New White Flight," *Wall Street Journal*, November 19, 2005, A1, http://proquest.umi.com, accessed March 3, 2007.
49. Ibid., A1.
50. The "Chinese Jordan" joke is indicative of the film's production before Yao Ming and Jeremy Lin became two of the NBA's most popular players. In their study of the "flexible marketing" of Yao Ming, Thomas Oates and Judy Polumbaum show that praise of his ostensible gentleness and discipline could imply criticism of the behaviors of black players. See Thomas Oates and Judy Polumbaum, "Agile Big Man: The Flexible Marketing of Yao Ming," *Pacific Affairs* 77.2 (Summer 2004): 187–210.
51. Jeffrey Paul Chan et al., eds., *Aiiieeeee! An Anthology of Asian-American Writers* (Washington, DC: Howard University Press, 1974), viii.
52. Celine Parreñas Shimizu, *Straitjacket Sexualities: Unbinding Asian American Manhoods in the Movies* (Stanford: Stanford University Press, 2012), 4.

53. Ibid., 125. In addition to Shimizu's book, other critical works on *Better Luck Tomorrow* have emphasized its dialogue with stereotypes of Asian men as asexual and Asian women as readily available sexual objects. See Margaret Hillenbrand, "Of Myths and Men: Better Luck Tomorrow and the Mainstreaming of Asian America Cinema," *Cinema Journal* 47.4 (Summer 2008): 50–75; and Ruthann Lee, "Ambivalence, Desire and the Re-imagining of Asian American Masculinity in *Better Luck Tomorrow*," in *Pimps, Wimps, Studs, Thugs and Gentlemen: Essays*, ed. Elwood Watson (Jefferson, NC: McFarland, 2009), 51–67.

54. Josephine Lee, *Performing Asian America*, 91.

55. Daniel Y. Kim, *Writing Manhood in Black and Yellow: Ralph Ellison, Frank Chin, and the Literary Politics of Identity* (Stanford: Stanford University Press, 2005), 211.

56. Ibid., 212.

57. In the film, Virgil refers to his friends as his "niggers," and the mock website created for him to publicize the movie drives the point home: http://www. betterlucktomorrow.com/character_sites/virgil/homepage.htm, accessed November 29, 2003.

58. Manohla Dargis, "Death of the 'Model Minority,'" *Los Angeles Times*, April 11, 2003, http://www.betterlucktomorrow.com, accessed November 29, 2003.

59. D. Y. Kim, *Writing Manhood*, 211.

60. The work of social psychologists on the impact of stereotypes on educational testing, policing, criminal sentencing, and other areas makes a compelling case for how racial representations deeply influence life possibilities. For example, see Claude Steele, *Whistling Vivaldi: And Other Clues to How Stereotypes Affect Us* (New York: Norton, 2010).

61. Josephine Lee, *Performing Asian America*, 196.

62. Palumbo-Liu, *Asian/American*, 398.

63. Berlant, *Cruel Optimism*, 199.

64. Lauren Yee, *Ching Chong Chinaman*, in *Asian American Plays for a New Generation*, ed. Josephine Lee et al. (Philadelphia: Temple University Press, 2011), 314. Subsequent citations in text.

65. Josephine Lee, "Introduction to *Ching Chong Chinaman*," in Lee et al., *Asian American Plays*, 266.

66. From 1988 to 1990, the Department of Education's Office for Civil Rights conducted investigations to determine whether or not universities had discriminated against Asian American applicants. Several universities also conducted self-studies in the 1980s, with some acknowledging unconscious bias and others denying discriminatory practices. For more on these investigations, see Dana Takagi, *The Retreat from Race: Asian-American Admissions and Racial Politics* (New Brunswick, NJ: Rutgers University Press, 1992).

67. The briefs for *Fisher v. University of Texas*, including those in support of the petitioner and the respondent, were published on the website of the University of Texas at Austin: http://www.utexas.edu/vp/irla/Fisher-V-Texas.html.

68. Maxine Hong Kingston, *The Woman Warrior: Memoirs of a Girlhood among Ghosts* (New York: Vintage, 1989), 5–6.

69. My thanks to Tabitha Kenlon for a useful discussion of the possible significance of Desdemona's name at the 2013 ASTR Everyday Life working session.

70. The report is available online at http://www.pewsocialtrends.org/2012/06/19/the-rise-of-asian-americans/.

71. Association for Asian American Studies, "Association for Asian American Studies Response to the Pew Center Report: 'Rise of Asian Americans'" (press release, July 16, 2012), http://aaastudies.org/content/index.php/77-home/117-whats-new, accessed July 29, 2013.

AFTERWORD

1. "Good Hygiene Gets Girls," YouTube video, 4:30, posted by Wong Fu Productions, January 18, 2010, https://www.youtube.com/watch?v=WZfAYWbhQP8.

2. "Good Cooking Gets Girls," YouTube video, 4:23, posted by Wong Fu Productions, January 14 2011, https://www.youtube.com/watch?v=14HjPdvV8go; "Working Out Gets Girls," YouTube video, 5:23, posted by Wong Fu Productions, September 12, 2012, https://www.youtube.com/watch?v=Ub_ltTBnCtE.

3. A 2011 study by the Pew Research Center reported that more Asian Americans use the Internet than any other racial group. Lee Rainie, "Asian-Americans and Technology" (Pew Internet and American Life Project, January 6, 2011), http://pewinternet.org/Presentations/2011/Jan/Organization-for-Chinese-Americans.aspx, accessed May 25, 2012. I consider criticism of these reports later in the chapter.

4. Austin Considine, "For Asian-American Stars, Many Web Fans," *New York Times*, July 29, 2011, New York ed., ST6, accessed October 27, 2013. Videos are available on their respective YouTube channels: www.youtube.com/user/nigahiga; www.youtube.com/user/MichellePhan; www.youtube.com/user/kevjumba.

5. Jean Burgess and Joshua Green, *YouTube: Online Video and Participatory Culture* (Cambridge: Polity, 2009), 57.

6. "Yellow Fever (2006)—Re-release Official," YouTube video, 20:32, posted by Wong Fu Productions, January 28, 2010, www.youtube.com/watch?v=vC_ycDO66bw.

7. The company name comes from the nickname of Philip Wang, one of the three founders. See interview by Ho Chie, "From East to West with Wong Fu Productions," http://taiwaneseamerican.org/ta/2008/11/14/from-east-to-west-with-wong-fu-productions/.

8. Chan et al., *Aiiieeeee!*, viiii.

9. Ibid., viiii.

10. Frank Chin and Jeffrey Paul Chan, "Racist Love," in *Seeing Through Shuck*, ed. Richard Kostelanetz (New York: Ballantine, 1972), 65–79.

11. Shimizu, *Straitjacket Sexualities*, 15.

12. David Eng, *Racial Castration: Managing Masculinity in Asian America* (Durham, NC: Duke University Press, 2001), 21.

13. I use the term "ethnic" here rather than "racial" to borrow a distinction made in Hazel Rose Markus and Paula Moya's *Doing Race: 21 Essays for the 21st Century* (New York: Norton, 2010). Stressing that in practice this distinction does not always hold, Markus and Moya conceive of ethnicity as a "more mutual, power-neutral, and positive process" than race, which is connected with the perpetuation of hierarchies and inequalities (21–23). As this chapter argues, the cultivation of a nonhierarchical concept of *ethnicity* can nevertheless perpetuate hierarchies based on gender or sexuality.

14. For example, see "Elbow Zit," YouTube video, 2:10, posted by KevJumba, May 18, 2009, www.youtube.com/watch?v=9czIVC9p8BA; and "Dear Ryan—Klondike Bar," YouTube video, 1:43, posted by Nigahiga, July 2, 2012, www.youtube.com/watch?v=eQvdOLxkGco.

15. "Expectations vs. Reality: Romance," YouTube video, 4:56, posted by Nigahiga, February 15, 2013, www.youtube.com/watch?v=EvAJt3VMouk.

16. Y. S. Lee, *Modern Minority*, 15.

17. Grace Wang, "A Love Song to YouTube: Charting a 'So-called Asian Movement' Online" (paper, Association for Asian American Studies Annual Conference, Seattle, April 18, 2013).

18. "I Have to Deal with Stereotypes," YouTube video, 4:54, posted by KevJumba, March 8, 2007, www.youtube.com/watch?v=nbZ9zJ22WfQ; "Dear Ryan—Can You Open Your Eyes?," YouTube video, 1:19, posted by Nigahiga, May 30, 2012, www.youtube.com/watch?v=IZsTBucXSFw.

19. "Draw My Life—Ryan Higa," YouTube video, 7:35, posted by Nigahiga, April 10, 2013, www.youtube.com/watch?v=KPmoDYayoLE; "Draw My Life—Michelle Phan," YouTube video, 11:25, posted by Michelle Phan, May 19, 2013, www.youtube.com/watch?v=05KqZEqQJ40.

20. For example, see "My Dad Is Asian Ep. 1," YouTube video, 2:08, posted by KevJumba, August 31, 2010, www.youtube.com/watch?v=yqSCOPvPJ7g; and "My Dad Is Asian Ep. 2," YouTube video, 1:50, posted by KevJumba, March 2, 2012, www.youtube.com/watch?v=Lw_vzLw4xyA.

21. Burgess and Green, *YouTube*, 81.

22. Lisa Nakamura, *Digitizing Race: Visual Cultures of the Internet* (Minneapolis: University of Minnesota Press, 2008), 178.

23. Tom Spooner, "Asian-Americans and the Internet" (Pew Internet and American Life Project, December 12, 2001), http://www.pewinternet.org/Reports/2001/AsianAmericans-and-the-Internet.aspx, accessed May 25, 2012; and Rainie, "Asian-Americans and Technology."

24. Nakamura, *Digitizing Race*, 179.

25. Nhi T. Lieu, "The Makeup Guru as Neoliberal Entrepreneur: Post-feminism, Self-Management, and Asian/American Women in the DIY Age of YouTube" (paper, Association for Asian American Studies Annual Conference, Seattle, April 18, 2013).

26. "Mulan Bride," YouTube video, 5:00, posted by Michelle Phan, June 18, 2011, www.youtube.com/watch?v=ebcc1WXJS6A.
27. Sianne Ngai, *Ugly Feelings* (Cambridge, MA: Harvard University Press, 2005), 125.
28. Ibid., 125.
29. "Acting, Acting," X8.

INDEX

Page numbers in italics indicate illustrations; page numbers in bold indicate major discussion.

Abelmann, Nancy, 130, 131
actor/character relationship: and alienation effect, 9, 135; convergence and disjuncture in *Kimchee and Chitlins*, 146–49; convergence and disjuncture in *Twilight*, 163–67; and role-doubling in *Tea*, 109–12; and theatrical performance, 8, 9–10
affirmative action: and Asian Americans, 214–15; and *Ching Chong Chinaman*, 214–15, 218
Ah Sin (Bret Harte and Mark Twain), 39, 43–44
Aiiieeeee! An Anthology of Asian-American Writers (Chan et al., eds.): compared with "Yellow Fever," 234; and racialized conceptions of manhood, 194–95
alienation effect, 9, 14, 54, 135, 149
American Dreams (Houston), 102–3
Anderson, Benedict, 79
The Arrival (Shaun Tan), 15
Asa Ga Kimashita (Houston): realist style, 102; summary, 102–3; use of the mundane in, 102–3
Asian American identity: complexity of concept, 75–76; and late twentieth-century social movements, 74–75
Asian Americans: and 2012 Pew Center report, 178, 227–28; and affirmative action, 214–15, 272n66; Internet use, 243;

and model minority stereotype, 3, 10, 12–13, 98, 173–74, 228; and online media productions, 231–32; and racialized conceptions of manhood, 194–95, 233–34; success associated with daily practices, 177–78
assimilation: as focus of sociological research, 35–37; as racialized, 187, 189, 215; racism downplayed in, 71–73; and resettlement policies, 73–74, 79, 81–82; as response to racism, 81–82, 83. *See also* racialization/assimilation dynamics
Association for Asian American Studies, response to Pew Center report (2012), 228
audience: and alienation effect, 135; participatory relationship in *Tea*, 117–18
audience perception: vs. actor's intention, 2; and Chinese immigrant performance of the mundane, 32–34; conditioned by everyday experiences, 68–70, 163–69; and racial stereotyping in *Twilight* performances, 163–65; and role-doubling in *Kimchee and Chitlins*, 151; shaped by racial identifications, 37–38; and theatrical performance, 2, 7–8, 21–22; *The Yellow Jacket* and *Our Town* compared, 60, 64–65
Aunt Emily (character in *Itsuka*): efforts to create community, 85–86; on Japanese Canadian self-erasure, 83–84; and redress movement, 92. See also *Itsuka*
Austin, J. L., 107

Lifton, Paul, 62

Light, Ivan, 128

liminality: and ritual, 104, 107–9, 113–14, 116–18, 122; of ritual in *Tea*, 104, 109–12; in theatrical performance, 111–12, 117–18

Lin, Justin, on *Better Luck Tomorrow*, 183–84

Los Angeles riots: differing perceptions of, 167–69; historical background, 127–28; media depictions, 124–25;

Lowe, Lisa, 185, 187

Lowry, Ira, 128

Lye, Colleen, 17

Lyons, Charles, and James Lyons, on Anna Deavere Smith, 156–57, 158, 161

Mackerras, Colin, 40–41

Mark Taper Forum (Los Angeles), 125, 154

McKenzie, Jon, 108–9

McKeown, Adam, 32

Michele, Mary di, on *Itsuka*, 118–19

Midgette, Anne, on *Tea*, 115

mimesis vs. imitation, 6, 7, 253n28

Miss Saigon: Velina Hasu Houston on casting of, 76; and yellowface performance, 76, 246

model minority's "others": in *Battle Hymn of the Tiger Mother*, 174–76, 179–80; in *Better Luck Tomorrow*, 18, 176, 180–82, 191–94, *193*, 200–204; and body/behavior disjuncture, 181, 190–91; in *Ching Chong Chinaman*, 18, 176, 180–82, 220–22; and convergence of stereotypes, 178–79; economic stratifications highlighted by, 181–82; as trope in Asian American cultural productions, 180–82

model minority stereotype: and Asian Americans, 3, 10, 11–13, 98, 173–74; and *Battle Hymn of the Tiger Mother*, 173–78; and civil rights issues, 98, 214–15, 228; convergence with yellow peril stereotype, 178–79; and doubling

as "others," 18, 174–76, 179–80, 180–82, 191–94, *193*, 200–204, 220–22; and economic anxieties, 178–79; efficacy of, 174; efforts to repudiate, 173–74, 228; and racialization of assimilation, 188–89; vs. "yellow peril," 3, 10

Modleski, Tania, on *Twilight*, 155, 164

Moon, Krystyn, 41, 42

Morgan, Harriet, 78–79

Morrison, Peter, 128

Mulroney, Brian, 91

the mundane: articulation of socioeconomic conditions through, 135, 136–37, 157–58; and Asian American racial formation, 3–5, 10–13; concept of, 3–4; and concept of the racial mundane, 3–10; defamiliarizing of, 14–15; in Internet video performances, 231–33; as mediator between conceptions of identity, 34, 122, 249–50; performance of by Chinese immigrant applicants, 32–34; vs. rituals, 78–79; and surrealism, 123. *See also* habitual behaviors; the ritualized mundane

Nakamura, Lisa, 243

Naomi Nakane (character in *Itsuka*): account of internment and dispersal, 82–83; disavowal of community, 83; homesickness of, 84–85; on Obasan's routines, 86–90; transformation of, 74, 80, 92–97, 262n40. See also *Itsuka*

National Association of Japanese Canadians (NAJC), 91–92, 94, 261n37

New York Times: on Asian American YouTube stars, 231; "Asians Are Going to the Head of the Class," 177, 178; "City Children Find 'Our Town' Alien," 68–70; on *Tea*, 115; on *The Yellow Jacket*, 48, 49, 50, 52, 53, 55, 56–57

Ngai, Sianne, 246

Nikkei International Marriage Society, 121

About the Author

Ju Yon Kim is Assistant Professor of English at Harvard University. Her research interests include Asian American performance and literature, modern and contemporary American theater, cross-racial and intercultural performance, and theories of the everyday.